Investigating
Sherlock Holmes

Library and Archives Canada Cataloguing in Publication

Nathan, Hartley R., author
    Investigating Sherlock Holmes : solved & unsolved
mysteries / Hartley R. Nathan and Clifford S. Goldfarb.

Issued in print and electronic formats.
ISBN 978-0-88962-992-9 (pbk.).--ISBN 978-0-88962-993-6 (epub)

    1. Holmes, Sherlock (Fictitious character). 2. Doyle,
Arthur Conan, Sir, 1859-1930--Characters--Sherlock
Holmes. I. Goldfarb, Clifford S. (Clifford Stanley), 1945- ,
author II. Title.

PR4624.N38 2014   823'.8   C2013-901854-9
                                            C2013-901855-7

Pubished by Mosaic Press, Oakville, Ontario, Canada, 2014.
Distributed in the United States by Bookmasters (www.bookmasters.com).
Distributed in the U.K. by Gazelle Book Services (www.gazellebookservices.co.uk).

MOSAIC PRESS, Publishers
Copyright © 2014, Hartley R. Nathan and Clifford S. Goldfarb
except as follows:
"Introduction to Sherlock Holmes" – Copyright © 2014, Hartley R. Nathan
"Prolegomenon" and "Regina v. Moran" – Copyright © 2014, John Linsenmeyer
"The National Rifle Association Guide to the Canon" and "Sherlock in Jerusalem" –
Copyright © 2014, Hartley R. Nathan, Clifford S. Goldfarb and Joseph Kessel

Printed and Bound in Canada.
Cover design and book layout by Eric Normann

ISBN: Paperback 978-0-88962-992-9   ePub 978-1-77161-009-4   ePDF 978-1-77161-012-4

We acknowledge the financial support of the Government of Canada through the Canada Book Fund (CBF) for this project.

Nous reconnaissons l'aide financière du gouvernement du Canada par l'entremise du Fonds du livre du Canada (FLC) pour ce projet.

 Canadian Patrimoine
Heritage canadien

Canada

Mosaic Press gratefully acknowledges the assistance of the OMDC (Ontario Media Development Corporation) in support of our publishing program.

MOSAIC PRESS
1252 Speers Road, Units 1 & 2
Oakville, Ontario L6L 5N9
phone: (905) 825-2130

info@mosaic-press.com

www.mosaic-press.com

Investigating Sherlock Holmes

Solved & Unsolved Mysteries

Hartley R. Nathan &
Clifford S. Goldfarb

 mosaicPRESS

CONTENTS

FOREWORD

The first thing we ever wrote together was published in a legal textbook. While we enjoyed writing it, we can't say that it left us with much of a sense that a lasting impression had been made on our colleagues. Neither of us can remember being cornered at bar association meetings by a breathless young lawyer, wanting to tell us how much he or she enjoyed our article on the use of trusts in business transactions. However, having survived all of the possible strains that writing jointly can put on a personal and professional relationship (one that has now comfortably exceeded 40 years), we decided to try something together in a Sherlockian vein.

Contrary to popular belief, we did not start out with a fixation on the 'Jewish connection' in the Canon. If anything, the early fixation was with Watson. One of Hartley's earliest papers was an attempt to prove that John Watson had emigrated to Canada and established himself in practice on Toronto's strangely-named Avenue Road. And so, our first joint paper, "Watson: Treason in the Blood", was an attempt to connect Dr. Watson with an ancestor named James or Jemmy Watson, implicated as one of the conspirators in the Regency Rebellion of 1816, thereby explaining why his spouse had apparently mistakenly called him 'James' in "The Man with the Twisted Lip".

We also didn't set out to do a series of papers on Sherlock Holmes' Jewish connection. In looking around for a subject, we realized that the possible Jewish roots of Irene Adler and her connection to the "Hebrew rabbi" referred to in Holmes' index in the very first of the Holmes short stories, "A Scandal in Bohemia", had not been extensively studied. "Who Was That Hebrew Rabbi?", in which we were able to establish these roots in a historical character and produce candidates for the rabbi, was well received. So we decided to continue mining this vein. A theme began to emerge that we have followed, but not universally, in our other papers – that is to seek out the non-Canonical origins of Canonical characters. After Irene Adler, we identified 'Old Abrahams' in "Lady Frances Carfax" and 'Ikey Sanders' in "The Mazarin Stone" with their Jewish antecedents. We deviated from that practice with the help of Joseph Kessel, when we followed Sherlock Holmes during the "Great Hiatus", as he secretly visited Jerusalem. We have dealt with a real person deliberately mentioned by Conan Doyle – Sir George Lewis, in "Illustrious Client" and another, Arminius Vambéry, in "The Musgrave Ritual". There may be one or two more papers left on that theme, but we have never been able to bring ourselves to tackle the ultimate question – was Sherlock Holmes Jewish? After more than 30 years of trying, we are just almost, but not quite, ready to concede defeat on that one.

For a change of pace, we ventured several times into the field of applied statistics, although our combined lack of understanding of this science would horrify any self-respecting statistician. Our first statistical paper was on restaurants in the Canon and the second on Canonical firearms, again with the help of Joseph Kessel. Our technical deficiency did not, however, prevent us from applying our own statistical methods to these two fields (not unlike the methods used by baseball statisticians, who can prove that Hufnagel bats .327 after the fifth inning against left-handed pitching in day games played on the East coast on Tuesdays). Some interesting conclusions emerged from these two papers.

Arthur Conan Doyle did not construct the Sherlock Holmes stories with all the care and checking that he might have employed if he were attempting to write one of his histories, or even his beloved historical fiction. In fact, a careful reader can find inconsistencies, not only between the various stories, but even within individual tales. How many wives did Watson have; where was his Afghan War wound – in the hip or the leg; why does his wife call him "James" when his name is clearly "John"; what happens to Watson's bull pup after its first mention in the very first story; how was Holmes related to the French artist Vernet (and which Vernet), where did Holmes go to school? The problems raised by trying to date the stories and put them in chronological order have spawned several bookshelves worth of scholarly books and pamphlets. Early in the twentieth century, aficionados of the stories began searching out and publishing these inconsistencies. From there it was but a short jump to seeking plausible explanations for them. Monsignor Ronald Knox in Britain, who was to become a prominent Catholic theologian, is generally considered to have started formal "scholarship" with the publication of "Studies in the Literature of Sherlock Holmes" in 1912, although there were other earlier scholars less well-known today. The essence of what was to become the "Great Game" or the "Sherlockian Game" is that Holmes was real, the four novels and 56 short stories published in the name of Arthur Conan Doyle (known as the "Sherlockian Canon" or the "Canon") were true, the stories were (with a few exceptions) written by Holmes' faithful Boswell, John H. Watson, and Conan Doyle played some role in having them published. Doyle became known in Sherlockian circles as "the Literary Agent". Dorothy Sayers pronounced that "the Game had to be played with one's tongue firmly in one's cheek, with all the seriousness of a cricket match at Lord's." But, at the same time, modern Sherlockians also play homage to the genius of Arthur Conan Doyle. So Sherlockian papers often straddle the line between pure playing of the Game, and seeking out externalities in the life and times of Conan Doyle that are reflected in the stories themselves. Our own papers frequently demonstrate this duality – we assume the events and people described in the stories really occurred, but they reflect people and events in the outside world which might have been in Conan Doyle's mind when he sat down to write the tales.

Most of these papers were first presented orally to The Bootmakers of Toronto, our local Sherlockian society, with varying degrees of acclaim (or otherwise). They have been lightly edited for publication, but we have not extensively updated them. Until 2005, a reference to the *"Annotated"* was to the *Annotated Sherlock Holmes*, compiled by William S. Baring-Gould and published in two volumes in 1967, which instantly became the most ubiquitous and hallowed edition of the Canon (often referred to as "Baring-Gould"). In 2005 Les Klinger's *New Annotated Sherlock Holmes* appeared and we began to use it in our papers. However, we have chosen not to update references to the *Annotated* in our earlier papers. In addition, in many instances we wanted to preserve the dialogue between us as the papers were delivered. Because of their oral genesis, those of you who, like us, move your lips while reading may find them more interesting than will more accomplished speed-readers.

Clifford S. Goldfarb
July 2014

ACKNOWLEDGEMENTS

We would be remiss if we did not express our profound appreciation to the Toronto Reference Library and especially to the three successive curators of its Arthur Conan Doyle Collection, Cameron Hollyer (who is no longer with us), Victoria Gill and Peggy Perdue, who went out of their way to provide us with helpful advice and much-needed reference materials over the years. Chris Redmond, Kate Karlson, Trevor Raymond, Barbara Roden and Mark and Joanne Alberstat, who have been the editors of *Canadian Holmes* (the journal of the Bootmakers of Toronto) over the many years of our writing partnership; Joseph Kessel, who joined us in several of our papers, and last of course, our very good friend John Linsenmeyer a true gentleman and scholar who provided us with the Prolegomenon and one paper, "Regina vs. Moran" with his usual panache.

To our long-suffering wives (Marilyn Nathan and Doris Goldfarb), who indulged us in our (to them) non-productive working breakfasts and lunches, patiently listened to us read numerous drafts, made constructive comments, came to Bootmakers' meetings to hear the papers presented and pretended to take seriously this inexplicable fascination of ours with the Sherlockian way of life and proofreading: Thank you!

Also a thanks to our children and grandchildren, who patiently put up with our idiosyncrasies.

Finally, our thanks to Lynda Clarke, Hartley's law clerk, who worked tirelessly on revising the material.

PROLEGOMENON

As Sherlock Holmes once said of himself, "Age doth not wither nor custom stale my infinite variety."[1] How true; superficially it already appears to be a crowded field and the Sherlockian world has been explored from Founding Father (later Monsignor) Ronald Knox's seminal 1911 paper though Sir Sidney Roberts, Dorothy Sayers, Christopher Morley, William S. Baring-Gould and others down to the monumental efforts of Leslie S. Klinger's three volume *The New Annotated Sherlock Holmes* and his ten volume Sherlock Holmes Reference Library. But two leading Toronto Holmesians, Clifford Goldfarb and Hartley Nathan have proved with their collected papers in this handsome small volume that ample room remains for careful scholarship and good writing.

Since it is possible that some readers might be unfamiliar with the subject, a word for their benefit is in order.

Apart from enjoyment of the four novels and fifty-six short stories comprising the Sherlockian "Canon," there are two broad categories. The first are what are called *pastiches*, novels or stories which take the characters of Holmes and Watson and create new tales, in some cases building on unreported cases mentioned by Dr Watson, such as "The Giant Rat of Sumatra" or "Colonel Warburton's Madness", and in others introducing Holmes into wholly new situations.

---

1 "The Adventure of the Empty House", Enobarbus to Caesar's friend Macenus, *Antony and Cleopatra*, Act II, scene 2 (Shakespeare)

Such novels range from well-written, entertaining tales of Holmes and 1888's "Jack the Ripper", or of an aging Holmes marrying a younger woman of comparable intelligence and toughness, to what Watson called "ineffable twaddle."

The other main stream of Sherlockian writing, the stream in which this book proudly sails, is what is sometimes grandly called the "Higher Criticism" (a term borrowed from Biblical scholarship and sharing a few of its characteristics, including in some cases tedious pedantry) and is otherwise called "the Great Game." The Great Game takes the Holmesian Canon as the factual accounts of real investigations, and seeks to apply genuine techniques of exegesis or historical, scientific and factual research to expand on the Canonical accounts. Sometimes names or situations which would be familiar to a High Victorian reader require explanation to a 21st century audience; sometimes the Watsonian chronology or reporting of the case is confusing or perhaps even deliberately misleading, as where dates or names are camouflaged to protect the innocent (or even the guilty); sometimes Canonical references to persons, places or events simply invite further research.

There is even a legitimate arena in the Great Game for scholarship seeking to establish that Holmes was wrong in his solution of a case: that snakes cannot in fact climb bell-pulls as suggested in "The Speckled Band" or that Jonathan Small is highly unlikely to have dumped the Agra treasure from the launch Aurora into the Thames as reported in *The Sign of the Four*. There is a paper at the back of this book "Regina vs Moran", which offers evidence that the solution of a murder in "The Empty House" by means of an air-gun, and the suggested motive, solo cheating at whist, are both impossible.[2]

---

2 The paper in this volume, "Regina vs. Moran", in this volume, an account of the trial of Colonel Sebastian Moran for the murder of Ronald Adair, fits into this genre of "Holmes was wrong" papers and was in fact written by me. It is based on the precise facts of the murder as set out in the Canonical "Adventure of the Empty House" evaluated in light of ballistic and other facts derived from the works of the leading Victorian firearms authority Mr William Wellington Greener and others. It is included in this volume for two reasons: First, Messrs Nathan and Goldfarb were consulted extensively during its preparation and rendered valuable advice on British criminal practice; and second, because Sir George Lewis, the subject of one of the most important papers in this volume, figures as instructing solicitor for defense counsel.

Messrs Nathan and Goldfarb have carved out their own specialty: the Jewish aspects and references in the Canon, and applied to it their combined skills in genuine research and clear expository writing.[3] It is not too much to say, in the jargon of 2014, that "they own this part" of the Great Game.

I realize my admiring comments may be discounted on the grounds of personal bias, since for decades I have been honoured to regard them both as close friends. However, I have been a duly-commissioned Baker Street Irregular for over forty years, and for five of those years edited the *Baker Street Journal*. Over those decades I have read, both for pleasure and from the stern call of duty, a great deal of Sherlockian writing so you may safely believe that I know good scholarship when I read it.

Seven of the papers are "The Jewish Connection" papers. One paper will suffice to show how useful this research is to a deeper appreciation of Holmes's life and times: "Oh Sinner Man", on Conan Doyle and the brilliant solicitor and all- around legal fixer Sir George Henry Lewis, Bart (1833-1911), who was a good friend of the Prince of Wales, later Edward VII. Mentioned in the Sherlockian "Adventure of the Illustrious Client," Sir George had many 'illustrious clients' and was like Holmes a friend in need even to royalty in peril from blackmailers, society toffs involved in card-cheating scandals and the like. He is also an exemplar of the turnabout in High Victorian and Edwardian days, that is, the days of Sherlock's prime, in attitudes toward Jews.[4]

---

3 Toronto, "no mean city" of which both authors are natives and lifelong citizens, is an appropriate venue from which to launch a compendium on Jewish connections in the Holmesian Canon. The city's Jewish population dates from the arrival of English-born Arthur Wellington Hart (1813-91) in 1832 when the city was still called York, Upper Canada. It became centred around Holy Blossom Synagogue founded in 1856 (whose curious name, unique so far as I know, comes from the Talmudic reference to young men preparing for the priesthood as 'holy blossoms', *pichay kodesh* in Hebrew. In its early days, Toronto's Jewish community was prosperous, Anglophone and Anglophile.

4 Queen Victoria's beloved Prime Minister Benjamin Disraeli, later Earl of Beaconsfield (1804-71) was born into an Italian Jewish family which had come to England, but following a dispute with his synagogue his father had him baptized in the Church of England. Born and remaining proudly Jewish, however, besides Sir George Lewis, were [i] Rufus Isaacs, first Marquess of Reading (1860-1935), who served as Attorney General, Ambassador to the United States, Lord Chief Justice of England, and Viceroy of India, and [ii] Nathan, Lord Rothschild (1840-1915), Cambridge school chum of Prince of Wales and powerful financier. Under the Prince's leadership, anti-Semitism had become rather *declasse*.

The succeeding sections of the book address various subjects, but not surprisingly concentrate on Canadian connections. The only Canadian who figures prominently in the Canon is Sir Henry Baskerville, who returned to give Holmes an adventure on Dartmoor with the hound. Sir Henry's purloined boot was made by a Toronto bootmaker[5] who gave his name to the leading Canadian society of Holmes devotees.

I am grateful for the honour of writing this Prolegomenon to this fine work of scholarship.

John Linsenmeyer
Baker Street Irregular
Pondicherry Lodge
Riverside, Connecticut

---

5 The 1896 Toronto City Directory lists, MEIER, JOSEPH, BOOT AND SHOEMAKER, 547 QUEEN STREET WEST (p. 1493). He is also listed with the same trade in the alphabetical section at p. 1038. It would require no mean level of quibbling to doubt that this is indeed the bootmaker patronized by Sir Henry Baskerville, Bart. before he returned to the land—and the curse—of his forefathers.

AN INTRODUCTION TO SHERLOCK HOLMES

This is an updated version of a paper presented by Hartley Nathan to the Academy for Lifelong Learning, University of Toronto on November 24, 2004

It is a safe assumption that enthusiasts for detective fiction, whatever their country or nationality, if asked to name the three most famous fictional detectives, will begin with Sherlock Holmes. In the long list of amateur sleuths down the last nine decades, he remains unique, the unchallenged Great Detective, whose brilliant deductive intelligence could outwit any adversary, however cunning, and solve any puzzle, however bizarre. In the decades following his creator's death in 1930, he has become an icon.[1]

According to *A Study in Scarlet*, the first Sherlock Holmes story,[2] Sherlock Holmes and his long time partner, Dr. John H. Watson first met in March, 1881 at the lab at St. Bartholomew's Hospital in London, England.

To the Sherlockians the meeting at St. Bart's was the start of a partnership that saw them through four decades of adventures which

---

1 P.D. James: *Talking About Detective Fiction* (Alfred A. Knopf, New York, 2009) at pp. 27 – 29.

2 Published in *Beeton's Christmas Annual* December 1887.

Dr. Watson faithfully recorded. Sherlockians say that Dr. Watson chronicled the stories and Sir Arthur Conan Doyle was the literary agent who saw they were published. There were a total of 56 short stories and 4 novels which Sherlockians affectionately call the "Sacred Writings" or the "Canon". There were, many more adventures which were not published.

Sherlock Holmes's creator Sir Arthur Conan Doyle

In "The Problem of Thor Bridge", Dr. Watson makes the following statement:

> Somewhere in the vaults of the bank of Cox and Co., at Charing Cross, there is a travel-worn and battered tin dispatch box with my name, John H. Watson, M.D., Late Indian Army, painted upon the lid. It is crammed with papers, nearly all of which are records of cases to illustrate the curious problems which Mr. Sherlock Holmes had at various times to examine.

Unfortunately, Cox and Co. was destroyed during the Second World War blitz, and the tin box disappeared.

Why is it that the stories and the character Sherlock Holmes appeal to so many people in every part of the world? Why are so many articles and books written, speeches given, debates conducted? Why do new societies spring up all over the world dedicated to the study of Sherlock Holmes? Why do people from all parts of the world to this day still write to Sherlock Holmes at 221 Baker Street, London, soliciting his help? Why would someone coin a phrase like: "It is said of Sherlock Holmes that he never existed, but will never die?" I have a few thoughts on the matter:

1. Sherlock Holmes himself is drawn as a unique individual with marked aloofness from commonplace affairs, a dedication to ratiocination, a disdain for the opposite sex (with one enthralling exception), and a hard edge to his character that permits no weakness except cocaine and nicotine addictions. Not the least of his attributes is a knowledge of medicine which appears to exceed that of his medical foil, the all too human Dr. John H. Watson.

2. The setting of the stories. The stories are set in late Victorian London, a time of gentility and adventure, an innocent age when all was right in England and the world. The British Empire was at the height of its greatness and England was the centre of the world. Dense fog lies low over the great city—a perfect setting for a mystery—dim figures scuttle through the gloom. The stories are a kaleidoscopic record of bowler hats, hansom cabs, fogs—few telephones to complicate the business of life—letters posted in the morning arrived in the afternoon.

3. Very compelling also is the sense of realism provided by graphic descriptions of real world geography and

climate and by references to actual events of the day and, in the medical areas, by the mention of instruments, hospitals, societies and publications (some fancied and some real).

4. But perhaps the greatest appeal for the modern day reader lies in the atmosphere that permeates the adventures. They are rich in the ambience of the Victorian era in England: a time when Britain ruled the seas, when the world was more tranquil, civilized, and manageable, and when humanity seemed poised on the brink of remarkable achievements in all areas of endeavour. So vivid are the narratives that one can almost hear the hansom cabs splashing through the rain and rattling down the uneven streets of London, shrouded in the yellow fog muting the flickering gas-lamps. It is this atmosphere especially which spawns an awesome sense of mystery and makes the meeting of evil face to face by Holmes and Watson seem all too real.

5. Lets face it, we are living in chaotic and discouraging times and everything seems to have a tendency to be going downhill, so it is rather pleasant to have a return in fantasy to days of much greater certainty, of a much greater spirit of optimism, an era in which there was a fixed belief that solutions existed to problems.

6. The methods of Sherlock Holmes are remarkable and are applied to specialized cases for the most part, fantastic crime. He makes it look so easy. He makes deductions and explains them in plausible detail. The characters are unforgettable.

7. Likewise there are the unforgettable cliches, the calls to adventure, the profound statements. "Come Watson, the game is afoot." *The Sign of Four* gives us examples of Holmes' wit: "Women are never to be entirely trusted -not the best of them" or "...when

you have eliminated the impossible, whatever remains, however improbable, must be the truth" or the statement he never makes, "Elementary my dear Watson" (shades of "Play it again, Sam" alleged to have been said by Bogart in *Casablanca*).

8. The universality of the stories, like the Bible there is something in the stories for just about everyone to relate to.

9. Sherlock Holmes himself. He is a hero that can be identified with. It is comforting to have him on our side. Through the adventures we learn the astonishing extent of Holmes' knowledge. We can admire all of his attributes but one, his habit of taking drugs. Fortunately he only took drugs when he was bored and after the Great Hiatus appears to have been cured of the habit.

I thought it might be informative if I gave you a brief chronology of the highlights of his life, and told you a little about his character. I would also like to tell you a bit about the people, real and fictional that Sherlock Holmes knew or read about and how they may have influenced him and the extent to which he has received worldwide recognition.

Sherlock Holmes was born on Friday, January 6, 1854 in Yorkshire, England, the third son of Siger Holmes and Violet Sherrinford.

In October of 1872 he entered Christchurch College at Oxford and it was here that Sherlock Holmes was asked by his classmate Victor Trevor to try his hand at solving his first case, one which was later recorded under the title of "The Gloria Scott."

On Monday, October 18th, 1879, Holmes made his first appearance on the London stage as Horatio in Hamlet.

As I mentioned earlier, it was in March of 1881 that Dr. Watson was introduced to Sherlock Holmes and thereafter they took rooms together at 221B Baker Street in London.

Many cases followed in the ensuing years.

One case of extreme importance took place on Friday May 20th to Sunday, May 22nd, 1887 and was chronicled under the name "A Scandal in Bohemia." It was then that Sherlock Holmes first met the "daintiest thing under a bonnet on this planet" namely Irene Adler, who to Holmes was always *the* woman.

Another case of note, particularly to Torontonians, took place between September 25th and October 20th, 1888 and is perhaps the most well known, namely *The Hound of the Baskervilles*. Here Sherlock Holmes in pursuit of Sir Charles Baskerville's killer reaches into the Grimpen Mire and pulls out an object. The Canon says: "He held an old black boot in the air. Meyers, Toronto was printed on the leather inside." I'll come back to this later.

It was in the spring of 1891 that Sherlock Holmes first talked to Watson about the evil genius Professor James Moriarty. It was on Monday, May 4th, 1891 that Sherlock Holmes and Professor Moriarty were locked in mortal combat at Reichenbach Falls, near Meiringen, Switzerland. Both appeared to have tumbled into the torrent and perished. It was then that Dr. Watson thought that he had lost the person who was to him "the best and wisest man whom I have ever known."

Between May 1891 and April of 1894, there occurred what is called the "Great Hiatus", during which time all the world thought that Sherlock Holmes was dead.

Then on that glorious day, Thursday, April 5th, 1894, a bookseller came into Dr. Watson's study and who should it turn out to be? It was Sherlock Holmes. He had of course a plausible explanation as to how he avoided being killed at Reichenbach Falls and where he had been for the three years. I quote from "The Empty House":

> I traveled for two years in Tibet, therefore, and amused myself by visiting Lhassa and spending some days with the head Llama. You may have read of the remarkable explorations of a Norwegian named Sigerson, but I am sure that it never occurred to

you that you were receiving news of your friend. I then passed through Persia, looked in at Mecca, and paid a short but interesting visit to the Khalifa at Khartoum, the results of which I have communicated to the Foreign Office. Returning to France I spent some months in a research into the coal-tar derivatives, which I conducted in a laboratory at Montpelier, in the South of France.

Many more adventures followed in the series called *The Return of Sherlock Holmes*.

In late October, 1903, Sherlock Holmes retired to keep bees in Sussex Downs.

In August of 1914 he came out of retirement to the aid of his country to capture the notorious German spy Von Bork in a case which was called "His Last Bow." It was after this adventure that Holmes and Watson parted, never to meet again.

As for his character he was a positive enigma. He did so many things so well and others not at all. If you read the stories, many things about him will become apparent to you. Shortly after they met, Dr. Watson made this list in *A Study in Scarlet*.

SHERLOCK HOLMES—HIS LIMITS

1. Knowledge of Literature.—Nil.
2.   "   " Philosophy. – Nil.
3.   "   " Astronomy.—Nil.
4.   "   " Politics.—Feeble.
5.   "   " Botany.—Variable. Well up in belladonna, opium and poisons generally, knows nothing of practical gardening.
6.   "   " Geology.—Practical but limited. Tells at a glance different soils from each other. After walks has shown me splashes on his trousers and told me by their col-

our and consistence in what part of London he had received them.

7.   "   " Chemistry.—Profound.

8.   "   " Anatomy.—Accurate but unsystematic.

9.   "   " Sensational Literature.—Immense, he appears to know every detail of every horror perpetrated in the century.

10. Plays the violin well.

11. Is an expert singlestick player, boxer and swordsman.

12. Has a good practical knowledge of British law.

Since then we have found out he was proficient in many other areas although it took other commentators on the stories to point some of these things out. For example, he was a skilled mountaineer, a linguist of some note, a gourmet extraordinaire, an oenophile and wrote monographs on many topics ranging from tobaccos to newspaper type.

The most outstanding attributes were his uncanny powers of observation—his methodology—and his logical mind.

"He was the most perfect reasoning and observing machine that the world has ever seen," according to Dr. Watson.

If I take the heretic approach and admit that Arthur Conan Doyle really wrote the stories, who did he base Sherlock Holmes on? For one, Dr. Joseph Bell. The famous Dr. Joseph Bell was a surgeon who practiced at the Edinburgh Infirmary, at the same time that Doyle was a student of medicine at Edinburgh University.

Dr. Bell had remarkable powers of reasoning and skills of perception. He had phenomenal diagnostic abilities. He would not only declare the identity of a patient's illness, but would also describe the patient's occupation and character simply from observation. Let us take an example. This is from *Lancet*, British medical journal for August 1, 1956.

A woman with a small child was shown in. Joe Bell said good morning to her and she said good morning in reply. 'What sort of a crossing di' ye have fra' Burntisland?' 'It was quid.' 'And had ye a guid walk up Inverleith

Row?' 'Yes.' 'And what did ye do with th' other wain?' 'I left him with my sister in Leith.' 'And would ye still be working at the linoleum factory?' 'Yes, I am.' 'You see gentlemen, when she said good morning to me I noted her Fife accent, and, as you know, the nearest town in Fife is Burntisland. You noticed the red clay on the edges of the soles of her shoes, and the only such clay within twenty miles of Edinburgh is in the Botanical Gardens. Inverleigh Row borders the gardens and is her nearest way here from Leith. You observed that the coat she carried over her arm is too big for the child who is with her, and therefore she set out from home with two children. Finally, she has dermatitis on the fingers of the right hand which is peculiar to workers in the linoleum factory at Burntisland.'

Compare this with the following dialogue between Sherlock Holmes and Helen Stonor from "The Speckled Band":

'You have come by train this morning, I see.' 'You know me then?' 'No, but I observe the second half of a return ticket in the palm of your left glove. You must have started early, and yet you had a good drive in a dog-cart, along heavy roads, before you reached the station.' The lady gave a violent start, and stared in bewilderment at my companion. 'There is no mystery, my dear madam' said he, smiling. 'The left arm of your jacket is spattered with mud in no less than seven places. The marks are perfectly fresh. There is no vehicle save a dog-cart which throws up mud in that way, and then only when you sit on the left-hand side of the driver.' 'Whatever your reasons may be, you are perfectly correct, 'she said. 'I started from home before six, reached Leatherhead at twenty past, and came in by the first train to Waterloo.'

But Sherlock Holmes went beyond Dr. Bell. He was a man who reduced the pursuit of criminals to an exact science. By the study of footprints, mud, dust, the use of chemistry, geology, he could reconstruct the scene of the crime as though he had been there—all of this when no system of scientific criminology existed and there were no crime scene investigation television programs as there are today.

INFLUENCES

I have already told you that his knowledge of sensational literature was immense. He read everything relating to early detectives such as the literature of Poe, Gaboriau and Collins, who set the pattern after which detectives were made.

The world's first full-length classical detective story was said to be *Caleb Williams* written by William Godwin, Mary Shelley's father and published in 1794.[3] It was followed by Edgar Allan Poe in 1841 in, "Murders in the Rue Morgue," featuring Auguste Dupin. Poe wrote two other stories featuring Dupin, namely "The Purloined Letter" and "The Mystery of Marie Roget."

Emile Gaboriau (1833 – 1873) was a French writer fascinated by police work, who had a working knowledge of the operations of the Sûreté. He created a policeman hero named Lecoq, who was adept at analyzing clues. He is able to tell his assistant in *Le Crime d'Orcival* that a man they are following is "of middle age and tall, wore a shaggy brown overcoat, and was probably married as he had a wedding ring on the little finger of his right hand". The points are explained: his "heavy and dragging step" shown in convenient snow, marked middle age, his height was marked by a block of granite on which he had leaned, the ring appeared through the imprint of his hand in snow, the colour of his coat was indicated by a few flakes of brown wool torn off by a wood splinter.

---

3 See P.D. James, *supra*, footnote 1 at p. 16

In more modern times, Wilkie Collins wrote his classical detective novel, *The Moonstone* in 1868 with the London detective Sergeant Cuff being called in to investigate the theft of a valuable diamond.

Sergeant Cuff appears only once in Wilkie Collins' writings, but makes a wrong guess as to "who dunnit". There is no question, however, that Collins and Gaboriau influenced Sherlock Holmes' development but the strongest influence is that of Poe. There are many similarities between Poe's Dupin and Sherlock Holmes which become apparent when the two characters are compared, but Sherlock Holmes is a more interesting person. Sherlock Holmes learned much from Dupin's methodology.

Sherlock Holmes also had much in common with Doyle himself. Let us compare some shared characteristics:

1. Both were partial towards old dressing gowns, clay pipes, keeping documents and lacking the time to arrange them.
2. Both worked with a magnifying glass on their desks and a pistol in the drawer.
3. Holmes' and Conan Doyle's ancestors were "country squires".
4. Both had the same bank.
5. Holmes refused a knighthood in the same year and month that Conan Doyle was knighted.
6. Both were respected criminologists. Conan Doyle interested himself in many real-life cases. He showed his own skill in the analysis of the case of Oscar Slater who was sentenced to death in 1909 for a brutal murder. Conan Doyle fought an intensive battle to prove his innocence, and won Slater his freedom in 1927. Likewise, he exposed the prosecution's weak evidence in the conviction and imprisonment of George Edalji in 1903 for horse maiming. After Edalji was released, Conan Doyle used his influence to mount a national campaign to establish Edalji's

innocence. He also agreed to serve on the Support Committee along with Sir George Lewis, perhaps the most famous solicitor of his day.[4]

ANALYSIS OF THE STORIES

Many writers feel that there is something hidden under the surface of the adventures. Martin Gardner in his Introduction to the *Annotated Alice in Wonderland* referred to G. K. Chesterton's "dreadful fear" that Alice's story had already fallen under the heavy hands of the scholars and was becoming "cold and monumental like a classic tomb". He says there is much to be said for Chesterton's plea not to take Alice too seriously.

He goes on to say that in preparing his annotated edition that he had done his best to avoid allegorical and psychoanalytical exegesis. Gardiner says that, like Homer, the Bible and all other great works of fantasy, the Alice books "lend themselves readily to any type of symbolic interpretation—political, metaphysical or Freudian. One commentator found Alice a secret history of religious controversies of Victorian England. The jar of orange marmalade for example is the symbol of Protestantism (William of Orange—Get it?), the battle of the white and red knights is the famous clash of Thomas Huxley and Bishop Samuel Wilberforce. The Cheshire Cat was Cardinal Nicholas Wiseman and the Jabberwocky could only be a fearsome representation of the British view of the papacy."

Much of the same can be said and has been said about the Sherlock Holmes stories. Conan Doyle has been described as a "highly compulsive, self-revealing allegorist who had artfully implanted a large number of clues among his stories. These clues profoundly associate Doyle and Sherlock Holmes and his companions with several "real life, fictional, legendary, and Biblical figures."[5]

---

4 See our paper "O Sinner Man: Who You Gonna Run o: Sir Arthur and Sir George."

5 See Samuel Rosenberg: *Naked is the Best Disguise*, The Bobbs-Merrill Company, Inc., Indianapolis & New York, 1946 at p. 144

Apart from having had a proper classical Victorian education, Conan Doyle was a voracious reader and a social animal who mingled with many of the important literary types of the day and was of course influenced by many of those that he met and talked with.

Joseph Marshall Stoddart was a Philadelphian and had for many years been the editor of *The Encyclopedia Americana*.

He brought Oscar Wilde to lecture across the States. He became Managing Editor of *Lippincott's Monthly Magazine* in January, 1889. Anxious to obtain distinguished contributors he sailed to London, contacted Conan Doyle and Oscar Wilde and invited them to supper at the Langham Hotel in London. Stoddart was a genial host and Wilde in good form told witty stories. The result of the supper was that Conan Doyle was commissioned to write *The Sign of Four*, while Wilde was commissioned and in due course provided *Lippincott's* with the immortal *The Picture of Dorian Gray*.

What about Oscar Wilde? There are oblique but identifiable references to Wilde in at least one of the stories. Oscar Wilde is described in a biography as having had "thick purple tinged sensual lips, uneven discoloured teeth..." and when he talked "he frequently put a bent finger over his mouth to show that he was conscious of his unattractive teeth."[6] (By the way it is thought his bad teeth resulted from mercury taken to cure syphilis in those days).

In *The Sign of Four* here is how Thaddeus Sholto is described:

> Nature had given him a pendulous lip and a too visible line of yellow and irregular teeth which he feebly strove to conceal by constantly passing his hand over the lower part of his face.

Just as a matter of interest, what was the significance of the name "Sholto"? Curious name "Sholto." The Marquess of Queensberry's name was John Sholto Douglas. The Marquess plagued Wilde who had

---

6 See Hesketh Pearson: *Oscar Wilde: His Life and His Wit*, Harper & Brothers Publishers, New York and London, 1946 at p. 144.

a torrid affair going with his son Lord Alfred Douglas. This of course led to Wilde charging the Marquess with criminal libel which started Wilde's downward spiral.

The Movies

The Sherlock Holmes that needs no introduction to you is the Sherlock Holmes that is the subject of numerous radio and television dramatizations, movies and plays. One of the most notable Holmes was, of course, Basil Rathbone, who together with Nigel Bruce who played Watson, made a total of 14 Sherlock Holmes' movies, two for 20th Century Fox and twelve for Universal, between 1939 and 1946. They also worked together in a Sherlock Holmes radio series during this period. Another early Holmes was Eille Norwood, who made 47 films in the 1920's which were faithful to the original stories. There have been other Sherlock Holmes, for example, a Canadian, Raymond Massey, 1931; John Barrymore, 1922—in one of the last silent films; Ronald Howard, son of Leslie Howard who made a series of 39 films in 1953-54; Peter Cushing, (1965) John Neville, *A Study in Terror* and Robert Stephens in 1971.

Another Sherlock Holmes movie was a Canadian film *Murder by Decree* in 1979 starring another Canadian, Christopher Plummer as Holmes and James Mason as Dr. Watson. Here, Sherlock Holmes helps discover the identity of Jack The Ripper.

There have been two hugely successful movies recently, *Sherlock Holmes* (2009) starring Robert Downey Jr. as Holmes, Jude Law as Watson, Rachel McAdam (Canadian) as Irene Adler and *Sherlock Holmes: A Game of Shadows* (2011) again starring Robert Downey Jr. and Jude Law, loosely based on "The Final Problem."

Plummer also played Holmes in a made for television version of "Silver Blaze." Plays also, such as *Baker Street* a musical, which was performed on Broadway in 1978.

The Speckled Band, which played in Toronto in 1976 at the St. Lawrence Centre, was written by Arthur Conan Doyle in 2 weeks in 1910 and was first performed in June of that year. The play *Sherlock*

Holmes, also here in 1976 at the O'Keefe Centre (now the Sony Centre) starred Robert Stephens. It was first performed in the United States in Buffalo in 1899 and in England in 1901, where one of the cast members was Charles Chaplin who played the part of Billy the page boy. This was written by William Gillette, an American actor who made a career out of portraying Sherlock Holmes.

There was also *The Incredible Murder of Cardinal Tosca,* which played at the St. Lawrence Centre in 1978.

Someone took a count and estimated there were over 150 movies, more than 75 television productions and 20 plays.[7]

Sherlock Holmes himself "loathed every form of society with his whole Bohemian soul" so it is not surprising he refused any part in the numerous dramatizations of his adventures on the stage and in films despite the fact he was an accomplished actor.

TELEVISION

From 1984 to 1995 Jeremy Brett portrayed Sherlock Holmes in a television series where David Burke portrayed Watson in 13 episodes and Edward Hardwicke in the remainder of the series which almost faithfully transferred some 41 episodes of the stories to TV. They actually covered 42 of the 60 stories of the Canon as the last one includes both "The Three Garridebs" and "The Mazarin Stone." In the latter, Brett appears only briefly, due to illness, so the detecting is done by Sherlock's brother Mycroft. Unfortunately, Jeremy Brett died in 1995 before another series could be televised. Many feel he had eclipsed Basil Rathbone as *the* Sherlock Holmes.

There are two new television series, one set in modern day London called "Sherlock" with Benedict Cumberbatch as Sherlock Holmes and Martin Freeman as Dr. Watson. Series one premiered in 2010,

---

7 Noted Sherlockian, the late John Bennett Shaw, so stated in "The Cult of Sherlock Holmes" in a lecture in 1975. See the "Norwegian Explorers Omnibus" 2007 published by The Norwegian Explorers of Minnesota. The number of television productions and plays has increased significantly in the past few years.

series two in 2012 and as third went into production in March, 2013. A second "Elementary", set in modern day New York, starring Johnny Lee Miller as Sherlock and Lucy Liu as Watson premiered on September 27, 2012 and is continuing.

BOOKS

As mentioned earlier, scatte and "Sherlock in Jerusalem" vanbered throughout the stories are references to some of the unpublished cases, some with fascinating names like "Ricoletti of the Club Foot and His Abominable Wife", "Vamberry the wine merchant" and "The Giant Rat of Sumatra".

Adrian Conan Doyle, Sir Arthur's son, wrote so-called accounts of six of these stories, the series being called the *Exploits of Sherlock Holmes*. He then collaborated with John Dickson Carr and wrote an additional six, this series being called *More Exploits of Sherlock Holmes*. They were all in the John H. Watson tradition. August Derleth in the mid 40's wrote a series of stories of Solar Pons and Dr. Parker, but stopped when the *Exploits* came out. After Adrian Conan Doyle's death Derleth wrote several more. There have been many other imitators, perhaps the most well-known being Nicholas Meyer, who wrote *The Seven Per Cent Solution*, which was a best seller, and was made into a successful movie starring Vanessa Redgrave and Sir Lawrence Olivier. He had written another book as well called *The West End Horror* involving Oscar Wilde, Gilbert & Sullivan, Sherlock Holmes and Dr. Watson. Others include *Dr. Jekyll & Mr. Holmes*, *Sherlock Holmes v. Dracula* and *The Stalwart Companions*, the latter brings Teddy Roosevelt together with Holmes and Watson. There were two recent best sellers, Lindsay Faye: *Dust and Shadows* (2009) and Anthony Horowitz: *The House of Silk* (2011). There are several Sherlock Holmes cookbooks. Vol. 31, No. 2 issue of *The Sherlock Holmes Journal* for summer 2013, the publication of the Sherlock Society of London, lists no less than 17 new books on Sherlock Holmes or Conan Doyle. All of these would have paid a royalty to Conan Doyle's estate. Now, however, more than 50 years has passed since Doyle's death in 1930 and the stories have fallen into public domain everywhere in the world except that some of the stories in *The Casebook of Sherlock Holmes* are still protected in the United States.[8]

SIR ARTHUR CONAN DOYLE

A talk about Sherlock Holmes would not be complete without a reference to Sir Arthur Conan Doyle, his creator. Born May 22, 1859 in Edinburgh, he died July 7, 1930. He was a graduate doctor. The Medical Directory for 1888 contains the following entry:

> Doyle, A.C. Bush Villa, Elmgrove, Southsea, M.D. 1885, M.B., C.M., 1881. University of Edinburgh. Author—"Action of a Gelsemium Sempervireus". Brit. Med. Journ. 1879. Notes on leucocythaema. Lancet 1885.

After unsuccessfully writing a few short stories, his first Sherlock Holmes story, *A Study in Scarlet* was accepted for publication in 1886 when Ward, Locke and Company purchased the same for £25 for the entire copyright. The story was published in *Beeton's Christmas Annual* for December of 1887. The first American edition was published in Philadelphia in *Lippincott's* magazine in March of 1890. *The Sign of Four* followed in *Lippincott's* magazine. In July of 1891, A "Scandal in Bohemia" was published in *The Strand Magazine* in England and the rest of the Sherlock Holmes stories appeared in the *Strand* with the 60th and last being "Shoscombe Old Place"", which was published in March of 1927. Doyle was a prolific writer having written more than 60 other books during his lifetime, many of which have become classics—just

---

8 At the time of publication, the US Court of Appeals had upheld a lower court decision limiting the scope of copyright in the U.S. to 10 tales in *The Casebook*, which expire between 2012 and 2018. Characters, plots and tales in stories published prior to 1923 are fully in the public domian in the U.S. The Conan Doyle Estate is seeking leave to appeal the decision to the U.S. Supreme Court.

to name one or two, *The White Company* and *The Lost World*. In addition, he published many, many short stories, horror stories, mystery stories and stories on spiritualism, with which he was closely connected until the time of his death.

He was throughout his long and eventful life a man of strong character, great patriotism, unlimited interests, active curiosity, droll humour, pervasive romanticism, intense sincerity, righteous humaneness, and surprising naivete. These diverse characteristics were unified by a keen sense of the past, the present, the future, and the spiritual. Quite understandably, therefore, the Sherlock Holmes tales are marked by the presence of vividly drawn characters and imaginative incidents. And as a result of his professional training, they feature an abundance of allusions of a medical nature as well. It is the extensiveness and variety of the latter that comes as a surprise to some when it is pointed out that there are mentioned in the 56 Stories and four novels a total of 68 diseases, 32 additional medical terms, 38 doctors, 22 drugs, 12 medically related specialties, three medical schools and two medical journals.

I was honoured in January, 2002 to address the Baker Street Irregulars at the B.S.I. dinner on "Sherlock Holmes in Canada." Let me give you some highlights. I tried to demonstrate that Sir Arthur Conan Doyle's visits to Canada, especially Toronto, had a profound influence on his writings in the Canon.

Sir Arthur visited Canada four times. The first visit was on Sunday, November 25, 1894. This was less than a year after Holmes was supposedly killed at Reichenbach Falls in "The Final Problem." This story was published in the December, 1893 issue of the *The Strand Magazine*. Sir Arthur crossed the border at Buffalo and went to Niagara Falls for a sightseeing trip en route to Toronto. After seeing the Falls, "he told his ailing wife that Niagara Falls and not those at Reichenbach should have been where Holmes and his enemy had met their deaths."[9]

---

9 Michael Coren: *Conan Doyle*, Stoddart Publishing Co. Ltd., Toronto, 1995, at p. 86.

I believe Sir Arthur had his "epiphany" then. My take on what he *really* said, was "after Niagara Falls, Reichenbach Falls was a piece of cake." It was then he realized that Holmes could have survived Reichenbach.

A little background to the 1894 visit. Goldwin Smith was once Regius Professor of history at Oxford, where he was a personal tutor to the Prince of Wales. He worked alongside Thackeray at the *Saturday Review* and dined with Dickens at the Athenaeum Club. He was one of the first professors at the recently established Cornell University. He showed little interest in the opposite sex. In fact the decision to admit women caused him to leave Cornell. However, he married the widow Harriett Bolton in Toronto and moved into her home, the Grange, said to be the most magnificent house in Toronto at the time. It is now part of the Art Gallery of Ontario. Unfortunately Sir Arthur had to decline an invitation to stay there when he arrived in Toronto on November 26, 1894.[10] That night, Goldwin Smith introduced Sir Arthur to an audience of 1500 people at Massey Hall, a facility still standing today. In his introductory remarks, Goldwin Smith stated on behalf of thousands of readers he hoped that Sherlock Holmes would enjoy "a speedy resurrection, for they all deplore his death."

Sir Arthur dined with Professor Smith on November 26, 1894. Joseph Meier (or Mayer) a boot and shoe manufacturer had his shop on Queen Street, one short block from the Grange. I believe Smith may have discussed how good a bootmaker Meier was. While there is no evidence Sir Arthur bought boots while in Toronto, I believe he named the bootmaker "Meyers, Toronto" out of deference to Smith.[11]

There is no doubt that Goldwin Smith was by this time Toronto's leading man of letters. Clearly his influence was so profound that Sir Arthur

---

10 Conan Doyle stayed with his friend Dr. Pickering on Sherbourne Street, in a house that is still standing. However, it is recorded that Doyle and other luminaries such as the poet Matthew Arnold and the biographer John Morley included Toronto in their North American speaking terms so they could be guests at the Grange.

11 See Donald A. Redmond: *Sherlock Holmes, a Study in Sources* (McGill-Queens Press, Kingston and Montreal, 1982) at p. 108 and "The Original Mr. Meyers" in *Canadian Holmes: The First Twenty-Five Years* at p. 209.

decided to resurrect Sherlock Holmes. A scant seven years after his visit to Toronto, *The Strand Magazine* published the first instalment of *The Hound*.

There are other indicators as to how much Smith and Toronto influenced Conan Doyle. To wit: the Grange was by far the most important residence in Toronto. "The Abbey Grange" was published in *The Strand Magazine* in 1904. "The Solitary Cyclist" with its reference to Chiltern Grange was also published in 1904. In "Wisteria Lodge" published in September, 1908, High Gable is called a "Jacobean grange". Most important, there are no references to "a grange" before 1894.

Conan Doyle would constantly comment on a variety of social and political issues. He took an active, personal role in fighting for the freedom of two men wrongly convicted, in part because one was a "halfcaste" (George Edalji) and the other a Jew (Oscar Slater). He lobbied to establish an appellate court system to quash false verdicts, championed divorce reform, and urged the development of education for deaf children. His political activism included support for Irish Home Rule, exposing Belgian atrocities in *The Crime of the Congo,* warning about the danger of German submarine warfare, and lobbying for all sailors to be equipped with "inflatable rubber lifebelts" and all soldiers with metal breastplates or body shields.[12]

THE SOCIETIES

Sherlock Holmes used several of the local street urchins in the neighbourhood to ferret out information for him. He called them "The Baker Street Irregulars". The Baker Street Irregulars is now the most prestigious of the Sherlock Holmes societies. It was created in the offices of the *Saturday Review of Literature* by Christopher Morley some time in 1933, its purpose was to study the 60 tales recorded by Dr. Watson. Like other learned and scientific societies the members

---

12 See Michael Keen: "Dickens, Conan Doyle and Holmes ": (2012) Vol. 62, No. 4 *Baker Street Journal* 14 at pp. 15-16.

exchanged notes of research and contributed papers to the general knowledge on Sherlock Holmes. The first formal meeting took place in June of 1934. Now an annual dinner is held close to the anniversary of Holmes' birth, which Christopher Morley had worked out as falling on January 6th. The dinner itself usually takes place on the first Friday night in January, and, since 1991, includes women as invitees among the 160 or so that attend annually. Each year up to as many as 17 persons, again including women, are made members of the Baker Street Irregulars and given an investiture also derived from the stories. An inductee is allowed to write a pseudonym after the initials "B.S.I.". I was investitured in January, 1980 as "The Penang Lawyer." which is a walking stick referred to in *The Hound of the Baskervilles*. The number 17, by the way, is said to be based on the number of steps up from the street to flat B at 221 Baker Street. For those Sherlockians who are not invited to the B.S.I. dinner there is a dinner held contemporaneously called the *"Baskerville Bash."*

From this well sprang many other societies in virtually every country in the world. In Canada we have societies in Halifax, Ottawa, Montreal, Toronto, Winnipeg, Saskatoon, Edmonton, Vancouver and more recently in Stratford. The name of the societies are often taken from the stories, as well. For example, The Sons of Copper Beeches in Philadelphia ("The Adventure of the Copper Beeches"); Dr. Watson's Colleagues of Lancaster, California; The Game is Afoot of Charleston, Virginia; and Toronto's chapter is called The Bootmakers of Toronto. You will recall my earlier reference to the *Hound* where Sherlock Holmes pulled out the old black boot and "Meyer's, Toronto was printed on the leather inside". Here is the full quotation:

> From amid a tuft of cotton-grass which bore it up out
> of the slime some dark thing was projecting. Holmes
> sank to his waist as he stepped from the path to seize
> it, and had we not been there to drag him out he could
> never have set his foot upon firm land again. He held
> an old black boot in the air. "Meyers, Toronto," was

> printed on the leather inside. "It is worth a mud bath,"
> said he. "It is our friend Sir Henry's missing boot."

Holmes was, of course, referring to Henry Baskerville, who had been farming in Western Canada. That was until he inherited a baronetcy from his uncle, Sir Charles Baskerville upon the latter's death as a result of the Baskerville effect. Unquestionably, Henry stopped in Toronto, at least long enough to buy a pair of boots from Mr. Meyers.

Today, the Bootmakers of Toronto is the best known Sherlock Holmes society in Canada. It was founded in 1972 by myself and six others, following a weekend Sherlock Holmes symposium at the Metro Toronto Reference Central Library (now the Toronto Reference Library) on December 4 and 5, 1971. The Bootmakers have been closely associated with the Library ever since.

The President of our club is called the Present Mr. Meyers and other officers derive their names from parts of the boot, The Treasurer is known as the Bootjack. The Bootmakers recently celebrated its 40th anniversary here in Toronto.

There are numerous journals that publish the various articles about Sherlock Holmes, *The Sherlock Holmes Journal* in London and the *Baker Street Journal* in the United States being the most prestigious. The December 1978 issue of the *Baker Street Journal* contains an article written by me where I proved that Dr. Watson lived in Toronto from 1905- 1932. Another paper I wrote based on "The Naval Treaty" was published in 1981 in the Journal. Here I proved Joseph Harrison one of the characters in that story was Jack The Ripper. Most scion societies have their own publications, *Canadian Holmes* being The Bootmakers' quarterly publication, which is sent to all members.

The Abbey National Building Society's headquarters in London occupied the spot where 221B Baker Street was located until 2002. They received mail daily from all over the world addressed to Sherlock Holmes soliciting his help.

COLLECTIONS

I would be remiss if I did not mention the Friends of the Arthur Conan Doyle Collection. Started in 1997, the Friends work closely with the Library to help maintain and enhance its substantial collection of Conan Doyle's writings. Its current Curator, the ever helpful Peggy Perdue, along with the Bootmakers, and the Friends help raise the Canadian consciousness of Sir Arthur Conan Doyle and his writings.

There are many private collectors of Conan Doyle's writings and letters etc. In May of 2004 thousands of personal papers belonging to Doyle fetched $1.7 million US at a Christie's auction.

The dispersal of these papers was controversial in the U.K. Richard Lancelyn Green, a former chairman of the Sherlock Holmes Society of London and the author of several books on Conan Doyle, was a vociferous opponent of the auction. In a mystery worthy of Holmes himself, Lancelyn Green was found garroted in his London apartment on March 27, 2004. At the inquest, his family said he had become increasingly agitated and worried for his safety in the days before he died. The coroner said that he could not rule out murder and gave an open verdict on the death.

By comparison, in late October of 2004, the world's finest private collection of books, letters and manuscripts relating to Oscar Wilde fetched more that £850,000 at Sotheby's London. A private buyer paid £72,000 for a handwritten manuscript of Wilde's novel *The Picture of Dorian Gray*.

I am often asked why a lawyer is attracted to the study of the Canon. The law is an ancient profession but for Anglo-Canadian lawyers the Victorian and Edwardian eras saw its maturation as a science. That is the era of most interest to me. Detection was in its infancy at this time and the Master (as he is often referred to), the undisputed master of detection. When I read the Canon my world becomes as it was then: a most acceptable time.

A final word about Doyle's character Sherlock Holmes. It has been said of him that "He was a most acceptable character. If he didn't exist he ought to exist."

WATSON: TREASON IN THE BLOOD?

Presentation to Bootmakers of Toronto, December 4, 1982,
34 Baker Street Journal *No. 04, December, 1984*

I

Who was John H. Watson, M.D., late of Her Majesty's Indian Army?
Apart from the fact that he had attended an English Public school
and graduated in 1878 from the medical school of London University,
that he served a brief spell as an army physician in Afghanistan, that
he had played rugby for Blackheath, that he suffered from a migrat-
ing wound (or two wounds, one explained and the other not), that he
had very little in the way of independent resources or income, that he
had an alcoholic brother who died in reduced circumstances, that his
long-deceased father was named H. Watson, that he was something
of a ladies' man who married a lass from Edinburgh (and may have
married four more times!), that his medical practice, when he had one,
was never very absorbing, we know very little.[1]

In part, this is due to his role as Boswell to Holmes.[2] As chronicler,
he reveals himself to us only to the extent that it is necessary in order
for him to properly pay his homage. What we can learn from him

---

1 Individual facts are documented in subsequent footnotes
2 The Boswell metaphor appears in "A Scandal in Bohemia"

we can learn only by gleaning relevant clues which may be scattered throughout the Canon.

Let us start with his appearance. Even if he did not describe himself to us, certain things can be deduced. We know that he is not stout because he tells us that he is reckoned fleet of foot.[3] By the same token, we know that he is not frail because he tells us that he played rugby.[4] For this reason we can also be certain that he was not a small person, although from the way he described Sherlock Holmes, the King of Bohemia[5] and Big Bob Ferguson of the "Sussex Vampire" we deduced that he was not unduly tall. We can then reasonably assume that he was a strong man of medium height. In fact, this is the description of him given by Lestrade in "Charles Augustus Milverton"—"a middle-sized, strongly built man—square jaw, thick neck, moustache…"—a description concurred in by Holmes. However, by the time of "His Last Bow", when Watson was in his sixties, his lifetime of bad eating habits had caught up to him, and he had become "heavily built".

We know that, from time to time, he walked with a limp, depending on whether the bullet wound that bothered him was in his leg[6] or left shoulder.[7] What else do we know of his appearance? Precious little! Perhaps we can assume a certain regularity in his facial features, beardless, but set off by a modest moustache[8] since he seems to have had some attraction for women.[9] Even Holmes remarks on his natural advantages with women, leading us to believe that he was what today we would call "movie star handsome".

Of his character, at least as it is revealed to Holmes, we know somewhat more—at their very first meeting, when he was recovering from the Afghanistan Campaign, he tells Holmes that he gets

---

3 *The Hound of the Baskervilles*

4 "The Sussex Vampire"

5 "A Scandal in Bohemia"

6 *The Sign of Four*, "The Noble Bachelor"

7 *A Study in Scarlet*

8 "The Adventure of the Red Circle"

9 "The Adventure of the Retired Colourman"

Watson (left) and Holmes, an illustration by Sidney Paget

up at all sorts of ungodly hours and is extremely lazy, though he has another set of vices when he is well.[10] Even when well, he has a natural Bohemianism of disposition,[11] though never so much as that of Holmes himself, with his cigars in the coal scuttle, tobacco in the toe-end of a Persian slipper and unanswered correspondence transfixed into the very centre of his wooden mantlepiece—faced with such an example, Watson gives himself virtuous airs.[12] Yet Holmes himself complains of the potent blend of "ships" tobacco that the good Doctor, a heavy smoker, puts in his pipe[13] and of his irregularity at meals.[14] Fortunately, his bad habits are somewhat compensated for by a sense of humour, however pawky.[15]

Of Watson as doctor, we also know very little. He appears to have limited enthusiasm for his profession, as if it were expected of him to

---

10 *A Study in Scarlet*
11 "The Musgrave Ritual"
12 *Ibid*
13 "The Three Students"
14 *Ibid*
15 *The Valley of Fear*

become a doctor, not as if he had chosen the profession himself. For several years after he first meets Holmes, he appears to have ignored his profession altogether,[16] perhaps a reaction to the horrors of his war service. Even in later years, when he has married and deserted Baker Street for his practice, we know that, although he started off with the best of intentions, he never found his medical practice very absorbing.[17] At times the practice itself was quiet, at other times it was busy, but even then he was ready to drop it in an instant at a mere word from Holmes, who was not fooled by Watson's assertions that he had not very much to occupy him.[18] One wonders at Watson's source of income during all these years—we can be reasonably sure that it is not entirely from his medical practice. We must assume that his literary agent, Dr. Doyle, was able to negotiate satisfactory royalties for him, and that medicine was almost a hobby for Watson—something to do when he was married or Holmes was otherwise engaged himself.

Was he a good doctor? The controversy rages among Sherlockians. In part it depends on what is meant by "good doctor".

He does not appear to have been by any means brilliant, at least as a diagnostician. His character appears to be somewhat ingenuous—not a man to make an insightful deduction or leap to a dazzling conclusion based on a handful of symptoms.[19] Yet, he must not be written off for all that. Medicine is as much the ability to obtain the confidence of the patient as it is an abstract science, and in Watson we have the epitome of the bluff, solidly reassuring persona—just the man to treat the masses of Englishmen and women who passed through the surgery of an English doctor.

He is a man who can, for the most part be trusted with a secret—he is a good listener, with a grand gift of silence,[20] yet when there is a real secret to be kept, Holmes leaves us in no doubt that Watson is not to be

16 "The Missing Three-Quarter", "The Retired Colourman", "The Resident Patient"
17 "The Redheaded League"
18 "The Stockbroker's Clerk", "The Final Problem"
19 See "The Dying Detective", "The Stockbroker's Clerk", "The Resident Patient", and "The Golden Prince Nez" for further information on Watson's medical knowledge
20 "The Man with the Twisted Lip"

brought fully into his confidence—we see this in the Canon time after time, in *The Hound of the Baskervilles*, "The Empty House", "The Dying Detective". Undoubtedly other examples abound. With his limited imagination and air of constant surprise at every deduction Holmes makes, he is the perfect foil: "A confederate to whom each development comes as a perpetual surprise, and to whom the future is always a closed book, is indeed an ideal helpmate."[21] What Holmes prized him for most was his common sense and practicality but above all for his steadiness, calling him "the one fixed point in a changing age."[22]

We do not fare so well when we try to pin down his background. On the surface, our man is an English gentleman and a true Victorian at that. However, he does not appear to be of the landed gentry, for his only income when he first met Holmes was a very modest military disability pension of eleven shillings and sixpence a day.[23] We know he is at least from the middle class, because he attended one of the lesser public schools with the likes of Percy Phelps[24] and that he is a gentleman of sorts because he played rugby.[25] (We need not remind you of the classical description of rugby as a game for ruffians played by gentlemen to distinguish it from soccer, which is described in exactly the opposite manner.) Yet, if he were of the gentry or the scion of a wealthy family, he would undoubtedly have gone to Cambridge or Oxford rather than to London University for his medical school and it is likely that he would have entered the army in some role other than as a campaign surgeon, given his obvious athletic ability and exemplary character. Yes, what we have here is a man who has not risen one inch above the social station of his forebears—the descendant of a line of doctors, apothecaries, school teachers or the like—a man of gentility but limited means and no property. In fact, it is this very absence of property which allows us to rule out successful mercantile activities as the living of Watson's forebears.

---

21 "The Blanched Soldier"
22 "His Last Bow"
23 *A Study in Scarlet*
24 "The Naval Treaty"
25 "The Sussex Vampire"

Apart from what has already been said of his father and brother,[26] we know very little of his family. He tells us he has neither kith nor kin in England.[27] Not even a close cousin or nephew? He tells us,[28] and Holmes confirms, that he had no close friends,[29] and particularly that no one would call on him during the days of his recovery from his war wound.[30] But he is not entirely friendless—his old friend Colonel Hayter invites him down to his place at Reigate in Surrey,[31] and there was young Stamford[32] and Percy Phelps.[33] He was, obviously, not a gregarious man, despite the image of some of the various movie Watsons (e.g., Nigel Bruce).

And so, it might seem we have pinned our man down and arrived at a specimen not too distinguished, somewhat humdrum, somewhat stodgy, not the least bit exceptional, conventional even in his eccentricities, interesting only because of his association with the Master—shining only in the light reflected from the best and wisest man he had ever met.

If we are not sadly mistaken, this is the view which most of his readers have and this is the view which Watson is determined that his readers shall take. But it is not our view.

Consider this. This is the epitome of the Victorian gentleman, patriotic, moral and sedate in his ways -the last bastion of English respectability, "Good old Watson." Yet this is also the man of whom Holmes said, "I never get your limits, Watson ...there are unexplored possibilities about you".[34] It is also the man who has a vast experience of women on three different continents and in many countries.[35] He is a man who had three, four or possibly even five wives[36] who

---

26 *The Sign of Four*

27 *A Study in Scarlet*

28 *Ibid.*

29 *The Hound of the Baskervilles*

30 *A Study in Scarlet*

31 "The Reigate Squares"

32 A *Study in Scarlet*

33 "The Naval Treaty"

34 "The Sussex Vampire"

35 *The Sign of Four*, "The Second Stain" ("the fair sex is your department")

36 See entry on Watson in Jack Tracy: *The Encyclopedia Sherlockiana*, Doubleday & Company, Inc., Garden City, New York, 1977.

writes with rare penetration, incisive wit, brilliant recall (subject to his discretionary changing of names, dates and places to protect the confidentiality of the detective-client relationship) and great modesty with respect to his own bravery, devotion and perspicacity. This is man who suffered a wound in mysterious circumstances—not in Afghanistan, for we know how he suffered that wound. This is a man named John whose wife calls him "James"[37]—not by mistake and not because she was seeing another, but for a reason. What that reason is, we will not reveal to you just yet; you shall hear it in due course. Moreover, Watson, the healer and civilized Victorian, had and displayed a great attachment to his trusty pistol—almost, if not actually, a fetish—and fired it with great relish.[38] In short, we are faced with a man of contradiction—even, one might say, a man of mystery. Was Watson the respectable Victorian British Gentleman through and through as he would have us believe from his own words and those of Holmes, or was he perhaps something more or less? Was there a skeleton in his closet? What was that skeleton? Treason in the blood—what strange forms it is liable to take.

II

Treason was rife in England at the close of the Napoleonic era. Inextricably intertwined with this treason are the roots of the Watson family. Some background is necessary.[39]

Although the defeat of Napoleon brought peace to Europe it was followed by much hardship in England. For nearly 20 years the British Government had been fighting a major war, spending vast sums of money in the process, and now it was over. Manufacturers who had thrived on war contracts went bankrupt, while thousands of discharged soldiers and seamen came home to look for work, rates and taxes rose,

---

37 "The Man with the Twisted Lip"

38 *The Hound of the Baskervilles, The Sign of Four*

39 See generally David Johnson, *The Regency Revolution: The Case of Arthur Thistlewood* Compton Russell Ltd., 1974 ("Johnson")

wages fell, unemployment soared. By 1816 the English economy was on the point of collapse.

The writings of Cobbett also stirred up discontent against existing institutions. The King, the mentally incapacitated George III, had then reigned for 56 years, but the true ruler of England was his son George, Prince of Wales, the Prince Regent (and later George IV). It was against this background that, on December 2, 1816, an extreme faction of reformers now for the first time known as "radicals" in alliance with a body of socialists called "Spenceans" first came into open collision with the forces of the law. The Spencean Philanthropists met chiefly in public houses in London to talk about land reform and other radical ideas. "The land is the peoples' farm" was a favourite Spencean slogan and they advocated sharing out all of the land in the kingdom equally, reckoning that there was enough to give every man, woman and child seven acres each.

The Society's best known members were James Watson and his aggressive young son, also named James, who was usually referred to as "Young Watson" or "Jem" or "Jemmy". Watson Sr. was a 50 year old apothecary who styled himself as "Doctor and Surgeon". He appears to have practised in many places and had been quite prosperous at one time, but later fell on hard times and when one of his 10 children died in infancy he claimed that the bed on which the child lay dying had been taken away because he could not pay the rent. There appears to be some question as to whether he was Lincolnshire-born or born in Scotland.[40] We would like to believe he is the James Watson who in 1787 published a dissertation in Edinburgh called *Dissertatio Inauguralis Medica de Amenorrhea* (which, literally translated, means "A Dissertation on the Medical Aspects of Abnormal Menstruation"). In the autumn of 1816, Dr. Watson began to put together his cabinet or inner circle. A rally was held in Spa Fields, Islington on November 15, 1816 and a strong body of police made sure that the crowd acted peacefully. A petition was prepared which Henry Hunt, a radical orator, agreed to present to the Prince Regent and a further meeting was arranged for December 2, 1816.

---

40 Johnson p. 3 and *The Dictionary of National Biography* Vol XX (1917) "Dictionary" at p. 921

By late November, some alarming predictions about the second rally were reaching the Home Office. The petition was not received. The rumours were that the general objects were to burn all the jails in the metropolis and let out the prisoners. There were warnings of large bodies of workmen moving towards London and an anonymous note to the Home Office declared that the appearance of troups would occasion the destruction of London. "20,000 Englishmen can set any city in such flames as no engines can extinguish". By the time December 2nd rolled around, the Home Office was expecting attacks on the Tower of London and the artillery ground at Bunhill Row, Headquarters of the Honourable Artillery Company, where 4 cannon and 250 stands of small arms were kept. It was said the signal for an attack upon the Tower and the other planned acts of atrocity was to be when Hunt started his address. Before Hunt even appeared, the mob, headed by the younger Watson, broke into gunsmiths' shops, carried off a large number of firearms, marched to the Royal Exchange, but were courageously met by the Lord Mayor with a few assistants and were soon dispersed. That night as the two Watsons and Thistlewood, one of the other leaders, were walking through Highgate, they were met by the Bow Street Horse Patrol. Thistlewood and Jemmy Watson both fired pistols and managed to escape, but the Doctor was arrested and locked up. The next day he was questioned by John Stafford, the Chief Clerk at Bow Street. Watson refused to identify the two men who had tried to shoot at the Patrol. Stafford was sure that one of the men must be the Doctor's son, who was now the "most wanted man in London". During the riot a man named Platt tried to restrain Young Watson from looting a gunshop near the Old Bailey and Young Watson had shot him in the stomach.[41]

Evidence then began to be gathered with respect to the organizers of the rally and evidence of visits to Watson's residence at 9 Greystoke Place, Fetter Lane disclosed the names of most of the members of the Spencean Society.

---

41 Johnson pp. 7-8

Watson was lodged in the Coldbath Fields House of Correction at Clerkenwell and his conversations were eavesdropped upon by a police spy, one Dowling. Word got out that all the leaders of the riot had agreed to leave for America in the event of failure." Watson said: "My son's rashness spoiled all," he added: "If he had waited we would have had a greater force to accompany us to the City.[42]

In due course a reward of £50 was posted for the arrest of young Watson.[43]

TRIAL OF DR. WATSON ET AL

In April, 1817 a true bill was found by the grand jury of Middlesex (including one G. Musgrave, Esquire) against Dr. Watson and four others who were charged with four counts of High Treason. It is interesting to note the opening words of the indictments as reported in the State Trials[44] (verbatim and with the same punctuation):

> The jurors for our lord the king upon their oath present that Arthur Thistlewood late of the parish of St. Andrew Holborn in the county of Middlesex gentleman James Watson the elder late of the parish of St. George Bloomsbury in the same county surgeon James Watson the younger late of the same place surgeon Thomas Preston late of London cordwainer and John Hooper late of the parish of Saint Ann within the liberty of Westminster in the said county of Middlesex labourer...

(The indictment continues on for many tightly packed pages totally free of any punctuation, even periods, to detail the various alleged conspiracies).

---

42 Johnson p. 10. The writer indicates that Dowling regarded the Doctor as a crackpot.

43 Johnson at p. 15 quotes the police description of Jemmy:

He must have been a grotesque sight: the police described him "as having smallpox scars on his face, the left eyelid rather dropping over the eye, and very black teeth. His face was further disfigured by vain attempts to remove a mole with caustic."

44 (1824) Vol. XXXII

We see that both James Watson the elder and James Watson the younger were described as surgeons.

All of the prisoners were arraigned and pleaded not guilty (Young Watson, having fled the country, was, of course, not present at the trial). They were remanded, having been informed that their trial would take place on June 9, 1817.

The Court of Kings Bench convened on Monday June 9, 1817 for the trial, unusual in that it was a jury trial presided over by no less than four judges. The trial lasted one week and was faithfully reported in more than 650 pages in the State Trials. The conspiracy and the goings on at the rallies were described in great detail.

Some of the points which were brought out at the trial are worth referring to:

1. As noted in the indictments, both Watson senior and junior were described as surgeons.
2. They lived at 9 Greystoke Place, Fetter Lane.[45]

Both of the Watsons were obviously articulate. Their addresses to the crowd are repeated in full at the trial. It is worth repeating some of their thoughts:

> Was there ever a more calamitous time in this country than at this moment? It is not only this country which has been thus oppressed—our sister Ireland has

---

45 The Greystoke Place address deserves some diversionary comment. Philip Jose Farmer wrote *Tarzan Alive: A Definitive Biography of Lord Greystoke*, Doubleday & Company Inc., Garden City, New York, 1972, and refers to the Holdernesse Greyminister Greystoke connection and analyzes the connection in a criss-cross fashion. The analysis is summarized in Farmers's *The Adventure of the Peerless Peer* written in 1974. The latter chronicles an adventure where Holmes and Tarzan combine forces to defeat the nefarious Von Bork. Farmer's theory is that Watson inadvertently wrote "Holdernesse" for Greystoke in "The Adventure of the Priory School" and Greyminister in the "Adventure of the Blanched Soldier" but used Greystone for *The Peerless Peer*. Farmer says "Watson left no note explaining why he had substituted one pseudotitle for another (p. 11 *The Peerless Peer*). Surely the answer must be tied in with the Greystoke address where Watson's grandfather and great-grandfather resided—a throwback to his roots where the Spencean Society plot had been hatched (see Johnson p.12)

shared in our misfortunes—there the climax of misery has been brought to a close—there their sufferings cannot be extended further. Have we not been in a state of bondage longer than the Israelites? They were in bondage but four hundred years but we have been longer, ever since the Norman Conquest—kings have been admitted by you to do as they liked—they have in many instances converted you to their own wicked purposes, but this must not last any longer.

Mr. Watson stood down, his son then, in the presence of his father, addressed the meeting At that time we agreed to present a petition to his royal highness the prince regent; this petition we had been told was presented, but answer there was none, except that the prince regent nor any of his family ever attended to the prayers of the people, unless through petitions from the two universities of Oxford and Cambridge, or from the corporation of the City of London; in a word, he will not attend to the prayers of the people; this man calls himself the father of his people; is it not the duty of a father to protect his children? Does he do so? No. He (the Prince Regent,) treats your complaints with indifference, and tramples on your rights. There is no luxury which he spares, because he knows the expenses must come out of your pocket. Are we to submit any longer to this? will Englishmen any longer suffer themselves to be trod upon, like the poor African slaves in the West Indies?

When given the opportunity to address the jury, Watson Sr. said:

My lord, after the very able defence I have received from the gentlemen who have spoken in my favour it would be presumption in me to say a single word to the jury, any more than to disclaim that I had any intention whatever against the established form of government, by King, Lords and Commons.

Though these words ring hollow to us today, they must have influenced the jury because he was acquitted, demonstrating once again the great strength of the British legal system, which gives the benefit of the doubt to someone accused of the most heinous crime.

3. Both of the Watsons had pistols and Jemmy used his on at least two occasions.

Watson was tried first. The whole proceedings against him lasted a week and in due course he was acquitted. The prosecution of the remaining prisoners was then dropped. Noted legal authorities have commented that had Watson and his associates been indicted merely for riot, they would probably have been convicted.

The opinion that was generally held of Watson was that he was a "half crazy creature" and his son a "wild profligate fellow as crazy as his father". The elder was said to be a man of loose habits and wretchedly poor and he continued his life as an agitator.[46]

III - AFTER THE TRIAL

What happened to the Watsons after the trial?

Dr. Watson Senior – It appears that afterwards he went to America where he died in poor circumstances in New York on February 12, 1838.[47]

Jemmy Watson – It appeared that when the reward of £500 was posted for young Watson and anyone who had harboured him, he escaped from England in a ship called *The Venus*. In view of his singular escape, many people thought of him as quite a daredevil figure.[48]

---

46 Dictionary p. 922
47 Dictionary p. 922
48 Johnson p. 35

However an Englishman who met him at Pittsburgh that autumn found him short in stature, mean in appearance and rather stupid. Thank goodness this is hearsay and can be rejected out of hand. He was said to be employed by a school at a salary of £50[49] a year.

What can we make of all this? Let us summarize the few points that appear to be known about each of them again.

Watson (right) and Holmes, an
illustration by Sidney Paget

James Watson Sr. 1766(?) – 1838

1. Probably a Scotsman
2. He published an important medical dissertation
3. He is described as "a surgeon, late of Bloomsbury".
4. He had very little practice as he was in very poor circumstances.
5. He went to America after the trial.
6. He died in New York, February 12, 1838.

---

49 Dictionary p. 923

James Watson Jr.– born(?) – 1836

1. He is described "as a surgeon"
2. He fled to the United States when the reward was posted for his arrest.
3. He died in 1836.

We can conclude that Jemmy could not possibly be the father of our Dr. John H. Watson. We assume that Jemmy was born in 1798, married around 1822 in the U.S. and we know he died in 1836, whereas *our* Dr. Watson was born August 7, 1852.[50]

In our opinion Jemmy was our Dr. Watson's grandfather. Jemmy had a son born sometime between 1824 and 1828. This son, H. Watson married around 1850 and our Dr. Watson, his second son, was born in America in 1852.

IV – CONCLUSIONS

H. Watson (first name otherwise unknown), followed his father's and grandfather's profession of medicine. Having made some money, he sent his younger son, James, to an English public school. There, for the first time, from the taunts of his classmates, he learns the shameful history of his family, and, to buy anonymity, changes his first name to John. After spending several active years in America, acquiring the first instalment of an experience of women (could Canada have been one of the many nations?) he returned to England to attend medical school.

Lest you think our conclusion is unfounded, we submit the following evidence:

1. Dr. John H. Watson had neither "kith nor kin" in England— his closest English relative in direct descent would be the great grandson of the elder Dr. Watson—in legal terms six degrees removed—hardly a close relative and in view of the family

---

50 W. S. Baring-Gould: *Sherlock Holmes of Baker Street*, Bramwell House, New York, 1962 at Appendix I.

shame, probably the name had been changed by those Watsons who remained in England.

2. Dr. Watson, Sr. had 10 children—certainly a man of whom we can say he had an experience of women—using the plural as inclusive of the singular (if authority is required for this interpretation see the *Interpretation Act*, R.S.O. 1980, Section 27(j) and (k)).[51]

3. This explains why our Watson married a Scotswoman—no Englishwoman would marry somebody with traitorous blood in his veins—even though we know Watson was as loyal a subject of Her Majesty as ever lived, with the possible exception of Holmes, of course.

4. Like his violent grandfather, Jemmy, he was fond, perhaps too fond of his trusty pistol. We need only refer you to the famous telegram from Holmes to Watson in the "Bruce Partington Plans": "Am dining at Goldini's Restaurant, Gloucester Road, Kensington. Please come at once and join me there. Bring with a *jemmy*, a dark lantern, a chisel, and a revolver". Clearly Watson was an open book to Holmes.Watson's mysterious second wound—surely he would not wish it known that he had fought a duel in his American days to avenge insults to his ancestry. Perhaps, alternatively, a more charitable explanation is available. We find that a private James Watson was decorated in the Red River Campaign[52] of 1870, ironically per-

---

51 Now the *Legislation Act, 2006*, s.o. 2006, c. 21,but this section no longer appears:
In every Act unless the contrary intention appears:

(j) words implying the singular number or the masculine gender only include more persons, parties or things of the same kind than one, and females as well as males and the converse;

(k) a word interpreted in the singular number has a corresponding meaning when used in the plural.

52 Neale & Irwin: *The Medal Roll of the Red River Campaign of 1870 in Canada,* The Charlton Press Toronto, 1982. The Red River Campaign was part of the Riel Rebellion, which actually consisted of two uprisings led by Louis Riel in what are now Manitoba and Saskatchewan in 1869 and 1885.

For a discussion of the involvement of Private James Watson in the Battle of the Little Big Horn and the theory that "the other wound" was suffered there see "There was not a finer lad in the Regiment" by John W. Ely Jr. *Baker Street Journal.* (NS) 32(June 1982) 83

haps suffering a wound in his left leg at the hands of one of Louis Riel' s rebels.

5. It was after suffering this wound that Watson returned to England and entered the medical school of London University.[53]

6. Watson changed his name to John, yet kept the initial "J" because, subconsciously, he admired the strength of character and purpose of his great grandfather, Watson, Sr., and the altruism of his motives, though he condemned the violent actions of his grandfather, Jemmy. In his heart he knew Watson, Sr. wanted legal revolution, not revolution with violence. Morever Watson Sr. was acquitted of the charges of treason. Watson's wife, Mary, knew his real name and, no Englishwoman, but a true Jacobite Scotswoman, proudly called him James at home.

7. Watson chose, perhaps out of a sense of tradition, perhaps at his father's urging, to follow his family profession—medicine.

8. Watson managed to overcome the revolutionary urges in his blood—*the strange form it took in him was super-patriotism.*

---

53 An institution of which both the authors are alumni.

THE RESTAURANT
GUIDE TO THE CANON

Presentation to Bootmakers of Toronto, May 24, 1986, Canadian Holmes, *Vol.12, 1988*

INTRODUCTION

There are plenty of references to food in the Canon. Numerous articles have been written on Holmes' taste in wines, and other equally diverting topics. One has only to refer to John Bennett Shaw's paper, "Alimentary, My Dear Watson", which appeared in 1967.[1] Shaw identified no less than 198 references to meals or food and 108 references to drink other than water (there was one reference to drinking water—in "The Five Orange Pips"). One may also refer to the numerous quasi-canonical recipes in *Dining with Sherlock Holmes – A Baker Street Cookbook*, by Julia Carlson Rosenblatt and Frederic H. Sonnenschmidt.[2] There are several other Sherlock Holmes recipe books. None of them, so far as I have been able to discover, addresses the question of where Sherlock Holmes and John Watson ate when they were not at home. Incidentally, eating seems to be the only one of the bodily functions mentioned in mainstream Victorian

---

1 *Baker Street Journal* Vol. 17 No. 2 1967, pp. 98–99

2 The Bobbs-Merrill Company Ltd., Philidelphia and New York, 1976.

literature! One searches in vain for any reference to a water closet at 221B Baker Street! However, while there is ample literature on food in the Canon, there is almost nothing, at least of a catalogued nature, on the subject of dining out in the Canon. Thus, paraphrasing a title from a popular work of science fiction, here is "The Restaurant Guide to the Canon."

A STUDY IN STATISTICS

When doing a serious study of this nature, the first thing to do is to define one's parameters. I have chosen to include all references in the Canon to eating commercially prepared food. I therefore excluded all references to dining at 221B Baker Street, with one important exception to which I will shortly refer, and all references to dining in the home of a client, of which there are several. A review of the 56 short and four long stories of the Canon discloses that no less than 23 of them contain references for this study. In fact, since some stories contain more than one reference, there are, altogether, 29 occurrences in the collection—more than enough to be deemed significant by the amateur statistician. I should add that the study methods have been derived from those used in the most widely-known branch of applied statistics—sabermetrics, or the study of baseball statistics. Applying this method to the 29 references results in some interesting discoveries. The following list is set out in an order derived from the mathematical sequence published by Professor James Moriarty in his "Treatise Upon the Binomial Theorem". The significance of the order will, of course, be obvious to anyone possessing the requisite knowledge:

1. Of the 19 stories in Volume I of the Baring-Gould *Annotated Sherlock Holmes*, five or 26.3%, contain dining-out references.
2. Of the 41 stories in Volume II of the *Annotated*, 18 or 43.9%, contain dining-out references. Volume II has 1.67 times as many references per story as Volume I.
3. If one considers stories with multiple references, of which there is only one, *Valley of Fear*, in Volume I, and four, "Naval

Treaty", "Final Problem", "Illustrious Client" and *Hound of the Baskervilles,* in Volume II, the ratio becomes even greater: six references per 19 stories in Volume I, to 23 references per 41 stories in Volume II. This increases the ratio to 1.78 dining-out references per story from Volume to Volume. The conclusion is obvious: Holmes dined out more frequently in Volume II of the *Annotated* than Volume I.[3] There are several possible reasons for this: he may have had more money or more time. Possibly, he found Mrs. Hudson's quasi-Scottish cuisine somewhat limited or less appealing as time went by.

4. One story, "The Illustrious Client," actually has three references to dining out—showing that Holmes, like the

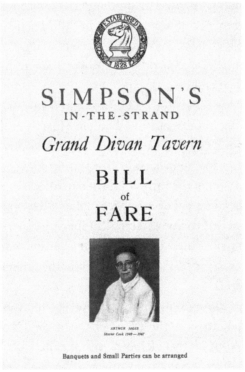

Bill of Fare from Simpson's In-The-Strand

experienced investigator he was, knew how to take advantage of an expense account. When I tell you that two of these

---

3 Holmes's fees were "upon a fixed scale" ("Thor Bridge"), but his disbursements obviously were not.

dinners were at Simpson's in the Strand and the third at the Cafe Royal, Regent Street, you will appreciate the accuracy of the above comment. When working for a poor or middle class client of modest means, Holmes was more likely to dine at a railroad station buffet or local inn.

5. Holmes had eclectic tastes in food. On five occasions, or 17.2% of reported meals, he can be found eating in station buffets: "Naval", "Crooked", "Final" (twice, once at Canterbury or Newhaven, and once at Strasbourg) and "Abbey Grange". Yet, on other occasions he can be found eating at some very snooty places, such as the Cafe Royal, referred to above, or the somewhat garish Italian restaurant, Goldini's, Gloucester Road, Kensington, in "Bruce-Partington Plans"; not to mention the three references to Simpsons, two in "Illustrious Client" and one in "Dying Detective". Holmes even manages to dine at the Vegetarian Restaurant in Saxe-Cobourg Square, Aldersgate, in "Red Headed League".

6. Twelve of his meals, or 41.4%, are eaten in inns, pubs and hotel dining rooms outside London. Just over half of all meals, 15 of 29, or 51.7%, are eaten outside of London.

7. Two meals are eaten outside Britain, a quick snack in the salle-a-manger of the railroad station in Strasbourg ("Final") and another in a cabaret in Montpelier ("Disappearance of Lady Frances Carfax"). Actually, there is no reference to Holmes having eaten in either place, but one assumes that he would not enter a restaurant with the intention of not eating there.

8. Two of the dining out references are not to Holmes dining out at all. Watson is the first person in the Canon to dine out—lunching at the Holborn Restaurant with his friend, Stamford, after leaving the Criterion Bar, and before he has ever met Holmes (*A Study in Scarlet*). As well, Watson spent an entire day at his club, where he must have dined, in *The Hound of the Baskervilles*.

9. Not all commercially prepared meals were eaten in restaurants. Holmes orders, from an unknown confectioner, what must surely be one of the first take-out meals in English literature in "Noble Bachelor". And what a meal it was—not the ubiquitous pizza or Chinese dinner—Holmes displayed his true, elitist tastes in the menu, which consisted of a couple of brace of cold woodcock, a pheasant and a paté de fois gras pie accompanied by a group of ancient and cobwebby bottles of wine. This, of course, is another example of Holmes' masterful way with an expense account. The second example of take-out food in the Canon can be found in "Naval Treaty", where Holmes filled his flask with tea and his pocket with a paper of sandwiches from an inn at the pretty little village of Ripley in Surrey. Here, of course, he had to economise because he was on government business, and knew that his account would be audited by the one man he could not hope to fool—his brother, Mycroft.

RESTAURANTS REAL AND FICTITIOUS IN THE CANON

Cliff has referred already to John Bennett Shaw's article. Shaw only briefly turned his attention to the number of restaurants and was not specific as to which ones they were. He said: "only a few restaurants and inns and bars are mentioned by name (less than two dozen) and once, God forbid!, Holmes mentioned a vegetarian restaurant. This curious lack of mention of dining out I attribute to Watson's disinterest: he had his meals it matters not where."[4] John doesn't make my job easier because he doesn't name the less than two dozen restaurants. One can, of course, for some guidance refer to Michael Harrison's charming and largely un-canonical discussion on London cafes and restaurants with which Holmes and Watson were likely familiar, in *The London of Sherlock*

---

4 "Alimentary, My Dear Watson", *supra* footnote 1 at p. 99

Holmes.[5] Cliff and I made our own search for these restaurants. Let me be selective in discussing these as otherwise this essay will take as long to read as it took to eat an average English dinner in Victorian times. We cannot identify the "vegetarian restaurant" but at least we found out what *Punch* for August 2, 1884 had to say about The Gay Vegetarians:

> A successful dinner was given at the "Healtheries" to Mr. Weston, on diet-reform principles, by the Society for the Study and the Cure of Inebriety.

> Come hither, all ye Alderman! For say who would decline
> To eat, when so delightfully the Vegetarians dine;
> 'Tis true no mutton's there to grace the feast, nor veal,
>   nor beef,
> But fruits and salads come to give the dinner due relief;
> While as to all the list of wines, why many folks may think
> They show that e'en Teetotallers are too well off for drink.

> First came a choice tomato soup, or green pea you
>   might try,
> Then followed "vegetable steak and onions" and a pie;
> The cauliflower *au gratin,* and the macaroni too,
> Were both pronounced by *connoisseurs* of admirable goût;
> While cabbage graced the festive board, and folks
>   were hard to please
> Who didn't like the well-cooked new potatoes and
>   the peas.

> Then came the Sweets, which would have much
>   delighted childish hearts,
> Fig pudding, ay, and hominy, and charming apple tarts;
> Stewed apricots and gooseberries—but endless task
>   were mine

---

5 Drake Publishing Inc., New York, 1972.

To tell the fruits, so here's the list of unfermented wine:
With Muscat and Vesuvius, Bordeaux and Fruit Champagne,
It seems the gay Teetotaller would never dine in vain.

So we must give up half the things we generally eat,
The mutton cutlets and the beef, in fact all kinds of meat;
The chicken or the toothsome game must ne'er adorn
    the dish,
Also it appears we must forswear the harmless fish.
Thus dine and walk like Weston—though that stalwart
    man, methinks
Did not indulge in that long list of unfermented drinks![6]

Let me start at the genesis of the Canon, *A Study in Scarlet,* which takes place in March of 1881. Dr. Watson is standing at the Criterion, when young Stamford taps him on the shoulder. The Criterion was a well-known dining establishment of the day and occupied about half a block lying within a rectangle formed by the Haymarket, Jermyn Street, Piccadilly Circus and Lower Regent Street. The building still stands as Lillywhites, a department store.

Watson then asks Stamford to lunch with him at the Holborn. The Holborn Restaurant, now demolished, stood at the west corner of Kingsway and High Holborn. It was described "as an example of Victorian classicism at its worst", so perhaps it is no loss that it has been demolished. Baring-Gould in *The Annotated Sherlock Holmes* points out that Watson took Stamford there because the Holborn was considerably cheaper.[7]

In "The Dying Detective" Holmes and Watson reward themselves for a job well-done. "When we have finished at the police-station I think that something nutritious at Simpson's would not be out of place".

Baring-Gould shows a picture of Simpson's Tavern and Divan (also known as Simpson's Cafe Divan or Simpson's Divan Tavern, 103 Strand) prior to its demolition in 1900 and its rebuilding in 1903-1904

---

6 no author given.

7 Baring-Gould, Vol. I, p. 146 ("B-G")

as Simpson's-in-the-Strand.[8] Baring-Gould assumes, of course, that the Master is talking of what we now know as Simpson's-in-the-Strand. It should be noted that there were other "Simpson's" in operation at that time. In particular, there was Simpson's Restaurant in Cornhill[9] as well as Simpson's Cheapside. The latter was described as a "Fish Ordinary" in Bird-in-Hand Court in Cheapside, and was bombed out in World War II.[10] On the assumption it was Simpson's as in Simpson's-in-the-Strand there is a second visit there during the case of "The Illustrious Client" in September of 1902 where Watson meets Holmes "by appointment that evening at Simpson's where, sitting at a small table in the front window, and looking down at the rushing stream of life in the Strand[11] ... The next time they meet is the following evening when they dined again "at *our* Strand restaurant" (emphasis added).[12]

Rosenblatt and Sonnenschmidt[13] point out that in "The Illustrious Client" Watson refers to Simpson's as "our Strand restaurant" yet that adventure is said to have begun on September 3, 1902.

The Cafe Royal on Regent Street was a popular restaurant in Sherlock Holmes' day. It was of course outside Cafe Royal in September of 1902 that Holmes was set upon by two of Baron Gruner's accomplices in "The Illustrious Client"[14] and suffered lacerated scalp wounds and bruises. While we are not told that Sherlock Holmes actually dined there, with his French background it would be surprising if he had not. Doyle was no stranger to the Cafe Royal. There is a reply in *The Times* on November 7, 1912 of a speech given by Doyle on November 6, at the Franco-British Travel Union dinner at the Cafe Royal. His

---

8 B-G Volume I p. 450. See the many references to Simpson's in the Strand in Michael Harrison's *The London of Sherlock Holmes* pp. 140, 141, 143, 159 and 160.

9 There is a photo of Simpson's in Cornhill in *The London of Sherlock Holmes* at p. 156

10 See H. V. Morton: *In Search of London*, Metheun & Co. Ltd. 1962 at pp. 34-35

11 B-G Vol. II p. 675

12 *Ibid.* p. 679

13 *Dining With Sherlock Holmes:* The Bobbs-Merrill Company Ltd. Philadelphia and New York, 1976 at p. 64

14 See the description of Cafe Royal in *The London of Sherlock Holmes*, p. 86-87 and opposite note B-G Vol. II p. 682.

topic was the need for a channel tunnel. Sounds like Doyle had tunnel-vision. Just a coincidence, I suppose that Baring-Gould notes that Watson presumably chronicled "The Illustrious Client" in 1912. This story could well have been written while Doyle was being introduced.

Lord Montagu of Beaulieu, as president of the Franco-British Travel Union, occupied the chair at the inaugural dinner which was held last night at the Cafe Royal. Among those present were Sir Thomas Elliott, Sir A. Conan Doyle, Sir George Reid, (High Commissioner for Australia), Mr. De Coppet (Consul General of France), M. Paul Doumer (ex-president of the French Chamber of Deputies) Sir John and Lady Cockburn, Sir C. Cartwright and Sir Thomas and Lady Barclay.

The Chairman in proposing the toast to "The Two Countries, Their Dominions and Colonies" said that if on their travels Englishmen did not see the Union Jack in a place they were delighted to see the Tricolor. Wherever they saw a French colony they observed the excellence of the roads. He had motored as many miles in France as any living Englishman and there was no finer holiday ground in the world.

According to *The Times*:

Sir Arthur Conan Doyle, in responding for the guests, whose health was proposed by Professor Salmon, expressed his opinion that the least intelligent thing which had been done in our generation was the refusal to build the Channel Tunnel. It was in his judgment a matter of such urgent national necessity that it should be pressed forward at once to completion, but it should be a Government undertaking. In peace the tunnel would bring an enormous tourist traffic to London, and it would be a cheap and complete insurance against national starvation in times of war. If the estimates given were correct, we could for the price of about three Dreadnoughts have an absolute insurance against the one great threat which another nation could hold over us.

Here's what one writer said about the Cafe Royal in the 1920's:[15]

About the first restaurant in the West End which provided a really good French dinner was the Cafe Royal Street (now being rebuilt), which, founded by M. Nichol over fifty years ago, has had a prosperous career ever since. During the Franco-German War 1870-71 and after the Commune it was a great rendezvous for French refugees, two of whom, Henri Rochefort and a talented artist, Piloteil by name, had a dispute which terminated in a scuffle outside. The large downstairs room at the Cafe Royal has always been an artistic and cosmopolitan resort where literary and artistic celebrities like to take their ease, while the unconventional dress and appearance of some of the habitues has struck a distinctive note which is struck nowhere else in London. M. Nichol, the founder, was an able man of an original turn of mind, who, once he had attained prosperity, collected fine wines as other people collect pictures. In all probability he was the finest judge of wine of his day. Under his management the cellar of the Cafe Royal attained a wide and well-deserved reputation. At one time, it is said, he had an enormous sum of money locked up in rare vintages.

In 1922 the owners were told it had to be demolished and rebuilt to conform with other buildings in Regent Street's Quadrant. The poet T. W. H. Crosland said of the news:

---

15 Ralph Nevill: *Night Life in London & Paris:* Cassell & Company, Ltd., 1926, p. 126

They might as well have told us that the British Empire
is to be pulled down and redecorated.
It took 4 years to rebuild.

The Cafe Royal was an obvious favourite spot for many of the artists
and writers of the day. It was Oscar Wilde's favourite haunt. George
Bernard Shaw is said to have been present in the Spring of 1894 in
the Cafe Royal just prior to Oscar Wilde's arrest when Frank Harris
begged Wilde to leave the country before it was too late. Charles
Higham in his biography of Conan Doyle says that the scene in "The
Illustrious Client" outside the Cafe Royal is "a specific reference to
Queensberry and his thugs chasing after Wilde."[16]

There are those who consider the writings on the writings to be
authentic in some way. Nicholas Meyer's *The West End Horror*,[17] set in
1895, brings Holmes and Watson into contact with George Bernard
Shaw, Oscar Wilde, Gilbert & Sullivan, and other literary and theatrical luminaries of the day. Here Holmes and Watson dine with Shaw at
the Holborn. Holmes states "What do you say to some Windsor soup,
beafsteak pie, rolypoly pudding, and a respectable Bordeaux? (p.59).
The Cafe Royal, was, of course, known for its fine wines. There are also
visits to Simpson's Cafe Divan and to the Cafe Royal where a meeting
between Watson, George Bernard Shaw and Harris took place.

It is in November of 1895 in "The Adventure of the Bruce Partington
Plans" that a messenger delivers a note to Watson, which reads in part:
"Am dining at Goldini's Restaurant, Gloucester Road, Kensington. Please
come at once and join me there ..." Goldini's was described by Watson
as a "garish Italian restaurant." "Garish"—it is defined: "unpleasantly
bright; glaring, showy, gaudy; adorned to excess".[18] Holmes asks Watson
if he has had something to eat and invites him to join him "in a cof-
fee and curacao". Obviously Holmes had eaten by then. The fact that

---

16 *The Adventures of Conan Doyle:* Pocket Books 1976 pp. 81-2. No mention of this incident is made
   by H. Montgomery Hyde in his biography of Oscar Wilde (Magnum Books, London 1977)
   and Lord Alfred Douglas (Methuen London Ltd. 1984).

17 E.P. Dutton, New York: 1976.

18 *The World Book Dictionary*

Watson says he "drove straight to the address given" meant that it was unlikely to have been a regular spot for Holmes. Obviously it was a place of convenience only since it was near to Caulfield Gardens, the former home of Hugo Oberstein. Prior to my recent trip to London, careful research had failed to locate a restaurant by this name in Gloucester Road, Kensington or anywhere else in London for that matter.

What has now become the recognized authority on sources of names in the Canon had confirmed this. Donald A. Redmond says of Goldini's: "...Goldini's restaurant, supposedly in the Gloucester Road...is unknown to the directory as either a restaurant or a personal name."[19]

Could the restaurant have been named after Carlo Goldoni the famous Italian playwright? Maybe this was another slip of Dr. Watson's pen.[20] I was determined to find Goldini's. My perseverance paid off, but I was disappointed to discover that it was closed.

What would it have been like to dine in an Italian restaurant in the days of Sherlock Holmes? One writer did not think it a very pleasant experience. This is what he wrote in a turn of the century issue of *The Strand Magazine*:[21]

> But the bad Soho dining place is better than the bad modern dining place in the City. This has every inconvenience of the old chop-house and not one of its excellences. Oh, that bad City dining place! Sometimes the proprietor is Italian, and you can always ascertain if this is the case by smelling the food, which always communicates a peculiar rankness not easy to describe but instantly recognisable if you have run against it once. These places usually have cellar gratings in the pavement, and through these gratings a certain atmosphere rises. I have heard it conjected that this

---

19 *Sherlock Holmes, a Study in Sources:* McGill-Queen's University Press, Kingston and Montreal, 1982 at p. 185

20 The inspiration for this comment came from a visit to Scaramouche Restaurant in the Benvenuto Hotel, in Toronto.

21 July to December 1902, Vol. XXIV, at p. 192.

atmosphere might be cut with a knife; but I have never tried, not having a knife I cared to risk. If I really wished to cut it I should try a saw—one belonging to somebody else. The cellar-gratings, you will observe, are firmly bolted into the stone; nothing else would keep them there. This atmosphere, against which any innocent citizen with a wife and family dependent on him may dash himself unaware, forms one of the greatest perils of the London streets. It is as bad as the soup inside the shop, and a great deal thicker.

The soup, by the way, is always of one sort in these places. It could easily be made by anybody with a barrel of bones and fat and the requisite patience to keep the contents ripening for six months before making the soup. When it is made it is any soup you please. Put it in a plate with a lump of bone in the middle, and it is ox-tail. Fish out the bone and substitute a lump of gristle, and it is mock-turtle. Throwaway the gristle and pitch in cayenne pepper till the diner's hair raises on end and his eyes stand out like hatpegs, and it is mulligatawny; and so on.

The potatoes are of one sort, too—the sort that when boiled present on one side the tender, delicate hue of a costermonger's black eye. There is a secret method of cooking them, too, known only in these places, whereby they are rendered more durable than when raw, and are given the general characteristics and appearance of fine old mottled soap. The general one-sortedness of these establishments extends also to the waiters—and their clothes. It is quite plain that they are not born in those dress clothes, else some of them would fit. But I am convinced that they put them on in early life and never take them off again, even to sleep. And just as the waiters keep the same clothes all their lives, so these dining places keep the same wait-

ers; though I once did hear of one being dismissed who
was suspected of washing his hands.

The message from Holmes inviting Watson to join him at Goldini's is
only partly quoted above. The rest reads: "Bring with you a jemmy, a
dark lantern, a chisel and a revolver."

The World Book Dictionary defines the word "jemmy": British slang.
A sheep's head cooked for food. Maybe Holmes figured Watson should
bring his own food. *The Dictionary* also refers to "jemmy" as a dialecti-
cal variant of a "jimmy" which was a short crowbar used by burglars
to force open windows etc. Maybe the jemmy-jimmy was to be used
to dislodge the cellar gratings. Maybe he wanted Watson to bring the
chisel to cut the atmosphere or the food.

An Italian restaurant of the 1880s which has received favourable comment was Gatti's. Located in the Strand, it was the first restaurant to
introduce music at meals in London. The restaurant was popular in the
1880s and many theatrical and literary celebrities were to be seen there.

UNCOMPLIMENTARY, MY DEAR WATSON

In *The Valley of Fear*, Holmes and Watson stay at the Westville Arms
in Birlstone, where the two take high tea at five o'clock one afternoon.
Holmes, displaying an excellent appetite, cheerfully explained the days'
events to Watson, through a mouthful of toast. The two breakfast there
again the next morning. Yet, scarcely hours later, Holmes suggests to
the official police that they take lunch at some suitable hostelry, but
specifically says that his ignorance of the countryside prevents him from
recommending one! Clearly, he must have been rather unimpressed with
his two meals at the Westville Arms. This is the first recorded Canonical
restaurant criticism, albeit the criticism is more implied than explicit.

Having begun his career as a food critic on a rather subtle note,
Holmes took the next step in "Priory", with his views of the Fighting
Cock Inn, in an unnamed village near Chesterfield. Watson described
the Inn as forbidding and squalid. Holmes, obviously fearing he was

going to be forced to dine there, feigned a sprained ankle. This enabled him to speak to the landlord outside the Inn, thus avoiding the distasteful possibility of having to sample the cuisine.

The next venture into criticism was in "Cardboard Box". Holmes and Watson ask their cabby in Wallington to drive them "to some decent hotel". While the hotel remains unidentified, Watson reports that they had a pleasant little meal together, during which Holmes talked at length about his Stradivarius, followed by an hour of anecdotes about Paganini over a bottle of claret. The combination of Stradivarius and Paganini, two Italians, leads me to believe that there existed in the suburbs of London, even in 1889, a decent Italian restaurant. One could perhaps surmise, given that this occurrence is reported under the name of "The Cardboard Box", that the menu of this particular restaurant included take-out pizza. On the other hand, I can vouch from personal experience that there was no such thing as a good pizza to be had in London as late as the 1970s.

Another pleasant luncheon, so good that no business was talked, took place in *The Hound of the Baskervilles*. Holmes, Watson and Sir Henry Baskerville dine at the Northumberland Hotel, no doubt at Sir Henry's expense (given Holmes' way with an expense account when acting for a wealthy client). The Northumberland, of course, is now the home of the Sherlock Holmes Tavern. One wonders how many clients ate with him there over the years of his active practice. Enough, apparently, for the owners to change the name of the place.

Perhaps the most telling of Holmes' restaurant criticisms can be found in "Disappearance of Lady Frances Carfax". Again, we are met with a display of great subtlety—Holmes delivers his opinions with a rapier, never a bludgeon, so unlike most of today's food critics. Having just vacated his table at a cabaret in Montpellier, Holmes cables "Mrs. Hudson to make one of her best for two hungry travellers…" Imagine, if you can, a traveller in France, gastronomic heaven, displaying impatience to return to the cooking of someone who at her best can only be as good a culinary artist as a Scotchwoman? *Larousse*, the Encyclopedia of French and other acceptable cuisines, doesn't even have an article on Scottish cooking! Clearly, Holmes was disappointed with the quality of French cooking to be found in Montpellier's cabarets. With French blood in his veins, he was not likely to be unappreciative of good French cuisine. Not wishing to harm Anglo-French relations, and knowing that Watson would likely publish any derogatory comments he might have about the quality of the local food, Holmes chose to cast his critical remarks in a discreet way.

On the other hand, it is probably not out of any dislike of the food that Holmes sends the above note to Watson in "Bruce-Partington Plans":

> Am dining at Goldini's Restaurant, Gloucester Road, Kensington. Please come at once and join me there. Bring with you a jemmy, a dark lantern, a chisel, and a revolver.

Interior cartoon from Simpson's

ASSESSMENT

Though Holmes preferences in his dietary habits are eclectic, he can be bafflingly obscure in his likes and dislikes. Perhaps his pipe-smoking somewhat dulled his sense of taste, preventing him from being quite as discerning in this area as in his observation of cigarette ash, footprints and other types of physical evidence. It is surely not to his credit that he seemed to dislike French cooking, or at least to prefer a Scottish cuisine. On the physical evidence, both Mycroft and Dr. Watson (the former being naturally stout and the latter having grown stouter as he aged) were more likely to be described as gourmets. One gets the impression that Sherlock fell more readily into the category of he who eats to live, while Watson and Mycroft were more of the live to eat type. Holmes, after all, was known to go without food for days when hot on a trail. Nowhere in the Canon is there any evidence that Watson ever missed a meal. Quite the contrary. On the other hand, whenever Holmes finishes a difficult case, he seems to head for Simpsons-in-the-Strand or the Savoy, or at least to order the home delivery of a good meal. He also seems to eat well whenever he is acting for a well-heeled client. Holmes the diner and food critic is obviously as mysterious and difficult for us lesser mortals to understand as Holmes the detective.

THE NATIONAL RIFLE ASSOCIATION GUIDE TO THE CANON

Presentation to Bootmakers of Toronto, October 26, 1991
with Joseph Kessel

PART I BY CLIFFORD S. GOLDFARB

1. INTRODUCTION

Some of you may remember a paper delivered to the Bootmakers of Toronto, on May 24, 1986, "A Restaurant Guide to the Canon"[1], in which, among other things, Hartley Nathan and I used statistical methods to analyze the frequency with which Holmes and Watson dined out in the course of their careers. Using a computer and searching the electronic version of the 56 short stories and four novels which comprise the complete Canonical text of Sherlock Holmes stories, we have now been able to locate all of the references to firearms in the Canon. Because of the complexity of the subject matter, and because this was really Joe Kessel's idea, we have decided that our usual two-part presentation would be insufficient. We are therefore today presenting a

---

1 See our previous paper, "The Restaurant Guide to the Canon"

two-part paper in three-part harmony, which we entitle "The National Rifle Association Guide to the Canon". The first part of the paper deals with statistical matters. Hartley Nathan will take some pot shots at Canonical airguns and their makers in Part II. Finally, Joe Kessel will shed some light on two specific firearms referred to in the Canon.

2. STATISTICAL ANALYSIS OF THE REFERENCES

The most refined and interesting method of statistical analysis available for dissecting firearms references is SABRMETRICS, the scientific method developed by the Society of American Baseball Researchers for the analysis of baseball. I have used these methods previously in Sherlockian studies and found them to be profoundly relevant to the study of the Canon. In fact, I have found these methods to be so appropriate, that I have now adapted them to create a separate statistical system for the Canon, which I call "Mathematically Objective Routines In Algorithmic Reiteration of Textual Interpretation", or "MORIARTI" for short. Since my first paper, outlining this process, was published in the Insomniac's Journal in 1988, a number of statisticians have begun using these methods. This group is now known among its practitioners as "Moriarticians".

3. REFERENCE DATABASE

A search was conducted on the entire Canon for the following words (the italicized words were not found):

> gun [including air-gun, *machine gun*, shotgun, *handgun*], cannon, rifle, pistol, firearm, revolver, musket, artillery, six-shooter, *matchlock, automatic* [the *Oxford English Dictionary* (O.E.D.), 1987 Supplement, gives the 1902 Sears Catalogue as the earliest reference to "automatic" as a type of gun], Smith & Wesson, Winchester [the repeating rifle - the place name also appears in several stories], *Webley, Colt, barker, roscoe* and *betsy* [all slang names]. Some additional words or phrases, not searched on, were discovered in the course of the search, includ-

ing "arsenal", "weapon" [appears in 27 stories], "Eley's No. 2" [which is a type of ammunition, not a gun], "fire-lock", "shooter", "heeled" [slang for "armed"], "arms" and "gunpowder". No full search was conducted on "piece", which, although now regarded as mainly U.S. slang for a handgun, has been in use as a synonym for firearm since the 16th century [O.E.D.]. Some 30 stories contain the word "piece", making it impractical to search for its possible firearm associations.

4. RELATIVE DISTRIBUTION OF RAW REFERENCES

This statistical analysis is based on the relative distribution of fire-arms references between Volumes I and II of the *Annotated Sherlock Holmes*. As you know, the *Annotated* represents the conclusions of William S. Baring-Gould as to the chronological order in which the events described in the stories took place. It is possible that a some-what different result might obtain if the stories were taken in the order of their actual publication. The total number of firearm references (relevant and irrelevant to the story-line) found was 273. The frequency of references for the major firearm synonyms is given in the following table:

WEAPON	VOL. I	VOL. II	TOTAL
Revolver	28	59	87
Pistol	33	28	61
Gun	33	20	53
Shotgun	13	0	13
Air-gun	0	10	10
Rifle	14	5	19
Musket	7	1	8
Firearm	1	3	4
All others	13	5	18
Totals	**142**	**131**	**273**

1 – Distribution of Firearms References

Thirty-nine of the 60 stories (65.00%) have a firearms reference. There are firearms references in 13 of the 19 stories in Vol.I (68.42%), and in 26 of the 41 stories in Vol.II (63.42%). In other words, there is only a small statistical difference, which may not even be significant, in the frequency of stories with firearms references in the two Volumes. Whatever slight bias may exist is in favour of Volume I. However, when we look at the number of references per story, the situation changes drastically. There are 273 total references in the 60 stories, or 4.55 references per story. But these references are distributed very unevenly. In Volume I, there are 142 references for 19 stories, or 7.47 firearms references per story. In Volume II, the 131 references are spread out over 41 stories, or 3.20 firearms references per story—42.83% of the ratio in Volume I. If we only count the stories in each Volume with firearms references, the variance stays relatively constant. In Volume I the ratio is 142 to 13, or 10.92 references per story. In Volume II, the ratio is 131 to 26, or 5.04 references per story, or 46.15% of the ratio in Volume I. In other words, Holmes (or Watson or Doyle, take your pick) had apparently become far less bloodthirsty in Volume II. In "A Restaurant Guide to the Canon",[2] we demonstrated that Holmes dined out far more frequently in Volume II than in Volume I. Since the arrangement of the stories in the two Volumes is chronological, maturity in Holmes improved his appetite for dining out, while apparently reducing his appetite for violence. Appearances may be deceiving, however, as I will soon demonstrate. At this juncture, I need only remind you of the famous quote by Benjamin Disraeli (sometimes misattributed to Mark Twain), no doubt anticipating the future development of the Moriarti System: "There are three kinds of lies - lies, damn lies and statistics."

5. DIFFERENTIATION OF REFERENCES

Before we can really begin to draw valid statistical conclusions, the raw references must be further analyzed to determine whether they are part of the story-line, descriptive of some architectural feature (the "gun-room"), proper nouns ("Bengal Artillery"), an unnecessary

---

2 See footnote 1, *supra*.

allusion, or a historical reference. A good example of the unnecessary allusion variety is Watson's description of his love-struck first conversation with his future wife, Mary Morstan, in *The Sign of the Four*:

> To this day she declares that I told her one moving anecdote as to how a musket looked into my tent at the dead of night and how I fired a double-barrelled tiger cub at it.

Another classical example is Watson's description of Holmes from the opening passage of "Dying Detective":

> ...his occasional revolver practice within doors, his weird and often malodorous scientific experiments, and the atmosphere of violence and danger which hung around him made him the very worst tenant in London.

Sometimes, the word is used not as a noun, but as an adjective ("revolver bullet"), and even sometimes as a verb ("pistolling"). "Rifle", of course, is used in numerous places as a verb meaning to go through someone else's property looking for something. I have not counted this particular usage for the purposes of my statistical conclusions. There is also the rather obscure usage "If I can help to put him where he belongs, I'm yours to the rifle...." from "Illustrious Client". This particular usage does not appear in the O.E.D., but appears to be used in the sense of 'my rifle is yours to command'. There are also several brand name references:[3] Winchester, Smith & Wesson and Eley's No. 2 (a cartridge type, rather than a gun).

6. RELATIVE DISTRIBUTION OF RELEVANT REFERENCES

In 26 stories, a firearm is actually used - i.e., fired, pointed, placed in someone's pocket for comfort, shown with menace or used in the context of the story in some other way, e.g., as a club. In the Moriarti System, these are known as "Relevant Firearms References", or "RFR's". In 25 stories (11 in Volume I and 14 in Volume II), there are

---

3 The T. Eaton Company, *1901 Spring-Summer Catalogue*, pp.140-141 (juxtaposition)

references to firearms which are not used in the manner described above. These are known as "Irrelevant Firearms References" or "IFR's". There is some overlap here with stories having RFR's, as only 39 of the 60 stories have firearms references. In other words, there are 21 stories without a single firearms reference and 13 more with only IFR's. These 34 stories are referred to by Moriarticians as "Statistically Off Base", or "S.O.B". A story without any I.F.R.'s or R.F.R.'s is sometimes said to be "completely SOB" There are, incidentally, 44 IFR's in Volume I and 32 in Volume II, for a total of 76.

Table 2 demonstrates the distribution of RFR's between the two Volumes and further differentiates the references by the type of use and the person by whom it was used. The distinction between "Miscellaneous Good Guy" and "Miscellaneous Bad Guy" is somewhat arbitrary and may not necessarily reflect unanimous agreement among Moriarticians. In these matters it is best to take one's cue from the Master. For example, the unknown woman who assassinates Charles Augustus Milverton, the despicable blackmailer, has been categorized as a Miscellaneous Good Guy, because Holmes saw fit to exonerate her, though she was likely guilty of murder. Von Schuetzke, in his recent article in the *Journal of Obscure References*, has argued for a third category, or "Miscellaneous Neutral Guys". Into this category, he would put such ambivalent parties as Carruthers, the bad guy, turned good guy in "The Solitary Cyclist", who shoots his erstwhile partner in crime, after the danger is over, but who will benefit from Holmes' good word, when it comes to trial and punishment.

PERSON	VOL.I		VOL.II		TOTAL
	Shoot	Other	Shoot	Other	
Holmes	2	4	1	1	8
Watson	1	12	0	0	13
Misc. Good	8	43	2	2	55
Misc. Bad	11	17	11	11	50
Totals	22	76	14	14	126

2 – Distribution of R.F.R.'s

We can derive some other interesting information from this Table. For example, Watson only shoots his gun once in the entire Canon (in *The Sign of Four*), while Holmes shoots 3 times. Watson is far more inclined to put the gun in his pocket than Holmes - twice as frequently. In other words, Holmes[4] is far more dangerous on average than Watson when he is armed! It can also be seen that Bad Guys are almost twice as likely to shoot as Good Guys (22 to 14, including Holmes and Watson as Good Guys).

7. REFINED STATISTICAL ANALYSIS

Now we are in a position to examine the data with more precision. It can be seen that the raw data we started with has already predicted the trend that we will now be able to see with more clarity. We find that in Volume I there are a total of 98 RFR's in only 8 stories, while in Volume II, there are a total of 99 RFR's in 18 stories. In other words, in Volume I, there are 12.25 references per non-SOB, while in Volume II there are only 6.18 references per non-SOB, a ratio of 50.45%. This would seem to lead to the inescapable conclusion that there is far more violence per story in Volume I than in Volume II. But, we must not be too hasty. Another look is in order. In Volume I, only 8 of 19 stories, or 42.11%, have R.F.R.'s. In Volume II, 18 of 41, or 43.90%, have R.F.R.'s, almost identical ratios. In addition, *The Valley of Fear*, which is in Volume I, is found to have 50 of the 98 R.F.R.'s in Volume I. If we eliminate this anomalous and particularly bloodthirsty story from the equation, leaving 7 stories with R.F.R.'s of a remainder of 18 stories in Volume I, we find that the average number of R.F.R.'s per story is only 6.86, or slightly more than the 6.18 in Volume II. There is no correspondingly bloodthirsty story in Volume II, "Thor Bridge" leading the way with only 20 R.F.R.'s. However, if we deduct this from the Volume II total, there are now 79 R.F.R.'s in the remaining 17 stories, or a slightly lower average of 4.65. In other words, even if we disregard Valley of Fear, in which most of the violence takes place in far-off Pennsylvania, apart from one particularly disgusting shotgun blast that is not witnessed by Holmes or Watson, there is still a significant violence variance of almost

---

4 Sherlock Holmes – Most Dangerous Man in London (Poster from *A Study in Terror*)

50% between Volumes I and II of the *Annotated Sherlock Holmes*. Happily we must conclude that, just as Holmes became more civilized in Volume II, at least when it came to dining out, he and his co-actors in the great canonical drama also became more civilized in relation to firearms violence in Volume II.

PART II BY HARTLEY NATHAN

Cliff has told you his statistical analysis has produced ten references to air-guns in the canon. These appear in three stories, one in "The Final Problem", six in "The Empty House" and three in "The Mazarin Stone."

In "The Final Problem" we read of perhaps the only one thing that Sherlock Holmes ever feared—an air-gun. Holmes walks into Watson's consulting room on April 24, 1891. Dr. Watson observed that he was looking even paler and thinner than usual. Holmes replies "I have been a little pressed of late. Have you any objection to my closing your shutters?" "You are afraid of something?" I asked "Well I am." "Of what?" "Of air-guns." This fear was so strong that Holmes reminds Watson three years later in "The Empty House" that this fear of air-guns helped to drive him from London. It is, of course, in "The Final Problem" that we meet up with Professor Moriarty face to face.[5] Of course, when Moriarty and Holmes were locked in mortal combat there were no air guns, but both men vanished into thin air at Reichenbach Falls. Who was Moriarty modelled after? One school of thought holds that Professor Moriarty was Friedrich Nietzsche. Who was Nietzsche? Friedrich Nietzsche was a German philosopher born near Leipzig who studied Philology (the science that deals with words or their history) at the University of Bonn. He was made a Professor of Classical Philology at the University of Basel, Switzerland in 1869 at the age of twenty-five. Soon Nietzsche

---

5 Our friend John Linsenmeyer in his paper "Regina vs. Moran" elsewhere in this book casts strong doubt as to the possible use of an air gun in either of "The Final Problem" or "The Empty House."

formulated his own distinctive philosophy, culminating in the glorification of the Uebermensch or Superman and in the doctrine of the ruthless will to power. Real philosophers he said are commanders and law-givers. They say "thus shall it be". All life for Nietzsche was will to power. If you will look at "The Final Problem" Sherlock Holmes says this about Professor Moriarty:

> His career has been an extraordinary one. He is a man of good birth and excellent education, endowed by Nature with a phenomenal mathematical faculty. At the age of twenty-one he wrote a treatise on the Binomial Theorem ... On the strength of it he won the Mathematical Chair at one of our smaller Universities, and had, to all appearance, a most brilliant career before him. But the man had hereditary tendencies of the most diabolical kind. A criminal strain ran in his blood, which, instead of being modified, was increased and rendered infinitely more dangerous by his extraordinary mental powers. Dark rumours gathered about in the University town, and eventually he was forced to resign ...

Moriarty resembles Professor Friedrich Nietzsche in numerous and striking ways. Both became professors in European Universities while still in their early 20s, both became insane and ultimately resigned from their posts under duress because of their acute medical and personality problems.

Sherlock Holmes had a profound involvement with branches of Philology similar to that of Nietzsche. In "The Adventure of the Devil's Foot" Watson says:

> The ancient Cornish language had also arrested his attention and he had conceived the idea that it was akin to the Chaldean, and had been largely derived from the Phoenician traders in tin. He had received

a large consignment of books upon Philology and was settling down to develop his thesis.[6]

Three years later, in April, 1894, in "The Empty House" his worst fears were almost realized. The would-be assassin, Colonel Sebastian Moran, sets up shop across the road and is, of course, foiled in his attempt to kill Sherlock Holmes with an air-gun.

> Holmes had picked up the powerful air-gun from the floor and was examining its mechanism. "An admirable and unique weapon" said he, "Noiseless and of tremendous power. I knew Von Herder, the blind German mechanic who constructed it to the order of the late Professor Moriarty. For years I have been aware of its existence, though I have never before had an opportunity of handling it."

Von Herder, the blind German mechanic. Who was this mechanic with a title of nobility?

There appear to be at least two candidates worthy of consideration. One of them is referred to by Baring-Gould when he quotes from an article about one Augustus Heinrich Friedrich Von Herder who was said to have been born in Vienna on April 1, 1803. It is worth reading the entire entry:

> Mother: Fräulein Schmutzi (which of course means "dirty") Liebelnhastic (which means "randy") von Herder. Father: unknown. Knighted by Friedrich Wilhelm IV (date unknown) for research into problems of using dehydrated water as a propellant in place of gunpowder. (By removing all traces of moisture from water, it could be concentrated into a very small place; when reconstituted, it expanded and forced the bullet

---

6 See our discussion of the Cornish language in our paper "Sherlock Holmes in Jerusalem."

from the barrel with explosive energy.) Blinded by acid in 1839 while experimenting with poisoned bullets. Died by gunshot wounds 1 April 1901, believed to have been inflicted by a jealous husband.

– Unpublished notes of Rudolf von Esche.

1901 T. Eaton Co. Ltd. Catalogue

There was *another* Von Herder, identified by Sam Rosenberg,[7] Johann Gottfried Von Herder, the famous blind German philosopher and scholar who was born in 1744 and died in 1803 (at age 95). He was one of Goethe's teachers, a leader of the Sturm and Drang movement and a friend of the Nietzsche family. When Holmes said "I knew Von Herder", it would not have been possible for Holmes to have known this Von Herder since Holmes was born in 1854, some 50 years after the death of this Von Herder. In view of the relationship with Nietzsche it seems to me that perhaps it *was* this Von Herder who was referred

---

7 *Naked is the Best Disguise*: The Bobbs-Merril Company, Inc., Indianapolis and New York, 1974.

to. The only explanation I have is the obvious one, that is another example of an error by Watson who meant to write that Holmes knew *of* him and not that he actually *knew* him.

To complete the triumvirate, let's look at "The Mazarin Stone" where Holmes foils the would-be assassin, Count Negretto Silvius. He had followed the Count to Straubenzee's workshop in The Minories, where Straubenzee made his air-guns. The Minories was a street in the East End of London. Jack the Ripper fans would know that the prime suspect, Montague J. Druitt, had a cousin, Lionel Druitt, a doctor living at 140 The Minories and there is some evidence Montague lived there at one time. Anyway, back to the story. The Count was about to strike Holmes, or actually a wax figure of Holmes.

"It's a pretty little thing" said Holmes advancing towards the image. "Tavernier, the French modeller, made it. He's as good at waxworks as your friend Straubenzee is at air-guns." To which the Count with an innocent air comments: "Air-guns sir! What do you mean?". This is of course a walking stick air-gun—I'll talk more about this later.

Having given you some idea who Von Herder could have been, can we identify Straubenzee? I can tell you he is not a cookie-cutter of Von Herder. Donald Redmond presents[8] his candidate, Maj- Gen Sir Casimir Cartwright Van Straubenzee 1867-1956, an expert on firearms and a member of an old army family who eventually retired in Kingston, Ontario. My instincts told me this was not our Straubenzee and with apologies to Don I felt I had to dig a little deeper. A German baker, Urban Napoleon Stanger, was last seen outside his bakery at 136 Lever Street, St. Lukes in the East End of London on November 12, 1881. This became one of the most widely publicized mysteries of the Victorian era. The manager of Stanger's bakery, one Franz Feliz Stumm, also a German, was eventually tried for murder. Michael Harrison in *A Study in Surmise*,[9] has a theory that Doyle got such a rise out of the mysterious disappearance of this German baker and the

---

8 *Sherlock Holmes, a Study in Sources,* McGill – Queen's University Press, Kingston and Montreal, 1982 at p. 201.

9 Gaslight Publications, Bloomington, Indiana, 1984.

trial of this German baker's assistant that it coloured his imagery and his choice of names and he set out to convert the St. Luke's mystery into *A Study in Scarlet*. Let me read from page 33 of *A Study in Surmise*:

Let us examine from which the "Baker" element in Conan Doyle's material came:

1. The BAKER ELEMENT in the actual proceedings against Stumm:

   The missing man: Urban Napoleon Stanger, BAKER.
   The anxious friend: George Geisel, BAKER.
   The accused: Franz Felix Stumm, BAKER.
   The gaoler: At Worship Street Police Court, where the charges against Stumm were summarily heard, the accused was taken into custody by the gaoler, Thomas BAKER!

2. The BAKER ELEMENT from other sources:

   The witnesses and friends: As *The Times* querulously remarked (12 December 1882), all were either German BAKERS or German millers.

Now what has this got to do with Straubenzee? Once you know the fascination of Doyle with bakers, whether they be Baker Streets or real bakers, it becomes a piece of cake to make the Straubenzee connection. We know that Doyle spent six months in Vienna studying opthamology in 1890-91, so he certainly knew German, A standard German to English dictionary defines Straube as "fancies" as in "fancy cookies" and Zee (see) as a sea or ocean. So clearly Straubenzee is a "sea of fancy cookies", paying lip service of course to the fact that Doyle had been a ship's surgeon at sea. Seamen, of course, affectionately call their cook "cookie". Sherlock Holmes summed it up well when he said ("Bascombe Valley Mystery"): "You know my method. It is founded on the observation of trifles."

Back to the Count's question—Air-guns sir, what do you mean? Jack Tracey in his *Encyclopedia Sherlockiana*[10] says this of the air-gun:

> Air-gun, a gun in which condensed air is used as a pro-pelling agent. The bore of the barrel is connected with a reservoir, enclosed within or attached without the stock, into which air is forced by a piston or plunger fitted to the bore, or by an independent condenser. When the trigger is pulled, it operates a valve which permits the sudden escape of the whole or of a portion of the condensed air into the barrel at the rear of the ball or dart, thus projecting the latter. In some forms the propelling agent is a compressed spring freed by the trigger; the reactive force of the spring compresses the air between it and the projectile, and the air acts upon and projects the ball.

Data upon either the Von Herder or the Straubenzee air-gun is not easy to obtain. Donald Redmond is *A Study in Sources*[11] points out that in 1903 (the year of "The Mazarin Stone") one of the principal London purveyors of air-guns was Martin Pulvermann & Co. of No. 26, Minories. Nearby was Wilhelm Von Gerber, a watchmaker. He concludes Martin Pulvermann & Co. was disguised in two stages, Von Gerber/Von Herder to make Moran's air-gun. Let us take a look at the historical development of the air-gun![12]

The first known example of an air-gun was a single shot model made by Güter of Nuremberg as long ago as 1530. Other German gun-smiths, such as Lobsinger (1550) and Mavin (1600), then developed a repeating air-gun. One maker at this period, Dumbler, even perfected a gun which could fire through a 1-inch plank, but he was forbidden to market it on the ground that it was "a murderous weapon with which

---

10 Doubleday & Company Inc., Garden City New York, 1977 at p. 7.

11 *Supra*, note 8 at pp. 114, 135.

12 William Percival: "Sherlock Homes and Air-Guns" (1962) Vol 6 *The Sherlock Holmes Journal* 15.

a man might be killed and yet not know what had hit him". Indeed so unsporting was the weapon thought to be that gunmakers made their air-guns resemble ordinary muskets as much as possible.

About 1740 all pretence of musket-like appearance was dropped, and magazine air rifles with rates of fire far in excess of conventional weapons were made in some quantities. The very successful Croat sharpshooters of 1790 were armed with air-guns right up to 1815, although if captured they were treated as assassins and immediately hanged. At this period too the Austrians introduced the air-gun as a service rifle; it had a high rate of fire and a capacity of no less than 40 shots. A very celebrated Austrian gunsmith, Staudenmeyer, came to London, and in his workshop in Cockspur Street made air-guns on these military lines until 1832. (Maybe *he* was the role model for Straubenzee?)

Up to this time all the guns were operated by pumping up an air chamber to a high pressure with an external air pump, but the 1850-60 period saw the introduction of the spring-loaded air-gun—and this type is still extensively in production at the present day.

But it was nevertheless the air chamber type of gun in which the most important developments took place. Between 1862 and 1889 a Frenchman, Paul Giffard, developed an accurate and very powerful rifle using liquefied carbon dioxide gas. It was a tremendous improvement on all its predecessors—and in fact the modern Crossman air-guns in America closely resemble Giffard's design.

This superiority of the air chamber, as distinct from the spring-loaded type, of air-gun is important in considering the air-gun used by Colonel Sebastian Moran in "The Empty House." Dr. Watson's description was that it "appeared to be a stick" which, when laid on the floor, "gave a metallic clang", but he soon noticed that it was "a sort of gun, with a curiously misshapen butt". Moran "opened it at the breech, put something in, and snapped the breech-block"; when he fired "there was a strange, loud whiz". We also know from Holmes that it fired soft-nosed expanding revolver bullets and was "noiseless and of tremendous power", capable of firing with deadly effect across the width of Park Lane and of Baker Street. The actual gun appears no longer to be embellishing the Scotland Yard Museum, but there can be little doubt that it was of the air chamber walking stick air rifle type.

The walking stick air rifle was an exclusively English invention, first made in the early 1840's. Messrs. Townsend and Reilby were the most prolific makers. These guns ceased to be made in the early 1900's and good examples are now both rare and expensive. They closely resembled ordinary walking sticks and would be murderous weapons in wrong hands. As there was no recoil, the firing position was to hold the knob against the cheek and sight along the stick, but some sticks (such as that used by Colonel Moran) had a crooked handle and were fired from the shoulder. They operated at a pressure of 400-500 lbs. per square inch or more, being pumped up manually by a separate pump. One pumping sufficed for at least 20 shots and, by means of compensating valves, the power did not greatly diminish as the pressure fell. The extreme range was about 350 yards, and at 50 yards bullets (soft-nosed expanding revolver bullets, if desired) would easily penetrate a one-inch wooden plank.

These air-guns were indeed powerful weapons, far more deadly than any ordinary air-gun—especially in the hands of "one of the best shots in the world". The usual calibre was .32 inch, but special guns are known to have been made and an experienced gunsmith (even a blind German one like Von Herder), with a normal type as a copy, could easily have made an even larger and more powerful model. Very little is now known about the Straubenzee air-gun in "The Mazarin Stone", but the indications are that it was a similar type to that in the Moriarty collection. It is an easy conclusion to draw that Moriarty got his air-gun from the expert on air-guns, Colonel Moran. Additional support for this view is afforded by the fact that the malefactor in Doyle's play *The Crown Diamond*, which appeared at the Colisseum in 1921, on which the story of "The Mazarin Stone" is known to have been based, was not Count Negretto Sylvius but Colonel Sebastian Moran.

It has to be queried whether Watson's description of Moran's method of loading did not indicate a spring-operated air-gun. The answer is probably that, in the semi-darkness, Watson confused the loading of the gun with the operation of the air pump. No spring-operated air-gun could have been of the requisite power. Holmes' expressed fear of these formidable weapons was not mere "hot air".

PART III BY JOSEPH KESSEL

This evening I would like to examine a little more closely two of the many weapons mentioned or hinted at in the Canon. One is mentioned on at least ten different occasions while the other is only alluded to in passing at the beginning of a short story—both will be clearly identi-fied. Let me begin with that intrepid medical adventurer, J.H. Watson.

1. DR. JOHN H. WATSON'S SERVICE REVOLVER.

It has always intrigued me that the good doctor frequently came armed with his formidable service revolver, while Holmes was usually less well armed, if at all.

Young John Hamish(?) Watson, newly graduated from my Alma Mater—King's College, London University—joined the Army Medical Department at its training establishment at Netley.

The Army was an acceptable way of life for a gentleman who needed only a good regiment, good companions and a good life on campaign to live his life to the full. There was some danger, of course, during conflict - but it was generally a sportive existence and all the expenses were paid.

It should be noted that in the 19th Century most of the wars in which the British and other European empires were engaged were colonial expeditions. Here the Geneva Conventions did not hold any water since the local tribesmen did not identify or respect any badges of rank or service.

Doctors were not averse to donning the mantle of Mars over the cape of Aesculapius. Many took command when regimental officers became casualties and many won awards for gallantry under fire.

No complete list exists of the Victorian wars, punitive expe-ditions operations and insurrections. It has been estimated that between 1837 and 1901 more than 200 major and minor actions were fought by the British army and their allies alone. No doubt Gross Deutschland, Russia, France and Italy added many more to that list.

The Army Medical Corps, little changed since the Crimean War 1854/56, had recently undergone major reorganization with the Prussian model being used for the British Army.

Recruits for the Medical Corps had to be literate, of excellent character and aged between 18 and 28 years. In addition to their usual function all ranks were trained to use arms ~ swords, revolvers being the usual equipment issued to officers.

Consequently, Surgeon-Lieutenant or Assistant Surgeon J.H. Watson would be kitted out as befitted an officer proceeding on active service. Since he was going to serve in India with the Northumberland Fusiliers he carried both sword and side-arm. The Fusiliers wore a sealskin cap rather than the pith helmet or topee as worn by other regiments in India. This is not to be confused with the British officers in Indian Army regiments who wore more colourful headgear—mostly turbans of various hues and materials.

While army issue of sword and revolver were considered adequate, most young subalterns of that period would most certainly try to outfit themselves with the best equipment available.

Living in London, young John or "Jamie" as he was known would often leave the College and stroll down the Strand toward the West End of town where the better stores were located.

An excellent sword could be bought from Henry Wilkinson & Son of 27 Pall Mall, known to this day as fine cutlers and razor manufacturers. Wilkinson reasoned that when an officer had a sword made for him in their workshops it seemed sensible to make him a revolver also. He therefore arranged for the arms manufacturer, P. Webley & Son to make him a special line.

This was the Webley-Pryse which was sold as a Webley-Wilkinson-Pryse. The differences were matters of ease of loading, accuracy, refinement and finish. It was manufactured in Belgium in the .450 calibre, fired six cartridges and had a barrel of 6 inches with 5 rifling grooves.[13] The model was particularly favoured by the army for accuracy and rugged reliability under adverse conditions. It had good stopping power with about 1000 foot-pounds of energy at 100 yards. Although later models were chambered for 0.455/0.475 calibre with slightly shorter barrels, the earlier Webley-Wilkinson-Pryse was still being sold many years later. Other writers have opted for the Adams six shot .450 or the .442/.450 solid frame Webley Double Action but I feel that the most obvious choice would have been to follow the trend of the other subalterns and purchase the weapons from Wilkinsons.

On a closing note, Dr. Watson transferred to the 66th Berkshire Regiment which was going to see action during the Afghan War of 1879/80. This was another one of those colonial situations which started with the interference into the internal squabbles of an independent country. Afghanistan was having a periodic power struggle and was vulnerable to a takeover by a superpower, Russia, and so another superpower, Britain, quickly sent a mission to Kabul. This mission was massacred by the Afghans. War followed, and at the disastrous battle of Maiwand on July 27th 1880 John Watson was wounded and was subsequently evacuated to England. At Maiwand an ill-trained Indian regiment fled, allowing the Afghans to overrun the position. However, here was one of the finest recorded examples of regimental discipline. The 66th Berkshires fought steadily back-to-back until nearly all lay dead. The Royal Horse Artillery fired from point blank range until the remnants of the army could withdraw. This was the type of action seen too often in colonial wars, where reliable men and arms saved the day.

Two Victoria Crosses were awarded that day and 8 Distinguished Conduct Medal. The battle honours of the British Army did not specify whether actions such as Maiwand were victories or defeats - as Kipling wrote:

For when the One Great Scorer comes / To write against your name
He marks - not that you won or lost / But how you played the game.

---

13 Our firearms expert John Linsenmeyer is of the opinion the Webley was a Birmingham made Royal Irish Constabulary (RIC) Webley.

2. Sherlock Holmes' Indoor Target Weapon.

In the opening paragraphs of the story "The Musgrave Ritual", Dr. Watson makes jocular reference to his friend's habit of indulging, from time to time in the pastime of target shooting. However, the target is the wall of their shared accommodation, and Sherlock Holmes has adorned this wall with the letters V R done in bullet pocks. Watson refers briefly to the hair-triggered pistol used by Holmes. At this point I would like to give four reasons why the good doctor is being less than accurate in his account.

a) The Canon gives us to understand that Holmes, while being a good shot with a rifle, was much less accurate with a revolver.

b) One cannot expect to achieve any kind of accuracy in explosive calligraphy using a pistol without some form of mechanical restraint, and Watson has Holmes idly plinking away while seated in his armchair.

c) The use of even the smallest calibre cartridge, 0.22, which has roughly 500 foot pounds of energy, would demolish the wall.

d) Indoor rifle shooting was an acceptable popular pastime during this period among the upper middle class, provided you used the right equipment.

While there are many circus and vaudeville acts which rely on skill and practise, there are many more which employ a combination of skill, trickery sleight of hand and clever diversion. Trick shooting falls somewhere between these two extremes.

This type of showmanship had been part of sideshows, no doubt since the days of Robin Hood or at least William Tell. These two apocryphal figures exhibited such feats of accuracy that have seldom been repeatable.

Closer to our own time, around the turn of the century, saw William F. Cody and his Buffalo Bill Wild West show. His star performer was the legendary Annie Oakley. My own father witnessed such a show in Berlin, where Kaiser Wilhelm volunteered to have a (long) cigar shot from between his lips. This no doubt increased the attendance considerably although he gave no repeat performance. What is not common knowledge is that the marksman often used special loads for special effects. For example, bird-shot for popping balloons or drilling playing cards. When a dollar coin was shot out of the air a substitute with a hole drilled through was shown to the enthralled crowd. Buffalo Bill believed quite devoutly that as P.T. Barnum pointed out, there is a sucker born every minute.

For that V.R. to appear on the wall as an exercise in explosive calligraphy we must look to a far simpler explanation than Dr. Watson's off-handed reference to hair triggered pistols.

During the latter part of the 19th Century and up to 1914, indoor rifle shooting, using small lead bullets, 4mm diameter and low power had enjoyed a wide popularity among the middle class households of Europe and Britain. The rifles were mainly of German, Belgian and Austrian manufacture, were capable of exceptional accuracy and had been specifically developed for use indoors only. They were equipped with peep sights or better, triple hair triggers to avoid any jarring when squeezing off a shot and had a punch of only about 25 foot pounds.

I firmly believe that Holmes would have equipped himself, or have been presented with such an instrument. The Martini, with its Tyrolese stock, massive breech block and compact overall size would have been an attractive acquisition for a dedicated shootist. The fact that their advertisement appears in English as well would indicate that they did have customers and even an agent representing the firm in Britain. Finally, the fact that the shooting produced pock marks and not the destruction of the interior wall definitely points to a very low power bullet such as is fired by the Martini indoor rifle.

In concluding I would like to share a follow up to the visit of the Wild West show to Berlin. In a biography of William (Buffalo Bill) Cody it tells of how the Kaiser spoke to him just after the trick shot that removed the cigar from the Kaiser's mouth. "Tell me Colonel Cody—just what would you have done if you had missed the cigar and hit me?" asked the Kaiser. Buffalo Bill looked hard and then smiled, he gestured toward the Royal box. "Waal Highness" he drawled, "I guess we would have had to find us another Dook for tomorrow's show."

WHO WAS THAT
HEBREW RABBI?

Presentation to Bootmakers of Toronto, March 24, 1984, Canadian Holmes *Vol. 33 No. 4 Summer 2011. Winner of the True Davidson Memorial Award for best paper presented to the Bootmakers of Toronto in 1984.*

To Sherlock Holmes she is always *"the* woman." We are all familiar with the opening words of "A Scandal in Bohemia", which, according to William S. Baring-Gould in *The Annotated Sherlock Holmes*, took place Friday, May 20, to Sunday, May 22, 1887.[1]

It is in this story that we are introduced to Irene Adler. The King of Bohemia tells Holmes that it was five years before, during a lengthy visit to Warsaw, that he had made the acquaintance of the 'well-known adventuress, Irene Adler.' Holmes then asks Watson to look her up in his index. Watson says: 'In this case I found her biography sandwiched in between that of a Hebrew Rabbi and that of a staff-commander who had written a monograph upon the deep-sea fishes.'

Before we turn to our own theories as to the identity of the Hebrew Rabbi, let us summarize the sparse extent of the current literature. (The identification of the staff commander will have to wait for another time).

---

1 Vol. 1, p. 346. Clarkson N. Potter Inc., New York, 1967.

Baring-Gould, in *The Annotated*, refers to Ruth Berman's identification of the Hebrew Rabbi as Hermann Adler, Chief Rabbi of the United Congregations of the British Empire from 1891 to 1911.[2]

Miss Berman gives cogent arguments why the likely Hebrew Rabbi was Rabbi Hermann Adler, as opposed to Rabbi Nathan Marcus Adler (who was Hermann's father). Irene Adler was sandwiched in between the rabbi and the staff commander, and this eliminated Nathan because his entry would come after Irene's. Based on this analysis, she concludes that, since the *Encyclopaedia Britannica* refers to Hermann Adler as 'a prominent figure in English public life,' he is the only one suitable to the position. Miss Berman does acknowledge that Holmes uses an unorthodox alphabetization in "The Adventure of the Sussex Vampire" (the word 'unorthodox' will become relevant shortly). In that story, Holmes asks Watson to get out the index volume for the letter V, and refers to the record of old cases and so on, starting with the voyage of the Gloria Scott and going on to Victor Lynch the forger, Venomous lizard or gila, Vittoria the circus belle, Vanderbilt and the yeggman, Vipers, Vigor the Hammersmith wonder, Vampirism in Hungary,

Hermann Adler

2 "On Docketing a Hebrew Rabbi", *Baker Street Journal*, NS 10:2, p. 80 (1960).

Vampires in Transylvania. The misalphabetization within the letter V is easily perceived.

It is not difficult to believe that Holmes could have been guilty of the same thing in alphabetizing Irene Adler after Nathan Marcus Adler, although one could probably agree with Miss Berman's second reason for discounting him: as Chief Rabbi in England from 1844 to 1879, he did little that would be of interest to non-Jews.

Miss Berman's article has not considered the possibility that the name of the rabbi might be something other than 'Adler.' When performing Sherlockian exegesis one is bound to emulate the methods of the Master himself, to observe as well as to see. One does not eliminate the impossible until one determines that there is something to be eliminated.

With all due deference to Miss Berman, her paper overlooks an opportunity to discuss the strongest argument in favour of Hermann Adler's candidacy as the Hebrew Rabbi. The most significant events of 1888 were the Jack the Ripper murders. One of the spurious side issues was the open conjecture that the murders might have been the work of a crazed Jewish ritual killer. A number, but not all, of the murders did take place on dates which were of religious significance to Jews. After the killings of Stride and Eddowes on September 30, 1888 (which was not a date of religious significance), there was a cryptic scrawl found on a wall near the scene of the murders: 'The Juwes are The men That Will not be Blamed for nothing.'[3] The press and public were rife with speculation and wild charges of an anti semitic nature. Rabbi Adler, in early October 1888, wrote to *The Times* and to the Police Commissioner to refute these calumnious charges. We know full well that Sherlock Holmes would never have missed such a letter in *The Times*.

This event alone would seem to make Hermann Adler a strong, if not the leading, candidate for the scrapbook, but for the timing. According to Baring-Gould in *The Annotated*, "A Scandal in Bohemia" took place between Friday, May 20 and Sunday, May 22, 1887. Watson

---

3 Richard Whittington-Egan: *The Casebook on Jack the Ripper*, Wiley & Sons Ltd., London, 1975, p. 139. There are several versions of the handwriting.

says in the story that it started May 20, 1888; Dakin says it was March of 1889.[4] It would only be by accepting Dakin's dating that the Ripper murders and Hermann Adler's strong response could have come to Sherlock Holmes' attention in time for "A Scandal in Bohemia."

The balance of the authorities, with whom we agree, favour the earlier dating for "A Scandal in Bohemia", namely either May of 1887 or March of 1888. While Rabbi Hermann Adler may eventually have made the scrapbook, his entry would have been sandwiched in after that of Irene Adler.

We have carried out an exhaustive review of all of the rabbis whose names start with A who could have achieved such notoriety that even Sherlock Holmes would have taken[5] notice. From this list we have chosen two candidates far more worthy of entry in Holmes' scrapbook. Paradoxically, but perhaps not coincidentally, one of them is named Adler.

Cliff Goldfarb says:

Who could the 'Hebrew Rabbi' be? First we must assume his name begins with A. Otherwise we would be faced with an impossible task. We must first eliminate the impossible, so that whatever remains, however improbable it may seem, will be the correct answer.

In my opinion, the Hebrew rabbi was Akiva (ben Joseph), a real, almost legendary figure in early post-Biblical Jewish history. Rabbi Akiva, as he is known, was born about the year 50 CE and, until he was 40, was an illiterate shepherd in the employ of Ben Kalba Savu'a, one of the wealthiest men in Jerusalem. Akiva fell in love with his employer's daughter, Rachel, and married her over the strong objections of her father. Encouraged by his new wife, Akiva began to study the Torah (the first five books of the Hebrew Bible). In time he became the greatest Jewish scholar of his age, one of the first authors of the Mishnah, the codification of the oral tradition of Jewish law, and father of rabbinic Judaism. His father-in-law now accepted him and left him half of his great wealth.

---

4 Martin Dakin: *A Sherlock Holmes Commentary* The Battered Silicon Dispatch Box, Eugenia, Ontario, 2012 at p. 42 (updated version)

5 *Encyclopaedia Judaica,* Vol. 2 (Keter Publishing House Jerusalem Ltd., 1972, pp. 268-90).

Perhaps an example of his writings will give some insight into the mind of this great man. In the Mishnah, he dealt with the eternal theological issue of free will versus determinism. For him there was no issue. He wrote, 'God foresees everything we do, yet we are given free will.' To many of you this will no doubt sound like a Zen proverb.

This is truly a great rags-to-riches story, an exemplary tale for those who say that old dogs and leopards are doomed to old tricks and perpetual spots. His story is an inspiration to those of us who still fervently hope that life truly does begin at 40. Exemplary, yes; but what in his life would have brought him to the attention of Sherlock Holmes and reserved for him a place in the scrapbooks?

To answer this you must understand a little about the times in which Akiva lived. The Holy Land had been a Roman province for more than 100 years when Akiva was born. During that entire time it had been a source of constant turmoil and trouble for the Romans. In the year 69 CE, when Akiva was a young man, the whole country rose up in bloody revolt against the Romans. Jerusalem was conquered and destroyed. The Temple of Jerusalem was destroyed and its treasures carried off to Rome by the triumphant general Titus. Thousands of Jewish slaves went with them. The revolt ended in 73 CE, when the defenders of Masada, the last stronghold, chose to commit suicide rather than be captured.

In an attempt to prevent further uprisings, the Romans banned the practice and teaching of the Jewish religion. Rabbi Akiva, though by nature a moderate person, defied this ban, and travelled about the country, clandestinely founding local religious academies wherever he went. There were in the land of Judea at that time two major religious parties, the Sadducees and the Pharisees. The Sadducees were the priestly party, wealthy aristocrats for the most part, representing the 'establishment' as we would call it today. The Pharisees, of whom Akiva himself was the pre-eminent representative, were humbler, sometimes a bit unworldly. They were known for their strict interpretation of the religious laws and their strong moral behaviour. They supported religious liberty, but also counselled observance of the civil laws of the land. There were also some smaller sects, such as the Zealots, a group whose beliefs were much the same as those of the Pharisees, but more aggressively nationalistic. You may also have heard of the Essenes, a small ultra-religious group that lived in the caves surrounding the Dead Sea are believed to be the authors of the literary works known as the "Dead Sea Scrolls."

In the year 132, when Akiva was already over 80, the emperor Hadrian began to rebuild Jerusalem as a Graeco-Roman city. Akiva decided that the time for revolt had arrived. He had met a charismatic young Zealot leader, Shimon bar Koseba. Akiva changed the young man's name to 'bar Kochba', meaning 'son of a star', and proclaimed him the long-awaited Messiah. Thousands of Akiva's disciples flocked to the banner of the new leader, and the revolt began. It lasted three years and it was a failure. Bar Kochba was killed, as were more than 500,000 Israelites. Akiva was arrested and imprisoned for his religious activities, but soon the Romans dragged him from his cell and he was flayed to death.

I believe that Rabbi Akiva was in the scrapbook because of his extraordinary life. He was a man of action and a brilliant philosopher. A spiritual leader, he defied the laws of the land and clandestinely carried on his activities under the very nose of the Roman authorities. In his extreme old age he was still capable of starting a revolution. One might easily describe him as "the most dangerous man in Jerusalem." Even after his death his disciples bore the seed that carried Jewish learning through the dark centuries of persecution. The remaining part of Akiva' s lifetime work of codification of the oral laws was completed, and the institution of the rabbi as a spiritual and moral leader, rather than religious intermediary between man and God, continued to develop. But, you may object, Akiva had been dead more than 1,700 years when Sherlock Holmes was born. Of what relevance could be his inclusion in a scrapbook intended to be of practical significance? You will recall that Holmes once said (in *The Valley of Fear*), "All knowledge is relevant to the detective." Perhaps Holmes felt there was some comparison to be made between the intellectual and physical capabilities of Rabbi Akiva and those of Professor Moriarty—a comparison that might give him some small advantage over his adversary. Certainly, Holmes must have admired Akiva.

Again, you might argue, Akiva was not contemporary—why put him in the scrapbook? "So what?" we respond. Neither Holmes nor Watson ever told us the criteria for inclusion of an item in the scrapbook. So far as we can tell from the information we are given, the only criterion seems to be that the item is of some interest to Holmes. Why question the inclusion of a "Hebrew Rabbi" when the same scrapbooks also contained a clipping on vampirism in Transylvania, a phenomenon of purely historical and fictional significance, since Holmes makes it clear (in "The Sussex Vampire") that he does not believe in such things?

Finally, in a last-ditch effort, you object that Holmes was not a religious person and would have no reason to know anything about a post-Biblical non-Christian scholar. Again, we refer you to the numerous references which demonstrate that Holmes not only was religious but may even have had some theological training. For an example of the former in "The Veiled Lodger": 'The ways of Fate are indeed hard to understand. If there is not some compensation hereafter, then the world is a cruel jest.' There are others in "The Retired Colourman", "The Cardboard Box", *The Sign of the Four*—and, of course, there is the reference to the Father of Evil in *The Hound of the Baskervilles*. The most direct statement he could possibly make on the subject is contained in "The Naval Treaty": 'there is nothing in which deduction is so necessary as in religion. Our highest assurance of the goodness of Providence seems to me to rest in the flowers.' In short, Holmes was a man of devout, but unorthodox, beliefs.

Why do we believe that he had some theological training? How many of you would know who Uriah the Hittite was without the assistance of the *Annotated Sherlock Holmes* or a Bible dictionary? Holmes knew, and displayed his knowledge in "The Crooked Man". What costume did Holmes choose to wear on the eve of the most momentous adventure of his life ("The Final Problem") but the garb of an Italian priest? And in the very story with which this paper is concerned, "A Scandal in Bohemia", didn't Holmes disguise himself as a Nonconformist clergyman in order to gain entrance to Briony Lodge?

Finally, I must say something about the use of the term "Hebrew rabbi." Rabbi can be loosely translated as 'teacher.' It also implies the duty of interpreting the religious laws, and has come to refer to the spiritual leader of a congregation, a position equivalent to priest or minister, although there are significant differences in religious authority. As there is, at least to my knowledge, no other religion which has rabbis, the use of the qualifier 'Hebrew' seems at first blush to be redundant. We choose to believe that the word is not superfluous. Holmes is telling us that we are not dealing with an English, British or American rabbi, but with one who lived in the Holy Land. We have already described Rabbi Akiva as the founder of rabbinic Judaism. He was, in fact, no ordinary rabbi. He was an ancient rabbi of the Hebrews—hence the designation "Hebrew Rabbi."

Hartley Nathan continues:

It is easy to refute Rabbi Akiva. Akiva is not contemporary, and it appears from the scrapbook that the entries are made with respect to people and items which might in future be necessary to assist in Holmes' vocation. Any notoriety Akiva has in the non-Jewish world is theological, historical and political, but hardly forensic. Akiva may be considered one of the fathers of the orthodox religious movement, whereas Sherlock Holmes was anything but orthodox. Everything from his unorthodox indexing to his disguise as a Nonconformist clergyman attests to this.

This paper has already alluded to the many religious references in the Canon. It has, of course, not been exhaustive, for one can bend the mind and find, as Samuel Rosenberg did in *Naked is the Best Disguise*,[6] many clues associating Sherlock Holmes and his companions with Biblical figures and scenes.

There is another rabbi who is worthy of attention and that is Samuel Adler, who is not mentioned in Miss Berman's article. A word or two about Rabbi Samuel Adler would be appropriate. Born in Worms,

---

6 The Bobbs-Merrill Company Inc., Indianopolis and New York, 1974

Germany in 1809 he became spiritual leader of the Congregation Emanu-El in New York in March 1857, where he remained as such until 1874, when he became rabbi emeritus.[7] He would be best known as a pioneer of the reform movement in the United States, which spread throughout Europe and probably saved the Jewish communities in many parts of the world from disappearance. As well, he advocated the rights of women in Judaism, in symbolic terms (with the levelling of the barrier separating the sexes in the ancient synagogue of Worms) and with his effort to have women take a more significant role in the religion. It was not until about 1970, however, that a woman was first ordained as a rabbi in the United States—and not until 1981 in Canada.

Another pioneer reform instituted as a result of Rabbi Samuel Adler's work was the policy of uncovering heads during worship in the temple. In May 1859, the Rev. Dr. Adler (as he is described) headed a committee which reported in favour of the propriety and lawfulness of attending divine worship with uncovered heads, and a resolution to that effect was presented by the president of the temple. Opinion was said to be sharply divided on the issue, and the matter was tabled for six months. However, in due course bareheadedness became an accepted part of the reform service.[8]

There is no shortage of reference to hats or their equivalent in "A Scandal in Bohemia." Dr. Watson describes Irene Adler as "the daintiest thing under a bonnet on this planet." Furthermore, when Holmes disappears into his bedroom and reappears in the character of an amiable

---

7 After graduating from Frankfurt Gymnasium, he entered the University of Bonn in 1831 and later studied at the University of Giessen, where in 1836 he received his degree of Doctor of Philosophy. In 1842 he was elected Rabbi of the Jewish Congregations in Alzey and its neighbourhood, and remained in this position until 1857, when he became Rabbi of Congregation Emanu-El in New York. He was not only a thorough Talmudic scholar, he was master of the entire field of knowledge concerning the Jews. He contributed scholarly articles to learned periodicals, and was an eloquent and passionate speaker in support of Jewish causes at home and abroad. He died in New York in 1891. See *The Jewish Encyclopaedia* (Funk and Wagnalls, 1901) at p. 199

8 Hyman B. Grinstein, *The Rise of the Jewish Community of New York, 1654-1860*. The Jewish Publication Society of America, Philidelphia, 1945, appendix IX, p. 507.

and simple-minded Nonconformist clergyman, there is a reference to his "broad, black hat." Now the definition of a non-conformist is "one who refuses to be bound by the accepted rules, beliefs or practices of a group."[9] One must consider the reform rabbi—the advocate of removing hats and of the mixed seating of men and women in the synagogue—as being one who was not bound by the accepted rules, beliefs or practices.

Now what would Samuel Adler have done to come to the attention of Holmes? One can assume that, if Irene Adler was sandwiched between the Hebrew Rabbi and the other fellow, she was an afterthought and may have been inserted much later than the entry for the rabbi. Alternatively, could one speculate that both were entered at the same time because of some connection?

What if Samuel Adler had a daughter? Given what we know about Samuel Adler, what might we say about his daughter? Let us digress and see what Sherlock Holmes tells us about Irene Adler:

"Born in New Jersey in the year 1858. Contralto ... La Scala ... Prima donna Imperial Opera of Warsaw. Retired from operatic stage ... Living in London."[10] Not much else is known about Irene Adler, other than the fact that she was married at the Church of St. Monica to Godfrey Norton, a London lawyer who resided at the Inner Temple and who fled London with her.

Our theory is that Irene's father, Samuel Adler, raised his daughter to become the first Jewish woman cleric. She was given musical training by the leading cantors of the day to develop her musical talent as a youngster. She was instructed in rhetoric and elocution by the leading contemporary orators. What a terrible disappointment when her hopes were dashed as the rabbinical body decided it was not yet time for a woman to enter the pulpit. Bitterness and cynicism followed, and

---

9 *The Heritage Illustrated Dictionary,* McGraw-Hill

10 Dr Julian Wolff has identified Irene Adler as Lily Langtry, whereas many other Sherlockians would prefer to believe that she was in fact Clara Stevens of Trenton, New Jersey. Clara is, of course, 'Aunt Clara' of musical fame: We never mention Aunt Clara / Her picture is turned to the wall / Though she lives on the French Riviera / Mother says that she's dead to us all. Chris Redmond identifies Irene Adler as Nordica (Lillian Norton): see *Canadian Holmes,* Vol. 7:2, Christmas 1983, p. 10

this led to her leaving the synagogue and rejecting its teachings—to join the opera, where her natural talents and training would serve her to greatest advantage. She so rejected her faith as to convert to Christianity and be married in a church. This is an ample measure of the degree of her bitterness. As further evidence of her rejection of the faith, one could also refer to the well-known theory that Nero Wolfe was the son of Sherlock Holmes and Irene Adler.[11] Nero was obviously named after the Roman emperor, whose cruelty to the Jews was well known.[12]

It is therefore respectfully submitted that the Hebrew Rabbi is, in fact, Samuel Adler. The timing is right. He came to New York, a short hop from New Jersey, in March 1857. Irene Adler was born in New Jersey in 1858. Rabbi Adler was well known for his progressive views on the role of women in Judaism. We are all aware of Holmes' views of women in anything. If I were to adhere strictly to the alphabetical order and accept Miss Berman's arguments, Samuel Adler would have to be rejected. I can, however, go back to the bottom line that there was always the unothodox alphabetization and what could be more appropriate for an unorthodox rabbi? More importantly, Hebrew is written from right to left and, accordingly, Samuel Adler would come before Irene Adler in any horizontal index.

I would be remiss if I failed to comment on the analysis of the "Hebrew" Rabbi as being one who lived in the Holy Land. My view is that we see yet another example of either a typographical error or a misreading of Watson's scribble by the typographer. What he obviously meant was the word "Reform" rabbi, not "Hebrew" rabbi. The qualifier "Hebrew" is clearly redundant, but it is easy to see how one could confuse the words. Both have six letters; a capital R can easily be mistaken for a capital H. The second letter in both is an E. The third letter, an F, can resemble a B, and the M at the end W if these letters

---

11 John D. Clark, "Some Notes Relating to Preliminary Investigation into the Paternity of Nero Wolfe". *Baker Street Journal,* NS, Vol. 6: 1. The theory is commented on by William S. Baring-Gould in *Nero Wolfe of West Thirty-Fifth Street* (Penguin), p. 83.

12 Nero ordered Vespasian to crush the Jewish revolt in 69 C.E. and destroy Jerusalem, all of which culminated in the tragic events at Masada in 73 CE

are not written carefully. The Reform Rabbi could only be the great German-American Reform Rabbi, Samuel Adler.

Cliff Goldfarb rebuts:

Apart from being an early and not overly well-known exponent of women's liberation, Samuel Adler had nothing in his life that would have been likely to bring him to the attention of a consulting detective half a world away. Nothing, that is, but a possible connection to Irene Adler. But if there were such a connection, surely the reference would not have been to "a Hebrew Rabbi," but to "her father, the rabbi." And if his entry was in connection with hers, both would have been made at the same time. In that case, her entry would not have been "sandwiched" between his and that of the staff commander. You may not be convinced, of this, but we are. We must dismiss the argument that "Hebrew" was "Reform." Is one suggesting that Holmes could not write, or that Watson was a poor reader?

There are the two theories. If one is right, we have found the Hebrew Rabbi, and maybe at the same time we have given you some insights into the psyche of Holmes, Irene Adler and (for you iconoclasts only) Arthur Conan Doyle.

Which theory is right? We leave it to you and posterity to decide. Only recovery of the scrapbooks themselves—an event about which we may have something to say when the world is more ready for it—would definitely settle the issue. That is, assuming that Holmes himself would not be willing, at this late date, to come forward and settle the question. One thing we can say for sure: we have eliminated the impossible. What we have left you are the probables. We ask only one thing. If you should discover the identity of the staff-commander—or why Holmes should have an interest in the subject of deep-sea fishes—don't call us. Write your own paper!

WHO WAS "OLD ABRAHAMS"? AND WHAT IS HE IN MORTAL TERROR OF?

Presentation to Bootmakers of Toronto, December 5, 1998,
Canadian Holmes *Vol. 24, No. 01, Michaelmass 2000*

In "The Disappearance of Lady Frances Carfax" (which we will refer to as "Carfax" henceforth), Sherlock Holmes tells Watson that he cannot go to Lausanne in search of the missing woman, and Watson must go in his place. Among the reasons he gives, one stands out:

"You know that I cannot possibly leave London while old Abrahams is in such mortal terror of his life.[1] This story was first published in the December 1911 edition of *The Strand Magazine*. However, Baring-Gould dates the events to 1902.

Who was Abrahams and what was he in mortal terror of? A search of the literature reveals that this question has *not* perplexed many Sherlockians over the years. In fact, we have located only two earlier efforts to solve the problem. The distinguished Sherlockian and Bootmaker Donald A. Redmond, writing in *The Holmesian Observer*[2] has suggested two candidates: Abraham Abrahams (1801–1880), a Jew who had fled to England in 1837 to escape pogroms in his native Poland, and Sir Henry Isaacs, Jewish Lord Mayor of London, 1889–

---

1 Baring-Gould, *The Annotated Sherlock Holmes*, Vol. II, p. 658

2 Vol. 4, No.2, June, 1974, pp. 10-12

1890, the target of anti-Semitic propaganda, some of it engendered by his support for liberal causes. However, Redmond is concerned with identifying candidates for Canonical characters among the acquaintances of Sir Arthur Conan Doyle or names Doyle might have seen in some newspaper story. Neither of his candidates would have been in any kind of terror, let alone mortal, in either 1902 or 1911. In addition, there is no need to look at potential candidates whose names were not "Abrahams."

The second attempt to identify old Abrahams was that of William E. Dudley, published in *The Baker Street Gazette*.[3] Disappointingly, this turns out to be a pastiche involving an elderly City grain merchant, Josiah Abrahams, who was being harassed by anarchists. No attempt is made to equate Josiah Abrahams to any living person.

Since the earlier attempts to identify Abrahams have failed, at least in our opinion, we must look elsewhere. Simple solutions are always the best. It seems to be common ground, and we certainly will not dispute it, that Doyle intended the person named "Abrahams" to be Jewish.

Computers make certain aspects of our scholarship easier than others. A search of Conan Doyle's works reveals that Doyle used the name "Abrahams" only one other time—surprisingly, in 1879, at the very beginning of his literary career. In *The Ghosts of Goresthorpe Grange*, a London con man uses "Abrahams" as a pseudonym. The narrator, Dodds, expresses his surprise when "a gentleman with a Judaical name," turns out not to share the stereotypical physical characteristics of the "sallow-faced, melancholy-eyed" Jew.[4] Even given Doyle's prodigious memory, he was unlikely to have been thinking of the same character in

---

3 No.3, Summer, 1989, pp. 49-55

4 According to John Dickson Carr and Owen Dudley Edwards, two of Conan Doyle's biographers, this story was written in or before 1879. Green and Gibson state in their *Bibliography*, that it was sent to *Blackwood's Magazine* under the title of *The Haunted Grange of Goresthorpe*. *Blackwood's* neither published it nor returned the manuscript, which is now in the National Library of Scotland with the Blackwood Archives. Doyle apparently rewrote it under the title given above, under which it was published in *London Society*, Vol. 44, pp. 681-682 (1883) and reprinted in *The New York Times*, December 23, 1883. The latter version was then republished in *Dreamland and Ghostland*, George Redway: London, 1887, (Vol. III, pp. 120-150), and subsequently in several other editions under this title and as *The Secret of Goresthorpe Grange*.

1911 as he had in 1879, though here, perhaps, one of Redmond's candidates might be a good selection.

We identified two candidates who are best qualified to be Holmes' client. We must admit, however, that there are other, in our view, less plausible candidates, whom we have chosen to leave to future scholars.

When we read the sentence in Carfax ("You know that I cannot possibly leave London while old Abrahams is in such mortal terror of his life."), two thoughts come to mind. First, was the name "Abraham" intended or "Abrahams"? Was this another handwriting mistake or a typo? More of this later. Secondly, perhaps Doyle might be up to his old tricks again? Perhaps he was considering events of the day, as reported in the newspaper or some historical event he had read about and was taking a name from one of the dramatis personae. We refer you to Michael Harrison's classic A Study in Surmise.[5] Harrison's theory was that Doyle used real cases as inspiration for names in the Canon. Doyle read of the arrest of a man connected to the disappearance of a German baker, Urban Napoleon Stanger, in The Times in September 1882. Harrison says Doyle modelled Holmes after an obscure private detective in that case and used the name Joseph Stangerson (and others) in A Study in Scarlet. Other tales in the Canon echoed events in that case. A more dramatic example of this theory was the murder trial of Edmund Galley and Thomas Oliver in 1836. Both were convicted. Oliver was hanged and Galley was transported to Australia. The efforts to vindicate him were carried on for more than 40 years. In 1879 a long article was published in *The Times*, Harrison concluded that, of the 64 characters who took part in the trial of Galley and Oliver, some 49.38 per cent of the names were used by Doyle in the Canon. There are many more examples used by Harrison. Those of you who were at the Bootmakers Lasting Impressions conference in June 1997, or read the Fall 1998 issue of Canadian Holmes, may recall Hartley's paper on "Sherlock Holmes and the Biblical Connection." This presentation demonstrated that

5 Gaslight Publications, Burlington, Indiana, 1984

Doyle utilized many characters from the Bible as role models and events as part of the plots in the stories. Hence, it would be easy to say that he has done this again in Carfax with "old Abrahams" or "old Abraham."

Keeping with Harrison's theory, let us cite a contemporary event. As noted earlier, Carfax was published in *The Strand Magazine* for December, 1911. In that same month, several anarchists were holed up in a commercial building in Sidney Street in London, resulting in a shootout and the death of five police officers. This was, of course, front-page news and continued to occupy that place for weeks after. It became known as "The Siege of Sidney Street".[6] Some of the anarchists or suspected anarchists (they were never convicted) and their associates were Peter Piaktow, known as "Peter the Painter," Josef Federoff, Jacob Peters, Sarah Rose Trassjonsky, Joe Levi (or "Josef The Jew") and Josef Sokoloff. One of the key witnesses was a 14-year-old boy by the name of Solomon *Abrahams*. The landlord of one of the suspected anarchists was also named *Abraham*. All of this could have been in Doyle's mind at the time Carfax was written and published in *The Strand Magazine* in that month.

Let us stop for a minute and look at the names. You will recall, biblically, that *Joseph* was Abraham's great-grandson; *Jacob*, his grandson and *Sarah*, his wife. There was also Peter the Painter. What about *Peter?* While not a relative of *Abraham*, Holy Peters was, of course, the villain in Carfax.

Now, onto what Hartley believes is the *real* story. It begins in 1880 in Russian Poland. In late 1880 and into 1881 the pogroms against the Jews were at their worst.[7]

---

6 See Colin Rogers: *The Battle of Stepney, The Sidney Street Siege: Its Causes and Consequences* by (Robert Hale, London, 1981).

7 The following is an extract from a biography of Morris "Two-Gun" Cohen describing a pogrom:

> The destruction of Jewish houses began. Window-panes and doors began to fly about, and shortly thereafter the mob, having gained access to the houses and stores, began to throw upon the streets absolutely everything that fell into their hands. Clouds of feathers began to whirl in the air. The din of broken window panes and frames, the crying, shouting, and despair on the one hand, and the terrible yelling and jeering on the other, completed the picture ... Soon afterwards the mob threw itself upon the Jewish synagogue, which despite its strong bars, locks

These pogroms resulted in the start of a wave of Jews leaving Russia and other parts of Eastern Europe to come to England, "a haven and protector of freedom."[8]

Let us take the case of one such immigrant by the name of "Issachar." The Biblical *Issachar,* incidentally, was one of the 12 sons of *Jacob* and the name of one of the 12 tribes of Israel. Issachar was also a grandson of *Abraham.*

Issachar leaves Russia and arrives in England, probably in December 1880 or very early 1881. In response to an enquiry, Hartley received a letter from the Immigration and Nationality Directorate in England confirming that Issachar was naturalized as a British subject on October 22, 1886, under Section 7 of the *Nationalization Act,* 33 Vict. c.14 of 1870. That act provided that an alien who "has resided in the United Kingdom for a time of not less than five years may apply for a certificate of naturalization." Issachar was 37 years of age when he

---

and shutters, was wrecked in a moment. One should have seen the fury with which the riffraff fell upon the (Torah) scrolls, of which there were many in the synagogue. The scrolls were torn to shreds, trampled in the dirt, and destroyed with incredible passion. The streets were soon crammed with the trophies of destruction. Everywhere fragments of dishes, furniture, household utensils, and other articles lay scattered about.

Bands of thirty to a hundred men armed with choppers, hammers, and bludgeons carried out the work.

"Their proceedings were watched by large crowds of spectators, and it was difficult to distinguish the rioters from the well disposed public," reported *The Illustrated London News.* "A crowd of people would be promenading a thoroughfare. Suddenly a whistle would be heard, and in a moment men would issue from the crowd and form themselves into a band, and an attack would be made upon a house...None were left unmolested. Warehouses were opened and sacks of flour poured out into the streets; tea-shops were entered, and the chests of tea emptied into the gutter; jewellers' shops were broken open, and gold watches and all manner of jewelry thrown by handfuls among the crowd.

Pogromists donned layers of suits and dresses as they went, carrying and carting away with stolen horses and wagons what they could not wear. They torched and destroyed about a thousand Jewish homes and businesses, tossing sobbing men and women through flaming doorways. They raped twenty girls and women, murdered others. Daniel S. Levy: *Two-Gun Cohen A Biography* (St. Martins, New York, 1997) pp. 10-11.

8 Lloyd P. Gartner: *The Jewish Immigrant in England 1870-1914* (Wayne State University Press, Detroit, 1960) p. 28.

arrived in London. According to informed sources, he became a pawn-broker's assistant.

Carfax is said to have taken place, according to Baring-Gould, between July 1, 1902, and July 18, 1902. Why was 1902 a particularly momentous year? First of all, it was, of course, the year after Queen Victoria died and the year of King Edward VII's Coronation. It was also the year of the completion of the national census in England. Taken as of March 15, 1901, the books were closed and the census completed in 1902. Hartley's father was born in 1901 in London, England, as *Abraham* Zelichowsky and his birth certificate showed his family's address in the East End of London. Based on this information, Hartley obtained from the National Census Office the names and ages of his grandparents and Hartley's father's siblings.

You will recall from *A Study in Scarlet* that Holmes and Watson took rooms together at 221B Baker Street in mid-January 1881. Watson recounts that Holmes narrated:

> "with great exultation how he had purchased his own Stradivarius, which was worth at least five hundred guineas, at a Jew broker's in Tottenham Court Road for fifty-five shillings."[9]

There seems to be a consensus that the Stradivarius was purchased in the very last days of 1880 or in early 1881.[10] In only one other incident in the Canon does it appear that Holmes had dealings with a Jewish merchant and that was in *A Study in Scarlet*. As Watson stated, after his first week in Baker Street there were numerous visitors.

One "afternoon brought a grey-headed, seedy visitor, looking like a Jew peddler, who appeared to me to be much excited ..."

The connection between the "Jew broker" and the "Jew peddler" is obvious. We believe that they are one and the same person. This is

---

9 Baring-Gould, *op. cit.* footnotes, Vol. II, p. 200.

10 See Jeffrey Alan Bradway, "Upon the True Provenance of Sherlock Holmes' Stradivarius", Volume 30, *Baker Street Journal*, September, 1996

what we believe happened: a review of the City Directory for London for the years from 1877 to 1885 shows only *one* pawnbroker on Tottenham Court Road, namely one James Smith at Number 23.

A foreigner, possibly an Italian, came to the only pawnbroker in Tottenham Court Road and pawned his Stradivarius violin. I am sure you know how pawnbrokers operate. A passage from the *Encyclopedia Brittanica* makes it clear:

> A typical transaction begins with a potential borrower coming into a pawnshop with the item he or she wants to pledge. The pawnbroker then determines how much to loan the patron for the item. Loans are paid out at a rate of about one-third to one-half of the price the broker can expect to receive for the sale of a good during the worst of times. This assures that a profit will be made.

In all likelihood the new shop assistant, Issachar, had no idea what the Stradivarius was worth. He was no expert. After the foreigner pawned the violin, Holmes came in and bought it from Issachar for 55 shillings and assumed he was the owner of the shop when he said he bought it at "a Jew broker's."

Why would Issachar be "much excited"? Possibly, the real owner came back to reclaim the Stradivarius, only to be told it had been sold. He demanded it be reclaimed or Issachar would suffer severe consequences. The violin had been in his family for years. He would return for it in two weeks when he came back to London. Issachar panicked and went to see Holmes to seek his advice. This would explain why this "grey-headed seedy visitor" appeared to be "much excited." Holmes told him to advise the foreigner who pawned the Stradivarius that the sale process was properly conducted in accordance with law and that he had no right to claim it back. Holmes' rather callous response was prompted by his passion for the Stradivarius.

Let's go back to Carfax again and the important sentence. We believe Issachar was "old Abrahams." If so, why was he in such "mortal terror of his life"? We will address that question later. Now, who was Issachar?

Hartley's grandfather's name was Israel Nathan Zelichowsky. In due course, Hartley's father, Abraham Zelichowsky, changed his name to Alfred Abraham Nathan. Israel Zelichowsky had a brother who married his niece Sarah, Hartley's father's sister, in France. He could not marry in England because it was and still is within prohibited degrees of consanguinity. From Hartley's grandfather's will, we know he was the executor of his brother Issachar's will. Hartley's grandfather's will refers to him as one of the executors of "the Will of my late brother Issachar Abrahams whose will was probated in 1908." According to his death certificate, Issachar died March 23, 1908.

Issachar's will left a legacy of £100 to Hartley's grandfather and a substantial portion of his estate to "his niece Sarah Zelichowsky," who was actually his wife. (You will recall that in *Genesis*, Abraham told Sarah to pretend she was his sister to fool the Pharaoh and the King of the Philistines.) Issachar's death certificate refers to Issachar Abraham and shows he died March 23, 1908, age 64 years. In 1902, the year of Carfax, Holmes, born January 6, 1854, would have been 48 years old. Abrahams would have been 59 years old in 1902. To Holmes, he would have been an "old man." In 1881, at 48 years of age, Issachar could well have been "grey-headed." According to the census report, Sarah was 20 years old in 1902 and Issachar was 59. Our theory is that Issachar was being cuckolded by a younger man. Here is what the death certificate says for cause of death:

> chronic hyperchondrical inclancholia 5 years, apo-
> plexy 2 days.

Basically, he died of a stroke but seems to have been in a depression for five years, which means since about 1903.

Depression. He was probably depressed because of what happened with the Stradivarius and his wife's affair. In fact, Sarah and one Reuben Goldfarb (apparently no relation to Cliff) were married not long after Issachar died. How convenient. We believe that Sarah and Reuben, her lover, conspired to kill Issachar in such a way that she would inherit his estate—if there were a divorce, she would get nothing. Hence, he was in "mortal terror of his life" and he had every reason to be. (By the way, Reuben was another son of Jacob and also one of the 12 tribes of Israel and also one of Abraham's grandsons.)

We submit one theory: that "old Abrahams" is Hartley Nathan's great-uncle, Issachar Abrahams.

Of the many other candidates we have identified, one name immediately stands out from the crowd: Israel Abrahams.

Israel Abrahams was born in England in 1858, one year before Doyle. In due course, he graduated from University College, London, with a BA and MA. In his early career, he taught English and Mathematics, as well as Jewish subjects. In 1902 he was appointed reader in rabbinic and Talmudic literature at Cambridge.[11] For many years he was the chief exponent of Jewish scholarship in England.

His home was the focus of Cambridge Jewish life. Though not ordained as a rabbi, he was a lay preacher who frequently led daily religious services in the synagogue.

His most important published works were *Jewish Life in the Middle Ages; Studies in Pharisaism and the Gospels; Hebrew Ethical Wills;* and *Notes to the Authorized Daily Prayer Book.*[12] For many years, he wrote a weekly literary and review column for *The Jewish Chronicle.* He edited *The Jewish Quarterly Review,* from 1888 to 1908, in association with Claude G. Montefiore, who became his close friend and supporter. He was one of the most important contributors to *The Jewish Guardian,* an anti-Zionist journal. However, at the same time, he was a passionate advocate of the establishment of a Jewish university in Jerusalem. Abrahams died in 1924.

While he remained essentially Orthodox in his own religious life, he supported extreme religious reform and provided the intellectual basis for the Jewish Religious Union, which was established in 1902,

---

11 Solomon Schechter, whom Abrahams succeeded, is best remembered today as the discoverer of the Cairo Genizah scrolls, the earliest known Hebrew texts until the discovery of the Dead Sea Scrolls

12 Edited by his father-in-law, S. Singer. He also produced numerous collections of essays on Jewish literature.

and of the Liberal Jewish Synagogue, equivalent to the Jewish Reform movement in North America, which developed out of it. Abrahams' general reputation and the publicity his religious stand engendered must have brought him to the notice of Doyle. As someone who was an iconoclast in religious matters himself, Doyle would have appreciated the strength and courage it must have required of Abrahams to take such an unpopular stand.

Note the two defining events in Abrahams' life in 1902: his appointment as reader at Cambridge and his role in the founding of the Jewish Religious Union. The appointment at Cambridge could not have aroused strong emotions, but the founding of the Union most certainly did. Montefiore, the movement's founder, greatly offended traditionalists with his radical views, including his entirely sympathetic view of Christianity and his belief that the future evolution of Judaism would and should encompass that which was good in Christianity. The founding of the Union led to strong reactions among the Orthodox, possibly intemperate or even physically threatening enough to put Abrahams, a peaceable man, in mortal terror of his life. If so, then Holmes may well have been called in to protect Watson's old friend, just as he had been called in to help out Watson's old friends Percy Phelps and Big Bob Ferguson.[13]

Why did Holmes call him "old Abrahams"? Because they were friends, not because he was "old." Abrahams was born in 1858 and attended the University of London, the same school from which Watson received his medical degree.[14]

They might very well have known each other at school, which is the usual reason why an Englishman, then and now, would preface his friend's last name with "old." Indeed, one of the senses of the word, from the *Oxford English Dictionary* is that it is:

> Used as an expression of familiarity in addressing or speaking of persons with whom one has an acquain-

---

13 "The Naval Treaty" and "The Sussex Vampire", respectively.

14 "In the year 1878 1 took my degree of Doctor of Medicine of the University of London ..." (*A Study in Scarlet*)

tance of some standing, or whom one treats as such, as in the colloq. Old boy, [old] chap, [old] fellow, [old] man[15]

In addition, the use of such a term of endearment implies that Holmes, as well as Watson, was familiar with Abrahams. This must have been because Watson had come across his old school acquaintance and introduced him to Holmes. Holmes and Abrahams had then become friendly, if not friends. Could this be because of Holmes' interest in the Chaldean roots of the Cornish language? As you will recall, in "The Adventure of the Devil's Foot", Watson says of Holmes, "The ancient Cornish language had also arrested his attention, and he had, I remember, conceived the idea that it was akin to the Chaldean, and had been largely derived from the Phoenician traders in tin." Today, Chaldean is known as Aramaic. Aramaic was, after all the spoken language of Israel at the beginning of the Rabbinic period. Israel Abrahams' scholarly expertise in this area, coupled with his wide-ranging, polymathic interests and engaging personality, must have endeared him to Holmes, who would have been starved for intellectual equals.

There is one other intriguing possibility that must be pursued. We think of a rabbi as one who is ordained to interpret the law and to perform marriages and other religious ceremonies. This is a modern usage. The term is properly used to describe someone who is deserving of respect because of his religious learning, authority, piety or office. Such a man was Israel Abrahams. You will recall that, in "A Scandal in Bohemia", Watson consults one of Holmes' scrapbooks for the entry on Irene Adler. He tells us:

> In this case I found her biography sandwiched in between that of a Hebrew rabbi and that of a staff-commander who had written a monograph upon the deep-sea fishes.

---

15 One example given, appropriately and coincidentally, of this usage is "1898 Doyle Trag. Korosk ix. 280 'There they go giving the alarm! Good old Camel Corps!'

We need not remind you that alphabetically the 'A-B' of "Abrahams" comes just before the 'A-D' of "Adler." Once before we asked, "Who was that Hebrew rabbi?"[16] I think we know now; it was, of course, Israel Abrahams.[17]

Admittedly, one hole in this theory is that there was simply no evidence of any violent threat against this "old Abrahams." In 1902, at age 44, he went to teach at Holmes' alma mater, Cambridge. He led an exemplary life. He was not in the rough and tumble of the pawnbroking game or anything close to it. He was an academic. Few academics or men of letters find themselves in compromising situations, thus, possibly, making Issachar our man.

We will once again have to leave it to our readers to determine whether either of us has found "old Abrahams."

---

16 See p. 83.

17 There is at least one other possibility, this one from the world of politics; Sir Lionel Abrahams (1869-1919). English civil servant and Anglo-Jewish historian, nephew of Israel Abrahams. In 1902 he became financial secretary for India, in which capacity he successfully reorganized the Indian currency. In 1912 he was appointed assistant undersecretary of state for India. Unfortunately, he would not be right. He is too young to have been at school with Holmes or Watson, or to be called "old" for his age. About the only advantage he would have is that of being in colonial politics, which could expose him to some kind of danger from Indian nationalists.

WHO WAS IKEY SANDERS?
AND WHO CARES IF HE PEACHED?

Presentation to Bootmakers of Toronto, May 15, 2004,
Canadian Holmes *Vol. 34, No. 2, Winter 2011-2*

I have the cabman who took you to Whitehall
and the cabman who brought you away. I have the
Commissionaire who saw you near the case. I have
Ikey Sanders, who refused to cut it up for you. Ikey has
peached, and the game is up.

So says Sherlock Holmes to the nefarious Count Negretto Sylvius in
"The Adventure of the Mazarin Stone."

The tale was published in *The Strand Magazine* in October 1921 as
part of *The Case-Book of Sherlock Holmes*. No internal date is given but Les
Klinger has placed it some time between 1902 and 1905.[1] The story is a
curiosity because it is one of a handful of the Holmes tales told in the
third person, not as one of the narratives of Dr. Watson, although he is
present at the beginning and ending of the tale. The Crown diamond
—the great yellow Mazarin stone—has been burgled. We first meet
Sylvius when he comes calling on Holmes. Holmes accuses the Count
of stealing the diamond. Holmes takes out his scrapbook and refers to

---

1 *New Annotated Sherlock Holmes*, W.W. Norton & Company, Inc., 2006.

the actions of the Count's "vile and dangerous life," the Count's pur-
ported murder of his benefactor, his robberies, the incident of a forged
cheque. The Count asks Holmes how all that is relevant with respect
to the jewel of which he spoke. Holmes then sets out the evidence, with
which this paper commenced, which he has amassed against Sylvius.

The Count's bully-sidekick, boxer Sam Merton, then shows up at
221B. Holmes absents himself, ostensibly to go into the other room
and play Hoffman's Barcarole on his violin, while the Count and
Merton decide whether to give up the stone and go free or keep their
secret and be handed over to the police. The Count brings Merton
up to date:

COUNT:	Ikey Sanders has split on us.
MERTON:	He has, has he? I'll do him down a thick'un for that if I swing for it.
COUNT:	That won't help us much. We've got to make up our minds what to do.

By the way, "peach" in underworld cant was to turn, inform, on one's
accomplices. "Split" has a subtly different meaning, implying spying
on; acting as an informant or a detective. We don't think that Doyle
was actually suggesting, in the second reference to Sanders, that he
was an undercover police officer or paid informant, although that
is possible.

Of course, Holmes is not in the other room. He has sneaked back
and hidden himself behind the curtain to listen to the two criminals.
Doyle has used the device of a phonograph record being played in the
other room to bring this off—something which seems so hopelessly
naive today that this story is not generally considered to be one of the
better ones in the Canon. When the Count takes the diamond out of
his secret pocket, Holmes leaps out from behind the curtain and seizes
it. The Count—a sportsman at heart—concedes that Holmes has
beaten him. Merton acknowledges that it was "A fair cop!" The two
are led away and Holmes returns the diamond to its grateful owner,
Lord Cantlemere.

Now, let's examine *The Crown Diamond: An Evening with Sherlock Holmes in one act* by Arthur Conan Doyle.

This play was first performed May 2, 1921, at the Hippodrome, Bristol, England, where it ran for a week, and then went to the Coliseum in London, where it played a short run from May 16, 1921. It lasted through August and then was shelved. If it has been produced anywhere else in the world since that date, we are unaware of it. According to Green & Gibson, the standard bibliography on Doyle,[2] it was commissioned by Oswood Stoll and a contract was signed with the producers, the Daniel Mayer Company, on April 18, 1921. The story was based on the success of Eille Norwood as Holmes in the Stoll Films series. Green & Gibson say "Norwood's disguises were remarkable and his sphinx-like countenance suggested the idea for the [play]." Here is an extract from the crucial scene in the play (with Colonel Sebastian Moran as villain, in place of Count Sylvius):

HOLMES: I have the cabman who took you to Whitehall, and the cabman who brought you away. I have the commissionaire who saw you beside the case. I have Ikey Cohen who refused to cut it up for you. Ikey has peached, and the game is up.

COLONEL: Ikey Cohen has split.

The play predated the story, which probably explains why it is told in the third person. Doyle clearly intended his Ikey, Ikey "Cohen," to be a Jew in *The Crown Diamond.* But between the play and the publication of the story in *The Strand Magazine,* he seems to have become sensitive about offending Jews and changed Ikey's surname to "Sanders" in "The Mazarin Stone." Cohen, after all, is the Hebrew name for a priest—a descendant in a direct line from Aaron, brother of Moses. While many people with this name had menial jobs and lived in poverty in London at that time, nevertheless, the name implied dignity

---

2 *A Bibliography of A. Conan Doyle,* Clarendon Press, Oxford, 1983. pp. 203 & 209.

and its use to describe an unsavoury character would have been doubly offensive to the Jewish community. We'd like to think, though we have no evidence to rely on, that Conan Doyle was responding to private criticism received from the Jewish religious authorities, possibly even to a complaint from Herbert Marcus Adler, grandson of Herman Adler, Chief Rabbi of England and consultant to Scotland Yard in the Ripper case. Herbert Adler was a lawyer and director of Jewish education in London at the time. But it is clear to us that, despite acquiring his new surname, Ikey Sanders was a character intended to be a Jew. Donald Redmond, in his *Study in Sources,*[3] agrees with us that the character was to be Jewish. Based on his occupation and the use of the name 'Ikey', there really can't be much doubt about this, as we will explain. "Sanders" itself is a common enough name in the London of the early years of the 20th century—Redmond found 19 private residents and 67 trade entities with that name in the *Post Office* list. But the name "Ikey" or "Isaac Sanders" does not appear in that list. However, Redmond did not have the advantage of the 1901 British census online. There were 23 Isaac Sanders in the U.K., a handful of them in London. There were also 19 Isaac Solomons living in London at the time of the 1901 census—one of them a bookseller, living in Whitechapel. No "Ikey" Sanders or Solomons is listed. Sanders, of course, is not an inherently "Jewish" name, nor is its variant "Saunders." In fact, neither surname appears in *Encyclopedia Judaica,* the standard reference work.

We have debated many Sherlockian points, esoteric and otherwise. This time we collaborated in our research to determine just who was this Ikey who peached.

WHERE DID SIR ARTHUR CONAN DOYLE GET THE NAME "IKEY "FROM?

We would like to discuss the derivation of the name "Ikey" and whether it was derogatory. Can we assume it was derogatory? Would

---

3 McGill-Queen's University Press, 1982, p.200

the contemporary audience have considered it to be derogatory? We start with the definition of "Ikey" from the *Oxford English Dictionary:*

Ikey: *sb* and a *slang* and *dial.* Also Ike, Iky, I. Familiar abbreviated form of the Jewish name Isaac (also Ikeymo f. *Isaac* and *Moses),* used typically for: a Jew or someone taken to be or resembling a Jew; also, a receiver, moneylender, etc.; *transfr.* a loafer; a tip, information; *(Austral.)* a bookmaker. As *adj.* **(a)** artful, crafty, knowing, 'fly'; (b) having a good opinion of oneself 'stuck-up'.

Derogatory and offensive in all uses as applied to persons.

1836 DICKENS *Sk. Boz.* (1836) 1st Ser. II. 44 'Let me alone,' replied Ikey, 'and I'll ha vound up … in five seconds.' 1870 LEYBOURNE in Farmer & Henley *Slang* (1896) IV, 2 My name is Ikey Bill, A Whitechapel Covey am I. 1874 HOTTEN *Slang Dict.,* 'Ikey,' a 'Jew' fence. 1881 *Punch* 10 Sept., 110/1 'Arf Ikey of course, put-up business.

1887 Parish & Shaw *Dict. Kentish Dial* 83, *Ikey,* proud. 1889 BARRERE & LELAND, *Dict. Slang, Ikey* (popular) a Jew; ..Also said of anyone who thinks himself knowing, smart; and has a great opinion of himself. 1892 CHEVALIER in Farmer & Hensley *Slang* (1896) IV, 2 Artful little Ikey little ways. 1894 ARTHUR MORRISON The child of the Jago. 1897 I. SCOTT *How I stole* 10,000 *Sheep in Austral. & NZ.* 33 Jim now hit on a rather 'Iky' way to do the ride to Wellington. 1906 RUSSELL & RIGBY *Making of Criminal* i. 7 His clothes are so very poor that he does not like… 'to show himself up' by appearing in them, especially if they are of a kind only affected by the professional loafer or 'ike'. 1911 D. H. LAWRENCE *White Peacock* vii 484, I haven't been to see them lately-can't stand Meg's ikeyness. 1913 D. H. LAWRENCE *Sons & Lovers* IX, 241 I want people to think we're awful swells. So look ikey.

Of course, we can't categorically state that "Ikey"—Sanders or Cohen—was intended to be a derogatory reference. Holmes does not say that he was implicated in the crime, merely that he was approached to cut up the stone and refused to do it. He may even have been an honest diamond cutter who recognized that the stone did not belong to the Count and did not want to become involved in a crime—hence he peached, or informed, on the culprits. However, against that interpretation, we have to point out that Holmes says "Ikey has peached," which clearly implies that he was involved in the underworld in some way but chose to sit out this particular crime. Ikey had to have been someone disreputable or who made a habit of working the criminal side—an honest man would not be trusted by criminals to do this and would not have 'peached.' Only a crook would peach. The best conclusion we can draw is that Ikey was an unsavoury character whom the Count and his associate had good reason to believe would assist them in carrying out the crime, even if only as an accessory after the fact. When Sherlock Holmes put pressure on him, it was second nature for Ikey to betray his client.

How did Ikey come to have this connotation of "crook", "sly" and, above all, Jewish? In the early 1800s, a man named Isaac or Ikey Solomons made quite a name for himself in the London underworld. He was a fence—a receiver of stolen goods. Starting, unsuccessfully, as a pickpocket, he returned to London after serving a prison sentence and became quite wealthy in his new profession, with a £20,000 establishment in Rosemary Lane. His subsequent arrest, escape, recapture, trial and transportation made his name a household word in London.

An interesting side issue on Solomons is whether Dickens based the character of Fagin in his 1837-8 novel, *Oliver Twist,* on him. Certainly he knew of him but scholarly opinion now is divided on this issue. JJ. Tobias, who wrote an excellent and highly readable biography of Ikey Solomons, *Prince of Fences: The Life and crimes of Ikey*

Solomons,[4] has presented an argument against Solomons being the model for Fagin, which we can summarize as follows: There is no physical resemblance between the two and Ikey does not seem to have engaged in the kinds of activities attributed to the totally evil Fagin, with his stable of young pickpockets. Fagin did not, as Ikey did, have a criminal wife—which would have been a wonderful character for Dickens to build into the story. Dickens never mentioned a connection to Solomons. He was distressed by the criticism of anti-Semitism in *Oliver Twist,* manifested by a protest at the presentation of the play in 1838, and wrote to Mrs. Eliza Davis, a Jewish friend, that this particular class of criminal was almost invariably Jewish, but without referring to Solomons. Tobias concludes: "Would it not have been the strongest possible argument that he could put forward, if he could say that Fagin was not entirely the creation of his own imagination but an adaptation of an existing and notorious Jewish receiver?"[5]

IKEY SOLOMONS,
From a Sketch taken at the Lambeth Street Police Office.

4 Valentine Mitchell: London, 1974

5 *Ibid,* p. 148.

Certainly the playbill for Dickens' play *Oliver Twist*, produced at the Royal Surrey Theatre in 1838, mentions Ikey Solomons but not as the inspiration for Fagin.

On the other hand, Tobias does not cite, or is ignorant of the reference to 'Ikey' as a Jewish fence in *Boz*, referred to in the OED definition above. In *A Passage in the Life of Mrs. Watkins Tattle*, from Dickens' *Sketches by Boz* (Ch. 2), "Ikey" is an attendant at a debtor's prison run by Solomon Jacobs—the implication is that Ikey is Jewish. However, in this case, he is not a criminal but merely a somewhat larcenous official. In Edgar Rosenberg's *From Shylock to Svengali: Jewish Stereotypes in English Fiction*,[6] the argument is made that Dickens would certainly have been aware of Ikey Solomons when he wrote *Oliver Twist*, either from recollection of the trial, or from the then well-known play *Van Diemen's Land* by W.T. Moncrieff, in which Ikey Solomons has a part in a convict plantation. Interestingly, the character was originally named "Barney Fence," but Moncrieff was induced to change it due to the publicity of Ikey Solomon's trial. It was very popular and there is little doubt that Dickens saw or read the play. It has been pointed out that Fagin lacks any stereotypical Jewish traits and Dickens, perhaps in an attempt to prove he had not meant to be anti-Semitic, ended up creating the almost too admirable Jewish

> **OLD BAILEY, Friday, May 13.**
> This being Friday, the day upon which our criminal courts endeavour to try the cases of murder, in order that the unhappy convicts may, by the intervention of Sunday, live for four-and-twenty hours longer than the severity of the law would otherwise permit, the court was crowded to hear the trials for this most heinous of all offences. The first case, however, was that of the demurrer upon the verdict of the notorious Ikey Solomons. The judgment and verdict of the trial were confirmed by the Court, and the prisoner was sentenced to be transported beyond seas for the term of 14 years.
> MURDER.
> *Thomas Gallagher, Edward Gallagher, Martin Moran,*

A listing from *The Times* of a case at the Old Bailey involving Ikey Solomons

6 Peter Owens: London, 1961

character, Riah, in his final novel *Our Mutual Friend,* published in 1864-5 (though why he would wait 27 years before trying to correct a false impression is difficult to understand). We simply don't have the time or inclination to spend on this point—it seems obvious to us that, whether or not Dickens based Fagin on Ikey Solomons, Ikey was the chief archetype of a particular class of criminal that Dickens was thinking of when he created the character. The scholarly debate is interesting but not germane to the question of whether Ikey Sanders is based on Ikey Solomons.

Let us now turn to "fences" as discussed in Kellow Chesney's *The Victorian Underworld.*[7]

'Ou' do', the plaintive yell of the barrow buyer, was a synonym for the Jew. In conventional minds there was also a strong connection between the Jew and the fence and, from Fagin downwards, the stereotype of the dealer in shady goods has a Semitic nose.

Ikey Solomons was a well-known convict in the 19th, century. Here is a brief chronology of his life taken from JJ Tobias' text,[8] *Prince of Fences: The Life and Times of Ikey Solomons.* Much of what Tobias relates is taken from the daily accounts of court proceedings reported in *The Times:*

> Isaac Solomons, the hero or villain of this book, reached the peak of his fame in July, 1830, when he stood in the dock at the Old Bailey facing thirteen charges of theft and receiving stolen goods. He had had a similar experience twenty years before: in June, 1810, he had been sentenced to transportation for life for picking pockets. He was not, in fact, sent out of the country as a result of this sentence, and in 1816 he was released from imprisonment. In the next ten years he built up for himself a position

---

7 London: Temple Smith Ltd. 1970

8 *Supra*, footnote 4

as one of London's leading fences ('the great Ikey Solomons', he was called), the bubble being pricked by a search of his home in 1826 and his arrest in 1827. This resourceful man then escaped from custody and managed to get out of England, eventually joining his wife in Van Diemen's Land (the modern Tasmania), where she had gone as a convict—for between Ikey's two trials at the Old Bailey, his wife and his father had stood in the same place. Both were sentenced on the same day in 1827, although their offences were not connected. Ikey was recognized as an escaped prisoner on his arrival in Van Diemen's Land and, after a great legal battle which attracted much attention, he was shipped back to England to stand trial. Convicted on two of the thirteen charges in July, 1830, he returned to Van Diemen's Land the following year as a convict. He and his wife were eventually reunited—but only to quarrel and separate. Ikey died a poor and lonely man in 1850. That, in outline, is the story of this book.

Here is one version of how Ikey escaped from custody, as reported in *The Times:*

> Once in Newgate, Ikey applied for bail, which meant he had to be taken in a coach to the Court of King's Bench in Westminster Hall. On May 25, 1827, bail was denied. However, on the return trip to Newgate, he managed to escape from the coach ... the coach was one owned, and possibly driven by his father-in-law. Somehow he was able to befuddle the turnkeys enough to get the coach detoured into Petticoat Lane, where he jumped out while a small mob of confederates kept the turnkeys from pursuing him, while he disappeared into the local maze of Whitechapel streets.

Compare this description of Ikey's escape with the trick devised by Holmes for Watson in *The Final Problem*. Watson is to take the third hansom cab, jump out and run through the Lowther Arcade, dash through and into a waiting cab at the other end, which is to take him to Victoria Station. The waiting cab was driven by a relative of Sherlock's—his brother, Mycroft. We're not suggesting that Conan Doyle got his inspiration for this device from Ikey Solomon, but...

SOME FURTHER IKEY REFERENCES

Thackeray used the pen name 'Ikey Solomons, Esq., junior' for *Catherine, a Story,* in *Fraser's Magazine* in seven parts in 1839-40. In his novel *A Child of the Jago,* 1896, Arthur Morrison refers to "the prince of fences, Ikey Solomons," without having to explain to his readers who he was. Morrison refers to Ikey's fixed prices for the same items in his own fictional fence. Morrison is perhaps better known to Sherlockian scholars for having created the private detective Martin Hewitt, who appeared in *The Strand Magazine* as one of its replacements for Sherlock Holmes after Reichenbach. It is at least possible, even likely, that Doyle would have read Morrison's work.

An appearance not unlike Dickens' *Boz* can be found in Watts Phillips, *The Wild Tribes of London,* 1855, in which the narrator and his friend tour a private debtor's prison and meet a functionary named Ikey:

> Melting down's what did him up; we caught him at it, and he got his seven year for it; didn't cure the old fence though. He is one of the worst of em now. A regular old sinner is Ikey, with cunning enough for a hundred.
>
> Hilloh, Ikey! how are you, old boy?
>
> Mr. Isaacs looks up, and discloses a very wicked-looking face, all wrinkled up and puckered into squares, like a pattern for Berlin wool, and to which

the white hair and beard seem scarcely to belong. He closes his book—a well thumbed ledger—and approaches the door, where, after kicking spitefully at the children on the step, he greets our friend as an old acquaintance.

Other modern references from the *Oxford English Dictionary*:

1927 T. PRENTICE *Music-Hall Memories* 16 Sez as I'm as ikey as the Dook of Boocle-Oo. 1934 *Bulletin* (Sydney) 18 Apr 11/1 She laid the odds, as smartly and acutely, I'll bet, as any trousered Ikey Mo. 1936 J.G. BRANDON *Dragnet* xiii 132 'E passed the ike, that there was somethink on there. 1941 *Penguin New Writing* Ill 69 Go indoors an' 'elp your sister with the washing up, you lazy young ike, 1942. P. ABRAHAMS *Dark Testament* I, xiii 72 Any guy his pal. Chink, ike. 1954 J. SYMONS *Narrowing Circle,* 135 I'm a Hackney Jew, Dave. At school they called us Ikeymoes and Jewboys. 1966 F. SHAW et. Al. *Lern Yerself Scouse* 36 *Yer very ikey* you are very dandified. 1969 *Private Eye* 6 June 14 *(caption)* Pull your head in, ikey *mo!* 1972 R. PLAYER *Oh! Where are Bloody Mary's Earrings* vi, 168 The Ikeys will win-you can stake your life on that. Hence Ike, I-ky v. (see quot. 1932); I-key-ness, the quality of, or an act of being, ikey. 1932 *Amer. Speech* VII, 401 *Iky* to jew down the price, to cheat, 'He ikied me out of my turn.' 1960 WENTWORTH & FLEXNER *Dict. Amer. Slang, Ike* v. to cheat; to lower the price by haggling; to 'Jew down'.

And, of course, we cannot overlook James Joyce, who in *Ulysses*, ch. *15,* part 1 [1922]: wrote:

"Three cheers for Ikey Mo!"

The quote comes shortly after Bloom sidesteps a ragman at midnight, saying that he is more likely a fence. After further accusations of impropriety against the ragman from two women:

> *-A crowd of sluts and ragamuffins surges forward.)*
> THE SLUTS AND RAGAMUFFINS

> *(Screaming.)* Stop thief! Hurrah there, Bluebeard! Three cheers for Ikey Mo!"

The reference is enigmatic, to say the least!

It is clear that Ikey Solomons was, if not a household name, certainly a very familiar element of the cultural literacy of any well-educated Victorian or Edwardian, even when this story was penned in 1921—just as much as his fellow master criminals Jonathan Wild (1683-1725) and Charlie Peace (1832-1879). Doyle has Holmes refer to Wild in *The Valley of Fear* (and mentions Fielding's novel *Jonathan Wild* in *Through the Magic Door).* Sherlock Holmes refers to Charlie Peace with affection in "The Illustrious Client". In the same story, he also refers to "Wainwright"— Thomas Griffiths Wainwright (1794-1847), almost a contemporary of Isaac Solomons, transported to Tasmania for forgery in 1837, and suspected but never convicted of murder by poison. In fact, Doyle may well have been reflecting on his own reading tastes when, in *The Valley of Fear*, he has Holmes lecture Inspector MacDonald:

> Mr. Mac, the most practical thing that you ever did in
> your life would be to shut yourself up for three months
> and read twelve hours a day at the annals of crime.

So, is this proof that Conan Doyle knew of Ikey Solomons and had him in mind when naming Ikey Sanders (formerly Ikey Cohen)? No. But it is most instructive. Nowhere else in his voluminous published writings does Conan Doyle mention the name "Ikey." The name is not a common one for him—it is deliberately selected to fit the need of this story. He had to invent an underworld character who could help dispose of a hot diamond and he chose the name of a man who was famous for his ability to do just that. Among his other activities, Isaac Solomons was said to have owned a jewelery shop. In fact, Ikey is still a well-known character today, thanks to the bestselling 1996 novel *The Potato Factory*,[9] by Bryce Courtenay and the 2012 Australian documentary film *The First Fagin*.

---

9 Little, Brown and Company (Canada) Limited, Boston, New York, Toronto, London, 1996.

SHERLOCK IN JERUSALEM

Presentation to The Bootmakers of Toronto, April 1, 2006, Canadian Holmes *Vol.34,
No. 1 Fall 2011. Winner of the True Davidson Memorial Award for best paper presented
to the Bootmakers of Toronto in 2006. Joseph Kessel was a co-presenter of this paper.*

PART I: HARTLEY NATHAN BEGINS THIS ARTICLE WITH AN INTRODUCTION

Many "Sherlockians," as we call ourselves, consider Sherlock Holmes and Dr. Watson to have been real persons who lived at 221B Baker Street in London. Dr. Watson was the scribe and Conan Doyle the literary agent who arranged for the stories to be published. This is known as "playing the game," and it can be a great deal of fun balancing what was going on in the real world against the events of the stories, as if they are real. To quote the great English mystery writer Dorothy Sayers: "[The game] must be played as solemnly as a cricket match at Lord's; the slightest touch of extravagance or burlesque ruins the atmosphere." Conan Doyle has been described, unfairly in my opinion, as a "highly compulsive, self-revealing allegorist who had artfully implanted a large number of clues among his stories. These clues profoundly associate Doyle and Sherlock Holmes and his companions with several "real life, fictional, legendary, and Biblical figures."[1]

---

1 Samuel Rosenberg: *Naked is the Best Disguise.* Bobbs-Merrill Company, Inc., New York: 1974. pp. 1-2.

This article will focus on two stories in the Canon: "The Final Problem," published in the December 1893 edition of *The Strand Magazine*, and which takes place from April 24th to May 4th, 1891, and "The Adventure of the Empty House", which took place on Thursday, April 5, 1894, and was published in *The Strand Magazine* in 1903.

Lithograph from photograph of Jerusalem by Horace Vernet

In November 1891, Doyle wrote to his mother: "I think of slaying Holmes, and winding him up for good and all. He takes my mind from other things."

In August of 1893, while Conan Doyle was in Switzerland, he confessed to some fellow travellers "that he was tired of his own creation"—"I intend to make an end of him. If I don't, he'll make an end of me."

Four months later, in December 1893, he did so. The nefarious Professor Moriarty and Sherlock Holmes engaged in a struggle and both supposedly fell to their deaths at Reichenbach Falls at Meiringen, Switzerland, as described in "The Final Problem."

In his memoir, "The Final Problem", written in 1893, Dr. Watson states:

> It is with a heavy heart that I take up my pen to write these last words in which I shall ever record the singular gifts by which my friend Mr. Sherlock Holmes was distinguished.

One of these singular gifts was the art of disguise.

Partly as a result of public outcry and offers he could not refuse for more Holmes stories, Doyle performed the difficult task of retrieving the great detective from his watery grave. He does this in 1903 with "The Adventure of the Empty House".

The manner in which Holmes occupied himself during the interval from Moriarty's death and Holmes' return—known to Sherlockians as "The Great Hiatus"—is a source of enduring delight to his admirers and is at the heart of this article.

In "The Adventure of the Empty House,"[2] Holmes tells us what he did during the Great Hiatus:

> I traveled for two years in Tibet, therefore, and amused myself by visiting Lhasa and spending some days with the head Lama. You may have read of the remarkable explorations of a Norwegian named Sigerson, but I am sure that it never occurred to you that you were receiving news of your friend. I then passed through Persia, looked in at Mecca, and paid a short but interesting visit to the Khalifa at Khartoum, the results of which I have communicated to the Foreign Office. Returning to France, I spent some months in a research into the coal-tar derivatives, which I conducted in a laboratory at Montpelier,[3] in the south of France.

The whole chronicle of his three years of travels is three sentences—117 words—and has inspired more commentary than almost any other Sherlockian event. There is no shortage of critical commentary devoted to this passage.[4] Les Klinger, in his masterful *The New*

---

2 "The Adventure of the Empty House" was published in *Collier's Magazine*, September 26, 1903 and in *The Strand Magazine*, October 1903.

3 The spelling of 'Montpelier' is incorrect in the Canon—One 'l' Montpelier is in Vermont. Holmes visited Two 'll' Montpellier in France.

4 See for example, Evan M. Wilson: "The Trip That Never Was or Sherlock Holmes in the Middle East," *Baker Street Journal*, Vol. 20, No. 2 (June 1970), p. 67 and the extensive treatment by Baring-Gould in *The Annotated Sherlock Holmes*, Vol. II, pp. 320-328.

Annotated Sherlock Holmes (2005) analyses the various theories and conjectures. He states:

> There is a distinct school of thought that "The Great
> Hiatus" never happened. The rationale for this view
> can be summarized as follows:
>
> 1. Tibet–was one of the most remote and inaccessible
>   places on Earth and was basically closed to Europeans;
> 2. Persia–travel was almost impossible; there were
>   no highways until the 1920s and no railways until
>   the 1930s;
> 3. Mecca–was barred to infidels. The Europeans
>   that visited Mecca and Medina were few and
>   far between, one of them being Johann Ludwig
>   Burckhardt in 1815. The most famous "visitor,"
>   of course, was Sir Richard Burton in 1853. Both
>   were fluent in Arabic and studied the Koran and
>   Islamic law. In fact, Burton was a convert to Islam.
>   Burckhardt disguised himself as a Syrian trader
>   and Burton as a Persian Sh'ia.[5]
> 4. Khartoum–by the time Sherlock Holmes could have
>   visited Khartoum in the Sudan, it had been levelled
>   by the Mahdi in 1885. Six months later, the Mahdi
>   was dead of typhus and his successor, the Khalifa, was
>   in Omdurman, which was more likely where Sherlock
>   would have gone.[6]

One writer[7] has suggested that Holmes may have visited the Holy
Land, rather than having gone in the impossible directions given by

---

5 Edward Rice: *Captain Sir Richard Francis Burton*. Charles Scribner's Sons, New York: 1990. pp. 181-4.

6 Any European would be in "mortal fear of his life" if he visited the Khalifa. See Rudolf E.
  Slatin: *Fire and Sword in the Sudan*. Edward Arnold, London: 1898

7 Wilson, footnote 4, p. 73.

Holmes and Watson and postulated "we should pursue our studies on the subject of Sherlock Holmes in the Middle East." This is too daunting a challenge to pass up.

Notwithstanding the above obstacles, let us assume Holmes did, in fact, do all that he said he did en route home to London.

PART II: JOSEPH KESSEL'S RENDITION OF THE RETURN JOURNEY HOME, 1893-4

Early in June 1893, as the snows retreated and the weather warmed up again, Holmes, as Sigerson, left Tibet and the city of Lhasa by the river route through the north-east Himalayas.

Following down the Dihong River, onto the Brahmaputra, and on through its tributaries, he reached the city of Calcutta.

Here he settled in lodgings near the centre to recover and resupply after the long and hazardous trip. Visiting the main branch of his bank—possibly Barclays—for funds as arranged with Mycroft back in London, he was handed a sealed envelope with the name Sigerson written on it. Inside were instructions (should he wish to follow them) from HM Government to search out a route along the Nile between Egypt and Khartoum in the Sudan which an expeditionary force might follow and possibly build a rail link, since the river route had failed in 1882.

In 1881, Mohammed Achmed, known as the Mahdi, led a rebellion in the Sudan against the Turkish-Egyptian occupiers. It plunged the Sudan into chaos. British attempts to withdraw from the region climaxed in General Gordon's ill-fated attempts to rescue officials, soldiers and Egyptian subjects from Khartoum. Gordon was killed at Khartoum on January 25, 1885, and the residents slaughtered by the Mahdi's army in the most cruel manner possible. The Mahdi died of typhoid fever a few months later and was succeeded by his loyal lieutenant, the Khalifa.

In England there was a rising agitation for another campaign in the Sudan. Revenge for the death of Gordon was, of course, a leading motive. International politics also pushed the British into contemplating action. In the general scramble for territory in Africa, they had supported the claims of Germany and Italy against the French and it was feared that France was preparing to move into the Sudan. To all this was added the fear that the Khalifa, who was cut from the same cloth as the Mahdi, might renew his attack on Egypt and the Suez Canal.

By July, Holmes commences his journey via the Indian Railway system across the subcontinent from Calcutta to Bombay on the west coast.

This is a well-established route, running via Sambalpur, Raipur and Nagpur. En route he spends some time studying the rail system, the construction of the numerous bridges and the track, and how it has improved and speeded up travel throughout the country. What name did he go by? Surely, not Sherlock Holmes. Apart from the fact that such use would instantly identify him as British or American, the name itself was by then well known throughout the world. Much too dangerous. And because he was widely thought to be dead, at best he would have been tagged as an imposter. The name he had been using in Tibet—Sigerson—was too Norwegian for Arabia or Africa. To emulate Richard Burton, he needed to pass as a Muslim and to get to Khartoum he had to get to Mecca first as a pilgrim. What better than to translate his pseudonym into Bin Sayaad (son of 'Siger' = 'seeker' or 'hunter')?

Arriving in Bombay he ascertains the onward route. He will travel to Bandar Abbas in Persia with the P&O line, transforming himself from the European explorer to Hafiz, a Persian merchant who is preparing, as a devout pilgrim, to make Hajj to Mecca.[8]

---

8 Disguise for the purpose of the Hajj consisted of: Colouring the skin to appear as an upper-class Persian merchant. Shaving the head, except for one lock at the rear. Growing a beard—the longer, the better. Could have started in India or Tibet, as the plan takes shape.

"Clothes make the Man." Zir-jamah-cotton pants. Ark-halik—skirts, karmarchen—tunic of Calico . Kafsh or slippers worn with heel folded down. Headgear and urussi—Russian shoes. Medical records show that on rare occasions some males are born already circumcised. This is considered a special blessing in the Jewish religion! It must be assumed that Sherlock Holmes was one of these rare males. Otherwise it would have been suicide to proceed on this perilous escapade.

In Bandar Abbas he changes his appearance, shaves his head, buys the necessary clothes and engages a servant ready for the Hajj, which in that year takes place from August to October. It is the year 1310 AH of the Muslim calendar.

From Bandar Abbas he makes his way by P&O steamer in September 1893, with hundreds of other pilgrims, to Aden, a transfer point en route to Jiddah, the port on the Red Sea closest to Mecca, which is reached by dhow, the traditional means of travel. The overland portion is a distance of 45 miles (72 kilometers) and is travelled in the company of many hundreds of Muslims from many lands and backgrounds—a good place to blend in without drawing attention to oneself.

At the end of the Hajj in October 1893, Holmes crosses the Red Sea by dhow to the port city of Suakin (now called Port Sudan). Camel caravans bring the returning pilgrims to Omdurman on the Nile.

Khartoum is in ruins and has been abandoned since the siege of Gordon. Here in Omdurman the Khalifa holds public gatherings for his multitude of followers. It would be a very brave Englishman who would dare to visit such a bloodthirsty tyrant. We believe he did. His disguise as a pilgrim was very convincing.

Leaving Omdurman (via Khartoum to Cairo), again by sailboat down the Nile, Holmes observes the terrain and the traffic moving steadily in both directions. How does one move a whole army the 700 km from the border with Egypt?

On arrival in Cairo, Holmes finally sheds his disguise and reappears as Sigerson once again. He meets with Sir Evelyn Baring, the British Pro-Consul for Egypt, the one man who will plan the expedition to retake the Sudan. But this will now take time and only start some years down the road. Holmes has made his report, fulfilled the task set him by HM Government and is now free to pursue his own desires.

He makes the short trip to Port Said, where there are regular 13-hour long sailings to the Port of Jaffa.

His new disguise, effected onboard, is that of Rabbi Shalom Bayit (peace on your home!), mild-mannered traveller to the Holy Land. While the Ottoman authorities are leery of potential Jewish settlers, they turn a blind eye to religious personnel of all persuasions visiting the area. Because of his undoubted fluency in German, we believe Holmes could speak a passable Yiddish. Jaffa is the terminal of the new rail link, completed in 1892, to Jerusalem. This is the most convenient way to make the journey through the coastal plain to Jerusalem, the City of David, in December 1893.

PART III -CLIFF GOLDFARB PONTIFICATES ON WHY HOLMES WOULD WANT TO VISIT JERUSALEM IN 1893.

Before giving you the reasons why Sherlock Holmes may have visited Jerusalem, let me give you a description of what he might have seen in December 1893. Jerusalem was a sleepy, decrepit hilltown with a population of about 45,000, consisting of 28,000 Jews; 8,700 Christian Arabs and Europeans and 8,600 Muslim Arabs (these numbers may underestimate the Muslim population).

Although the Zionist movement was officially established only in 1897, unofficially the idea of promoting a Jewish presence in Jerusalem had been underway since the middle of the century. Prior to 1858, when the modern building period commenced, Jerusalem lay wholly within its 16th-century walls, and even as late as 1875 there were few private residences beyond their limits. By 1893, several decades of construction had created a substantial community outside the walls.[9] Arabs also poured into the land, from what is now Syria and Lebanon, to take advantage of the prosperity and jobs created by the Jewish settlers. Both sets of immigration—Jewish and Arab— helped to create the Israel-Palestine demographic situation of today. As early as the 1860s, the English Jewish philanthropist Sir Moses Montefiore was financing the building of new Jewish neighbourhoods in and around Jerusalem, and there were German movements as well to encourage Jewish settlement in the city. Considerable new construction was being undertaken, especially in the Jewish quarter.

---

9 *Encyclopedia Britannica*, 1911, "Jerusalem"

This was the dawn of modern Jewish settlement in Palestine. In 1892 the Ottomans had prohibited the sale of land to foreign Jews. In 1893 the European powers pressured the Ottoman government to permit Jews legally resident in Palestine to buy land, provided they established no colonies on it.

Why did Holmes go to Jerusalem? Until his personal archives, the existence and location of which are known only to the writers and a select few others, are unsealed and made available for scholarly study, all we have to go on is the published works of his biographer, Dr. John Watson, whose own notes and papers have never, despite numerous claims, been found. And Watson is silent, even as to the very existence of this visit. So in the absence of concrete evidence, we must, to use the very words of Sir Arthur Conan Doyle, "make his visit."[10] Let us make it clear at the outset that none of us has the least bit of doubt that Holmes did, in fact, pay a visit to the Holy Land, and particularly Jerusalem, since he was already in the area. There are a number of compelling reasons for this conclusion. These fall under the following headings:

Archaeology
Philology
History
Sentimental
Politics
Adventure
Religion
Freemasonry

---

10 From *Through the Magic Door*, referring to "The Lost Special."

> The great writer can never go wrong. If Shakespeare gives a sea coast to Bohemia or if Victor Hugo calls an English prizefighter Mr. Jim-John-Jack -well, it was so, and that's an end of it. "There is no second line of rails at that point," said an editor to a minor author. "I make a second line," said the author; and he was within his rights, if he can carry his readers' conviction with him.

In letter 9 in the Arthur Conan Doyle Collection at the Toronto Reference Library, he wrote to his editor, Greenhough Smith, that "I should not hesitate at laying down a fresh line of rails—Or a fresh railway line as I did in [*The Lost Special*.]"

ARCHAEOLOGY

Because of the activities of the Palestine Exploration Fund, which had been excavating in Jerusalem since 1865, and publishing regular reports, as well as reports in the popular press, particularly *The Illustrated London News*, there was a high degree of awareness among the British public of the new discoveries. Some of the early excavators, including Captains Charles Wilson and Charles Warren and Colonel Claude Conder,[11] used their military engineering skills to drive long tunnels under populated areas, in order to expose earlier construction. Frederick J. Bliss (1859-1937), an American archaeologist who had been working at the seminal site of Tell el-Hesi, continued the work of the Fund in Jerusalem from 1894-1897, assisted by Archibald Dickie. Together they made important contributions to understanding the archaeology of the city. Bliss helped to delineate the city walls, often using the same tunneling methods of the first PEF archaeologists, to avoid causing friction with the religious inhabitants of the areas beneath which they were excavating. Bliss also excavated a Byzantine church in the area of the Pool of Siloam. In 1893, there were no prominent excavations going on in the city, although several of the monasteries were carrying on digs, literally in their own cellars.

Unfortunately, it is almost certain that Holmes did not come to Jerusalem, or anywhere else in Palestine, to offer his services on an archaeological dig. A comprehensive review of the literature, including an exhaustive survey of newspaper indices of the year 1893, reveals that there were no ongoing excavations in Jerusalem in that year. So apart from curiosity, and the opportunity to perhaps visit some of the remains of expeditions from the previous decades, we can safely conclude that archaeology was not a motive for his visit.

---

11 Professor A.H. Sayce, who was one of the early archaeologists to work in Palestine, was the great uncle of Kenneth Sayce, M.Bt, one of the early members of the Bootmakers. In Sept. 27, 1890 he had published an article in *The Illustrated London News* on recent discoveries at the Biblical sites of Lachish and Eglon. We believe Holmes would have been well aware of this article.

PHILOLOGY

What better place for Holmes to further his study of Chaldean, the language we now know as Aramaic? In the first century, Aramaic, which is closely related to Biblical Hebrew, was the spoken language of the common folk. But we believe that he was already well up in Aramaic when he arrived in Jerusalem, having been speaking it for weeks in the travels leading him there.

How would he get around without being discovered as an Englishman—both at Mecca, then at Khartoum and in between travelling in Arab lands? At Mecca he would do it as a Persian, elsewhere as a Christian, speaking Aramaic and passing himself off as a dweller from the hills of Syria. This would allow him to speak Arabic badly.

How do we know he could speak these languages?

Here is an extract from "The Adventure of the Devil's Foot":

> [I]n the spring of the year 1897 we found ourselves together in a small cottage near Poldhu Bay, at the further extremity of the Cornish peninsula...The ancient Cornish language had...arrested his attention, and he had, I remember, conceived the idea that it was akin to the Chaldean, and had been largely derived from the Phoenician' traders in tin. He had received a consignment of books upon philology and was settling down to develop this thesis.

Chaldean was, of course, what is known today as Aramaic. What Watson neglects to say is that Holmes already had a well-developed knowledge of Aramaic from his travels in the Middle East, acquired in the hills of Syria and refined among the Assyrian and Chaldean communities of Jerusalem.

As to Persian, or Farsi, here is an extract from "A Case of Identity":

> You may remember the old Persian saying, "There is danger for him who taketh the tiger cub, and danger

also for whoso snatches a delusion from a woman."
There is as much sense in Hafiz as in Horace, and as
much knowledge of the world.

Conan Doyle displays his own interest in the Persian language in *The Mystery of Cloomber*, a non-Sherlockian tale written in 1888. Possibly this interest came from his own contacts with Holmes.

HISTORY

If you think of history as important things that happened in an important place, that changed the way we live now, then no place is more important than Jerusalem. How could Holmes not go there, when he was so close?

The answer is that he had to go to Jerusalem, to walk its streets, visit its sacred sights, the churches, markets, burial grounds, pools and ruins that for 3,000 years have been at the centre of the events that shaped our civilization. Perhaps this was his only reason to visit Jerusalem—he was only a tourist! Perhaps, but ...

SENTIMENTAL

We know from "The Adventure of the Greek Interpreter" that Holmes' grandmother was a sister of the French painter Vernet. Which Vernet is something of which we are not certain. The consensus seems to be that it was Horace (1789-1863), who like his father Carl, also painted battle scenes. Horace Vernet, therefore, was Holmes' uncle. Horace was the first photographer in Jerusalem, in 1839 (with his nephew or student, Frédéric Goupil-Fesquet, and another nephew, possibly Holmes' cousin Charles Bouton, as well as with the Swiss Canadian daguerreotypist Pierre Joly de Lotbinière).

Unfortunately, none of the original plates taken by either Vernet or Goupil-Fesquet have survived and we are left only with lithographs published by Lerebours in *Excursions Daguerreiennes* in 1842, including a panoramic view of Jerusalem and another taken in Alexandria, of which more later. Holmes would likely have seen many photographs of Jerusalem, taken by other early photographers, including Horatio

Lord Kitchener in all his finery

Kitchener (later Lord Kitchener, the man who finally reconquered-Khartoum) as well as the romantic watercolours of David Roberts. He certainly would have wanted to see many of the world-famous sights of the fabulous city for himself.

POLITICS

In Act V of *Caesar and Cleopatra*, written from the vantage point of 1898, George Bernard Shaw has several Romans speaking in the harbour of Alexandria:

> Belzanor: A marvelous man, this Caesar! Will he come soon, think you?
>
> Appolodorus: He was settling the Jewish question when I left.

Was this why Holmes visited Jerusalem? Could he have had a commission from his brother Mycroft, directly on behalf of the Prime Minister, or perhaps for the Foreign Office, to check out the environment for Jewish settlement and the likely reaction of the local Arab and Bedouin populations?

The Dreyfus Affair, in 1894, was beginning to raise its ugly head in France, and, by galvanizing Theodore Herzl to seek a Jewish homeland, would result in the formal establishment of the Zionist movement four years later, and ultimately to the Balfour Declaration, which set out the British government's policy of establishing a Jewish homeland in Palestine.

Why does Holmes mention that he went to Mecca, but then his next stop is Khartoum? Why not mention passing through Jerusalem, or at, the very least, a side trip? Was it because in Jerusalem he was on an ultra-secret mission, one that was so sensitive that it could not be mentioned even 11 years later when Watson's account of the Great Hiatus was published? If so, that explains why Holmes could mention Khartoum, where he was likely also scouting for the British campaign that began in 1896 and culminated with the final victory over the Khalifa in 1898. There was no longer any need for secrecy.

ADVENTURE

Every English boy of Holmes' generation would have been thrilled by the stirring adventures of Sir Richard Burton, especially his famous 1853 trip to Mecca and Medina, disguised variously as a Persian prince and a wandering dervish. Burton succeeded because of his mastery of disguise, facility with languages, ability to think quickly in a dangerous situation and sheer audacity. Does this sound like someone else we know? Holmes must surely have believed that where Sir Richard had gone, he could go too, and maybe further. Under threat of death from the vestiges of the Moriarty organization, on a top-secret mission for the British government, the ability to blend into the native Jerusalem populace was at least as important as Burton's disguise at Mecca.

RELIGION

We believe that Holmes was not an actively religious man. However, a review of the 60 published Holmes tales turns up a few references to chapel attendances at college, evidence of divinity in his discourse on the nature of the rose, frequent Biblical references and allusions and even a willingness to impersonate a clergyman. From here we can infer that he was perhaps an agnostic who wished to explore the greater mysteries and where better to explore them than at the spiritual and geographic centre of the Judaeo-Christian world.

A first visit to Jerusalem is a powerful experience for anyone. The weight of 30 centuries of history, the parade of three major religions, the blood and faith that have washed the Jerusalem Stone which gives the City its distinctive appearance, makes it impossible for even the secular to deny feelings of religion. Holmes would have paid a visit to the Wailing Wall, as it was known in those days, the surviving Western Wall of the Herodian Temple Mount. He may even have approached the Wall, to stuff a handwritten prayer into a crack in the Wall, as Jews have done for centuries and continue to do. Holmes would have wandered through the churches of the Old City, especially the Church of the Holy Sepulchre, founded in the 4th century of our era by Helene, mother of the Byzantine emperor Constantine and said to be built over the burial place of Jesus. Holmes would have been well aware of the debate as to whether this site, or the nearby Garden Tomb, just outside of the City walls, was the correct burial place. This is another compelling reason why Holmes may have visited Jerusalem.

Hartley Nathan explains:

In "The Adventure of the Cardboard Box," Watson possessed a newly framed picture of General Charles Gordon. The location of the Garden Tomb, the supposed location of Jesus' burial place, has been the subject of much speculation. In 1883, Gordon arrived in Jerusalem, an event that proved to be critically important in the history of the Garden Tomb. Gordon, the son of a general, was the best-known and best-loved British soldier of his era. By 1883 Gordon had a worldwide reputation as a military figure surrounded by an aura of mystery. He was the grand representative of the Victorian era, the personification of heroism, duty and loyalty to the British Empire and faith in God. At the same time, he was an ambitious individualist, an adventurous crusader, and a captivating storyteller. Moreover, his deep religious consciousness went beyond the rational—indeed, reaching into spiritual hallucination. Motivated by a religious compulsion, Gordon came to Jerusalem to meditate on questions of faith that had perplexed him from his youth.

Gordon identified what he thought was the Garden Tomb's location. This caused, and still provokes, waves of controversy among pilgrims who wish to visit authentic sites of the Gospels. Even today the Garden Tomb is one of Jerusalem's best-known sites; it is visited by well over 100,000 tourists and pilgrims a year, visitors who imbibe its serene and sacred atmosphere. Indeed, the tranquility of the Garden Tomb provides a striking contrast to the city noise and tumult just outside.

His report on the location was published posthumously in 1885, after Gordon's courageous last stand at Khartoum, of which you have heard already. His identifications of this and other Biblical sites such as Golgotha gained fame and publicity, not for any scientific validity, but because of Gordon's compelling personality and his heroically tragic death.

In 1894, the cave and the surrounding garden were purchased by the Garden Tomb Association for £2,000 sterling raised by an influential group of Englishmen that included the Archbishop of Canterbury. This association still owns and maintains the site.[12]

We theorize that Holmes may have intended to verify Gordon's findings, or better still, he may even have assisted the Garden Tomb Association in its purchase of the site in 1894, a few months after Holmes arrived in Jerusalem.

FREEMASONRY: HARTLEY NATHAN (CONTINUES)

There are no less than five stories in the Canon where the Masonic science and symbols are recognized by Sherlock Holmes. These are "The Red-leaded League," "A Scandal in Bohemia," *A Study in Scarlet*, "The Adventure of the Retired Colourman" and *The Valley of Fear*.

---

12 Gabriel Barkay: "The Garden Tomb. Was Jesus Buried Here?", *Biblical Archaeological Review*. March/April, 1986, p. 40.

For example, in "The Red-Headed League", Holmes recognized Jabez Wilson as a Mason and asserted that "rather against the strict rules of your order, you use an arc and compass breachpin" (the emblem of a Master of a Masonic Lodge).[13]

Was Sherlock Holmes a Freemason? Statements in the Canon indicate that he was certainly knowledgeable about the order's beliefs. To be so knowledgeable, many commentators feel he actually had to be a Freemason himself. [14]

Conan Doyle himself was a Master Mason.[15]

What is Masonry all about and what has it to do with Jerusalem?[16]

The main rituals central to Freemasonry settled around the building of King Solomon's Temple in ancient Jerusalem and the murder of Hiram Abiff, the chief architect of the Temple.

Various accounts date the construction of the Temple to have begun between 1060 BC and 968 BC. This was the First Temple and was destroyed by Nebuchadnessar in 586 BCE. The so called Second Temple was rebuilt supposedly on the site of the First Temple during the reign of Darius the Persian King in 516 BCE after the Jews returned from exile in Babylon. The Second Temple was, in turn, destroyed in 70 CE under the Roman Emperor Vespasian.[17] What remains of the Second Temple is for many Jews the most significant place in Jerusalem and is known as the "Western Wall," "Kotel" or "Wailing Wall."

The exact location on the Temple Mount of the First Temple or the Temple of Solomon is unknown. Perhaps Sherlock Holmes came to Jerusalem to see if he could locate it through the use of his powers of deductive reasoning. To a Mason, visiting the supposed site of the

---

13 Barrett & Potter: "Sherlock Holmes and The Masonic Connection." 45 *Baker Street Miscellanea*, 1986, p. 28.

14 Cecil Ryder: "A Study in Masonry," *Sherlock Holmes Journal*, No. 3, Winter, 1973.

15 Yasha Beresiner: "Elementary, my dear brother—The Case of the Masonic Career of Sir Arthur Conan Doyle." *The Masonic Quarterly*, Issue No. 6 July, 2003.

16 The following is adapted from Michael Baigent and Richard Leigh, *The Temple and the Lodge*, Arcade Publishing, New York: 1989.

17 Flavius Josephus: *Wars of the Jews*. BK VI, Chapter V, Su 8.

Temple would be the equivalent of making the Hajj for a Muslim—not for religious reasons but to reflect on certain Masonic principles.

PART IV – CONCLUSIONS – JOSEPH KESSEL

His trip to Jerusalem over, Holmes continues on to Alexandria in January 1894. Before setting foot on board the cross-Mediterranean steamer in Alexandria, he undoubtedly paid a visit to the exterior of the Harem of Mehemet Ali, which had been photographed by his great-uncle, Horace Vernet, in 1840. This picture caused an uproar when it was published in Paris "because of its romantic/erotic connotations." In an article published in 1840, Vernet claimed he taught Mehemet Ali how to use the daguerreotype and thus gained entry into the harem.[18]

Lithograph from photograph of Harem of Mehemet Ali by Horace Vernet

Marseilles is the Mediterranean terminal of the MM or French Shipping Line where he takes passage to Marseilles. Holmes now assumes another role, that of the industrial chemist Sebastian Vernet (a graduate of École Technologique de Paris).

---

18 Nissan N. Perez: *Focus East: Early Photography in the Near East, 1839-1885.* Harry N. Abrams Inc., New York: 1988. pp. 228-9, citing F. Goupil-Fesquet: *Voyage d'Horace Vernet en Orient.* Paris: Callamel, 1843. *Journal des Journaux*, Vol. 1, January, 1940, n.p.

He soon finds his way to the laboratory in Montpellier (misspelled Montpelier in "The Adventure of the Empty House"), ostensibly studying coal-tar derivatives. In actual fact, he came to ascertain that there was an ample supply of creosote and other wood preservatives, suitable for coating railway sleepers should the British government ever get around to building the desert railway from Egypt to the Sudan. Montpellier was also the home of a famous yeshiva or religious academy, dating to medieval times. We're not suggesting that Holmes also went there because of the yeshiva but this is an angle which has not yet been explored.

Finally, in February 1894 he undertook the last stage of his return home by ferry to Dover, again assuming a new disguise upon reaching Dover, en route by train to London. He now became the quiet, unassuming bookseller who eventually surprised Dr. Watson in the story of "The Empty House."

Herewith ends the tale of the long journey back home.

It was undoubtedly true that Holmes was spying for the British government. He was their #00221(b), licensed to thrill. From the very first meeting with the British agent in Calcutta (sent by brother Mycroft?), he was under their orders to survey the route between Khartoum and the Egyptian border. His mission was to come up with a plan on how the avenging army was to travel across the desert to finally reach closure with the fact of Gordon's death back in 1885.

A decade later the British government began its efforts in the pacification and restoration of the Sudan—a mission led by Sir Horatio Herbert Kitchener that succeeded within two years at the battle of Omdurman in September 1898.

Did he first get a glimmer of an idea when he travelled by train right across the subcontinent from Calcutta to Bombay? He must have noticed that when traversing a series of diverse terrains that rail travel was the most obvious answer. But can you build a new rail line in the desert? He had to find out. By the time Holmes reached Cairo, his mind was made up and his report to Sir Evelyn Baring laid the foundation for the ultimate reconquering of the Sudan. The major problem which faced the British was that of getting an army into the heart of the Dervish country to face and destroy their forces.

It was about 1,000 miles (1,600 km) from Cairo to Omdurman, most of it hostile desert.

The one man who provided the means for moving the Anglo-Egyptian force under Kitchener into the Sudan was a young French-Canadian officer named Edouard Percy Girouard (1867-1932). He was a son of a judge of the Supreme Court of Canada, educated at Royal Military College and had worked for two years for the CPR before receiving his commission in the Royal Engineers. He was the railway traffic manager at the Royal Arsenal in Woolwich before being seconded to the Egyptian army.

The problems, as Holmes had pointed out to Sir Evelyn Baring in his report of 1893, were quite formidable. Hostile territory, inhabited by hostile tribesmen in a hostile climate, made for an impossible task.

But Kitchener was determined to succeed where the British had failed in 1884. Slowly, with numerous steam engines of various ages, men and supplies were moved into the Sudan, laying rails under the watchful eyes of army patrols, on wooden sleepers carefully protected by creosote preservatives against rot and insect infestation. In 1896 Conan Doyle himself, armed with special press credentials as an honorary war correspondent, traveled up the Nile to Wadi Halfa, where the British army was massing for the campaign. When he got to Wadi Halfa, the start of the campaign appeared to be on hold. Over dinner Kitchener told Doyle no fighting would take place for some time so a crestfallen Doyle sailed back to England.[19]

By 1897 the British army reached Abu Hamed, cleared now of the enemy and pushed on to Berber. By the end of 1898 they had reached a point south of Berber and defeated a large force of Dervishes that opposed their march. Finally in September of that year the bulk of Kitchener's army (including a young lieutenant named Winston Spencer Churchill) stood in a giant semicircle only 12 km from Omdurman with armed steamers protecting their rear on the Nile. Churchill himself described the campaign in his book *The River Wars*.

The rest is history!

---

19 Daniel Stashower: *Teller of Tales: The Life of Arthur Conan Doyle*. Henry Holt, New York: 1999, pp. 196-7.

And so the epic journey by Sigerson/Bin Sayaad/Shalom Bayit/ Sebastian Vernet/Sherlock Holmes, from the foothills of the Himalayas to the streets of London, ended triumphantly with Sherlock Holmes capturing Colonel Sebastian Moran, as chronicled in "The Adventure of the Empty House."

OH SINNER MAN WHERE YOU GONNA RUN TO?[1] SIR ARTHUR AND SIR GEORGE

SinS Conference, October 14, 2011, Canadian Holmes, *Vol.34, No. 4, 2012 & Vol. 35, No. 1, 2012. Winner of the Derrick Murdoch Memorial Award for best paper published in* Canadian Holmes *in 2012*

Religion does not appear as an important theme in Conan Doyle's works of fiction, with the notable exception of *The Refugees,* a novel about the persecution of the Huguenots. Although he was aware of the Jewish presence in England and had a number of Jewish acquaintances, Jews appear only incidentally in his fiction and Jewish themes not at all.[2] His Sherlock Holmes tales contain a number of Jewish characters but only in minor roles, or mentioned in unwritten tales. This article deals with a real Jewish person mentioned in the Canon. If you sinned in Victorian times—either civilly or criminally—then Sir George Lewis, solicitor, referred to in "The Illustrious Client", was the ultimate fixer and the man to run to for help.

"The Adventure of The Illustrious" Client took place from Wednesday, September 3 to Tuesday, September 16, 1902. It was first published in *Collier's Weekly Magazine,* November 8, 1924, and in two parts in *The Strand Magazine* in February and March 1925.

---

1 From the song by Nina Simone, © Warner/Chappell Music, Inc.

2 There is a very pro-Zionist letter dated Nov. 6, 1905, on file at the Jewish Archives in Israel from Conan Doyle to Israel Zangwill.

It begins with an envelope delivered to 221B Baker Street from the Carlton Club containing this message:

> Sir James Damery presents his compliments to Mr. Sherlock Holmes, and will call upon him at 4:30 tomorrow. Sir James begs to say that the matter upon which he desires to consult Mr. Holmes is very delicate, and also very important. He trusts, therefore, that Mr. Holmes will make every effort to grant this interview, and that he will confirm it over the telephone to the Carlton Club.
>
> "I need not say that I have confirmed Watson," said Holmes, as I returned the paper.[3]
>
> Do you know anything of this man Damery?
>
> "Only that his name is a household word in Society."
>
> "Well, I can tell you a little more than that. He has rather a reputation for arranging delicate matters which are to be kept out of the papers. You may remember his negotiations with Sir George Lewis over the Hammerford Will case."[4]

---

3 As lawyers we are accustomed to telling our clients when we are able to meet with them. It would be a very illustrous client indeed, who would tell us when we are to receive him!

4 A diligent search of the *English Law Reports* failed to provide any information on any Hammerford Will case. There was a *Hannaford et al v. Hannaford* et al wills case in the English Court of Queen's Bench in 1871 but neither Sir George Lewis nor his firm, Lewis and Lewis, were instructing solicitors. The absence of a law report is also capable of interpretation as evidence of Lewis' skill in hushing things up, although the fact that Holmes knew of his involvement in a case which, from the context, does not seem to have been one of his personal cases, does make it likely that the case was known to the general public. John Linsenmeyer theorizes that the Hammerford Will case was settled so it would not come to court. Fronia and Marc Simpson in "The Case of the Illustrious Aside" in Volume 13, No. 1 of Groans, Cries and Bleatings, Official Newsletter of the Baker Street Breakfast Club, cleverly point out the reference to Lewis cannot be fortuitous. They point to the opening lines of the story where Watson had asked Holmes "for the tenth time in as many years" for permission to report on it. While the story is set in 1902 it is chronicled in 1911, the year of Lewis' death. One might be tempted to say it could also be the year after King Edward VII died. Now that both were dead, it would be permissible for Dr. Watson, aka Conan Doyle, to relate the story. Klinger does not annotate the Hammerford Will case in *The Case-book of Sherlock Holmes*, part of the Sherlock Holmes Reference Library (Indianapolis: Gasogene Press, 2007).

Sir James attends at 221B Baker Street. The retainer is on behalf of an illustrious client whom Damery will not name.

Damery asks Holmes if he has ever heard of Baron Gruner, and Holmes responds:

"You mean the Austrian murderer?"

Sir James then asks Holmes if he has heard of General de Merville and again the response is:

"DeMerville of Khyber fame: Yes, I have heard of him."

Sir James then states:

"He has a daughter, Violet de Merville, young, rich, beautiful, accomplished, a wonder woman in every way. It is this daughter, this lovely, innocent girl, whom we are endeavouring to save from the clutches of a fiend."

"Baron Gruner has some hold over her then?"

We find out Baron Gruner is engaged to marry Miss de Merville.

We will talk later about who this "illustrious client" might have been.

Let us now introduce Sir George Lewis, the man we believe is Damery's real life counterpart.

Sir George Henry Lewis (1833-1911) was a unique figure in 19th Century England. He was the only solicitor ever to achieve the kind of fame bestowed on such great English barristers as Lord Carson and Sir Edward Marshall Hall. While the whole Victorian nation traced the progress of his courtroom dramas, Lewis himself strove to remain a mystery. He was Jewish—at a time of widespread anti-Semitism—yet he rose to take a distinguished place in the English establishment. He was a friend and confidant of Edward VII[5], Oscar Wilde, Lily Langtry and Edward Burne-Jones. Among his famous clients were Whistler, whom he advised on his bankruptcy after his libel battle with Ruskin in 1878; W.T. Stead, of whom we mention more later; and Charles Stewart Parnell.

---

5 The upper class disapproved of The Prince of Wales' friends, especially the affluent Jewish ones like Sir Thomas Lipton, the Sassoons, the Rothschilds and Baron von Hirsch. See Christopher Hibbert: *Edward VII: A Portrait*, Penguin Books Ltd (Harmondsworth, Middlesex, England, 1982) ("Hibbert").

Caricature from *Vanity Fair* of Sir George Lewis.

Some consider Parnell to be his greatest case. An Irish politician, Parnell, was accused of involvement in the notorious Phoenix Park outrages. Lord Frederick Cavendish, the newly appointed Chief Secretary for Ireland, and Thomas Henry Burke, the permanent undersecretary, were murdered in Dublin in May 1882. *The Times* published *Parnellism and Crime* with copies of letters said to be written by Parnell expressing approval of the murders. Parnell consulted George Lewis, who discovered the forgeries. A Special Commission sat for 128 days. After the flight and suicide in Madrid of Richard Piggot, who prevailed upon *The Times* to publish these forgeries, the Commission cleared Parnell in November 1889 of any involvement in the outrages.

Lewis acted in the most notorious society scandals of the day. He was, however, also known as a "poor man's lawyer," championing inhabitants of the slums of the Ratcliffe Highway and Seven Dials. He was knighted in 1893 and created Baron Lewis on the coronation of King Edward VII in 1902.

John Juxon in his biography of Sir George stated:

> He fought for his clients with a ferocity that verged on ruthlessness;[6] and he could be as single-minded in defence of the guilty as of the innocent.
>
> His second wife Elizabeth[7] was devoted to her fashionable salon—frequented by many artists including Hardy, Gilbert and Sullivan, Paderewski, Beerbohm, Ellen Terry and Henry Irving. Prominent artists painted members of his family—Burne-Jones,[8] Alma Tadema and Sargent among them. Lewis devoted much of his phenomenal energy to the campaigns for legal reform for which he is now perhaps best remembered—particularly in extending the rights of married women, which resulted in the *Married Women's Property Act* of 1870,[9] and in the establishment of the Court of Criminal Appeal in 1907.[10]

One writer described him:

> One of the key figures in late Victorian society, George enjoyed, for more than a quarter of a century, the prac-

---

6 John Juxon: *Lewis and Lewis*, Collins, (London 1983) at p. 13 ("Juxon").

7 His first wife, Victorine Kann, daughter of a German Jewish banker, died after two years of marriage in 1865. In 1867 he married Elizabeth Eberstadt, whose father was also a German Jewish banker.

8 *The Strand*, Vol. VI, July-Dec. 1893, at pp.650-1 describes a "picture of a little maiden lying at full length on a sofa, reading." (Sir George's younger daughter).

9 (33 & 34 Viet. c93).

10 *Criminal Appeal Act*, (7 Edw. 7, c.23) s.2.

tical monopoly of those cases where the sins and follies of the wealthy classes threaten exposure and disaster. The astute George Lewis was chiefly celebrated, in fact, for keeping things out of court.[11]

Oscar Wilde wrote: "Brilliant. Formidable. Concerned in every great case in England. Oh, he knows all about us and forgives us all."[11]

The Oxford Dictionary of National Biography on the Lives of the Law put it this way:

> More colourful is Sir George Lewis (1833-1911), who appears to have acted in every lurid high-profile case at the end of the 19th Century. It is said that "he cared for rules only so far as not to be caught breaking them" and that "he was a dangerous man to best." But he took up the cudgels on behalf of several well-known victims of injustice, including Adolf Beck and George Archer-Shee.[12]

---

11 Theo Arenson: *The King in Love,* John Murray (Publishers) Limited, (London, 1988) at p. 119. Lewis burned all his papers when he retired. This proved a relief to many individuals, but saddened the hearts of many gossip columnists and historians. His will was probated in 1912. *The New York Times* (February 6, 1912) titled its story "Lewis kept no diary—Famous lawyer left no memoirs either—good news for many." The will began with this preface: "In my professional career, especially during the last forty years, many matters have been confided to me of a delicate nature, which, apart from considerations of ordinary professional honor, imposed the necessity of absolute secrecy."

12 The Beck case led to the establishment of the Court of Criminal Appeal (and Edalji helped to push it over the line). See Juxon, pp. 290-295, esp. p. 294. C. H. O'Halloran's in "Development of the Right of Appeal, in England in Criminal Cases" (1949) 27 *Can. Bar. Rev.* 153, wrote: "Until the constitution of the Court of Criminal Appeal in 1907 the review of criminal cases in England was limited to a degree now hard to realize. That it was then revolutionized is credited in some quarters to the public-spirited activity of Conan Doyle in the *George Edalji* case (convicted in 1903), which quickly caught the mind of a public already aroused over the *Adolph Beck* case (convicted in 1896)."

Archer-Shee was the young boy accused of stealing a postal order in cadet school. Lewis engaged Sir Edward Marshall Hall, who established Archer-Shee's innocence. He was killed in the First World War and was the subject of the play and movie *The Winslow Boy.*

One cannot resist the following quote from *The Dictionary of National Biography*, even though it ends with a criticism of Sherlock Holmes' investigative techniques:[13]

> He possessed an unrivaled knowledge of the past records of the criminals and adventures of both sexes, not only in England and on the continent of Europe, but in the United States, which was peculiarly serviceable to him and to his clients in resisting attempts at conspiracy and blackmail.. . .audacious playing the game often in defiance of the rules, and relying on his audacity to carry him through... he had methods of investigation which were his own, and intuitions beside which the rather mechanical processes of Sherlock Holmes seemed the efforts of a beginner.

Lewis was lampooned in *Punch Magazine* as "Sir Lewis George" in a mock trial, satirized by Gilbert and Sullivan in *Trial by Jury* and characterized by 'Spy' in *Vanity Fair* in September of 1876. He is to be respected in that Lewis did not take notes and destroyed his personal papers so that no one would be able to discover who his clients were and what he did for them.

Sir George was well known to Conan Doyle both by personal interaction and by virtue of Sir George's reputation.

Both were involved in assisting the unfortunate George Edalji, who was wrongfully convicted of horse maiming in 1901. They were on the Campaign Fund Committee together. Sir George went on to help Edalji get reinstated to the Solicitors' Rolls.

Juxon comments:

> Lewis played a similar role in another case -not as famous as Beck's perhaps but notable in that it dis-

---

13 See James G. Ravin "The Most Famous Solicitor in England", (2002)52 *Baker Street Journal*. 23 at p. 25.

played an element of racialism rarely found in the nineteenth-century England;[14] and because not only Lewis but also the creator of Sherlock Holmes were among those who sought justice for the unfortunate George Edalji. Conan Doyle, then at the peak of his fame as a writer, took the role in the Edalji case played by George R. Sims, a respected journalist, in the Beck

George Edalji

Case, the only difference being that he wrote more eloquently and in greater bulk of Edalji than Sims did of Beck. Lewis supported Edalji by a campaign of letter-writing and private agitation -for there were establishment figures who would listen to Lewis while

14 But cf Anthony Julius: *Trials of the Diaspora: A History of Anti-Semitism in England*: Oxford University Press, (Oxford, 2010).

they would have dismissed Conan Doyle as a sensational novelist seeking publicity.[15]

We are not sure if many Sherlockians agree with this last statement.
Lewis was prominent in Victorian society as the pre-eminent fixer.
His involvement in numerous high-profile scandal cases such as the
Bravo Poisoning case in 1876, the Tranby Croft or "Baccarat Scandal"
in 1891, and the Oscar Wilde trials in 1895, when he was consulted by
the Marquess of Queensberry, were well known to the English public
and highly publicized.

Doyle certainly would have been familiar with these cases, due to
extensive press coverage. The following, from Michael S. Foddy's *The
Trials of Oscar Wilde*, gives us an idea of the role of the newspapers of
the late 19th century:

> By the time of Wilde's criminal trials, it can be
> claimed that the "sex scandal" was already well
> established as a sub-genre within the genre of crime
> reporting. W. T. Stead, maverick editor of the *Pall
> Mall Gazette*, had earlier pioneered an exploitative
> brand of investigative journalism in his 1885 expose
> of white slavery and child prostitution, entitled
> "The Maiden Tribute of Modern Babylon." From
> a historical perspective, the Wilde trials should be
> seen as a one in a long line of (mostly) sex-related
> scandals involving important persons that gripped
> the public imagination in the eighteen-eighties
> and eighteen-nineties: the divorce case of the rad-
> ical politician Charles Dilke in 1886; the unsolved
> Ripper murders of 1888; the divorce case of the Irish
> leader Charles Parnell in 1890; the scandal of the
> Cleveland Street homosexual brothel, 1889-90, said
> to involve the eldest son of the heir to the throne;

---

15 Juxon at pp. 297-300.

and the Tranby-Croft gambling scandal of 1891, which involved the Prince of Wales himself. Without a doubt scandals such as these and sex crimes in general, made excellent copy for the newspapers, and often boosted circulation to record levels.[16]

Another prominent person Lewis and Doyle both knew was William Thomas (W.T.) Stead.[17] In addition to being a maverick editor of the *Pall Mall Gazette* and a reformer, Stead was a devotee of the spiritualist cause. He was a contemporary of Doyle's and they were "kindred spirits," so to speak.[18] In 1885, Stead "bought" a 13-year-old girl from her mother for £5 and took her to Paris. He was charged with abduction when no record could be found of the payment. Stead was convicted and jailed for two months. George Lewis appeared in Bow Street briefly on Stead's behalf. In the trial proceeding, Stead conducted his own defence with a Mr. Lickford of Sir George's firm, Lewis and Lewis, attending to advise him on certain legal points. Ironically, at the Cosmos Club in 1909, Stead pictured himself as shipwrecked and drowning in the sea and asking for a rope. Three years later he went down with the Titanic.[19]

Lewis and Conan Doyle, certainly knew each other and had friends and acquaintances in common, including Oscar Wilde, but apparently did not move in the same social circles. For example, Lewis was not listed among those who attended Conan Doyle's second wedding on September 18, 1907, although George Edalji was one of the guests. Conan Doyle and Lewis were both at the funeral of Henry Irving on October 20, 1905.[20]

---

16 Michael S. Foddy: *The Trials of Oscar Wilde*, Yale University Press (New Haven and London, 1997) at p. 50. It would appear that in 1888, London had 13 morning and nine evening national daily newspapers. See Andrew Cook: *Jack the Ripper*, Amberly Publishing (Stroud, Gloucester, 2009) at p. 15.

17 1840–1912

18 Conan Doyle mentions Stead extensively in *A History of Spiritualism*, Cassell & Co., (London, 1926).

19 See Ruth Brandon: *The Spiritualists*. Alfred A. Knopf (New York, 1983)

20 Their names are next to each other in *The Times* report on Oct. 21, I 905.

Sir George Lewis was involved as an advisor or in some other capacity for parties involved in some of the major British scandals of the late 19th and early 20th centuries.

Some, but by no means all, of the scandals Sir George was involved in centred around indiscreet letters from lovers or jilted lovers which could be used for real or social blackmail purposes. The fact that so few of these cases caught the attention of the public is evidence of how successful Sir George was in protecting his clients' reputations. The full story of what he did for the Prince of Wales and for many other of his eminent clients in this direction will never be known.

One case was a near scandal of the Prince of Wales and his old boon companion, Lord Beresford, who shared the favours of Lady Daisy Brooke, the future 'socialist' Lady Warwick.[21] Lord Charles Beresford had had an affair with Daisy Brooke in late 1886. After his wife became pregnant and he reconciled with her, Lord Charles was then sent a letter of bitter reproach by Lady Brooke, claiming one of her children was his. The letter fell into the hands of Lady Beresford, who took it to the *eminence grise* of the day, the solicitor George Lewis. On this one occasion when he had to deal with the frantic Lady Beresford, he was unable to keep the matter quiet and the resulting publicity reflected poorly on all parties.

Lady Brooke regretted the letter to Lord Charles as soon as she had written it. Acting on Lady Beresford's instructions, Lewis wrote to Lady Brooke, telling her that her letter was in his possession and warning her against causing any further annoyance to his client. Daisy was furious. She wrote to Lewis, demanding the return of her letter. 'It is my letter. I wrote it, she declared. Lewis explained that she was wrong. Legally the letter was the property of Lord Charles Beresford,

---

21 She was later to be the attempted blackmailer of King George V. Following the death of Edward VII, and having large debts, she tried to blackmail his son, the new King George V. She threatened to make public a series of love letters written by Edward VII. It was the cunning expertise of Lord Stamfordham that managed to stop publication by arguing that copyright belonged to the King. See *infra*, footnote 22. Daisy found herself outmanoeuvred and died virtually penniless.

to whom it had been addressed.[22] Lady Brooke asked her lover, the Prince of Wales, to recover it for her.[23]

The Prince went to Sir George's house in the middle of the night and tried to recover the letter. Sir George let him read it but then sent the letter back to Lady Beresford. The Prince went to see Lady Beresford and threatened to banish her from the invitation list of Marlborough House, an action tantamount to social blackmail. She declared she would not destroy the letter, threat or no threat of ostracism. Instead, she then, through Lewis, spelled out the terms on which she was prepared to return the letter to Lady Brooke. Lady Brooke was to stay away from London for the entire season, again a form of social blackmail. Lady Brooke refused to agree to this proposal. In the end, the Prime Minister, Lord Salisbury, had to intervene and the parties reached an agreement.

On several occasions criminals sought to take advantage of Sir George's reputation. Here is the lurid headline in the *New York Times* for September 29, 1907 followed by a portion of the article:

AMERICANS CHARGED WITH BLACKMAIL-ING; said to have Personated Sir George Lewis, the Famous London Solicitor. USED HIS LETTER-HEADS Communications to which Sir George's Name was appended found in rooms—Now out on bail.

LONDON, September 28—There is probably no man in England who is the depository of so many scandalous secrets as Sir George Lewis. It has been said of this pleasant-voiced, white-haired, dapper little man that he holds the honor of half the British

---

22 Under copyright law the writer of unpublished letters has the right to control the first publication of those letters. While the writer owns the copyright in the text, the addressee owns the physical letter, but has no right to publish it. See John S. McKeown; *"Fox on Canadian Law of Copyright and Industrial Designs"*, 4th Edition, Carswell, (Toronto, 2009), Section 6:2(a).

23 The incident is reported in various books. See Hibbert *supra*, footnote 5 at pp. 155-6 and Pearson: *Edward The Rake*, Harcourt Brace Jovanovich, Inc, (New York, 1975) at p. 140.

peerage in his keeping and knows that the other half has no honor to lose. However exaggerated this epigram may be, it represents a widely prevalent opinion as to the character of the cases the handling of which Sir George has made his specialty.

This astute lawyer is considered to be even more proficient out of the Divorce Court than in it. The number of cases he has carried through that court, with the utmost possible advantage to his clients, is a tremendous tribute to his qualifications; but report will have it that he has been able to keep out of the Divorce Court even more cases than he has carried through it, and that, in other directions his great professional acumen, united with his consummate knowledge of the world, and his alert judgment of human nature has saved his clients legal expenses in comparison with which his fees have been insignificant—not to speak of the advantages accruing from the avoidance of publicity.

There was no little flutter in London devotees when the news first spread about town a few days ago that Sir George had appeared before a Magistrate in connection with an alleged case of attempted blackmail.

The accused man, Montagu Newton, forged a letter stating that Sir George had undertaken to pay a woman named Violet Fraser the sum of £3,000, using a reproduction of the Lewis and Lewis letterhead. He pleaded guilty to conspiring with Violet Fraser and another man by false pretences to defraud. Violet Fraser was found unfit to stand trial.[24]

---

24 Though the paper called it "blackmail", that term does not appear in the account of the trial: *Old Bailey Proceedings Online* (www.oldbaileyonline.org, version 6.0, 01 September 2011), October 1907, trial of NEWTON, Montagu (34, of no occupation) FISHER, Joseph D (35, engineer) (t19071021 <J8). It was actually a case of forgery and fraud.

Blackmail in the Royal Family was old hat to Sir George Lewis. D.J. Leighton in *The Ripper Suspect*,[25] trying to deflect suspicion away from Montague J. Druitt as the Ripper, says this of the Duke of Clarence:

> At Bonhams in March 2002 two letters from the Duke were auctioned for over £8,000. They were written in 1890 and 1891 and were to his solicitor, George Lewis, about paying off two prostitutes with whom he had become involved.
>
> He wrote: 'I am very pleased that you are able to settle with Ms. Richardson, although £200 is rather expensive for letters. I presume there is no other way of getting them back. I will also do all I can to get back the one or two letters written to the other lady.' This predicament encapsulates the Duke's naivety.

The most prominent case of blackmail in the Canon is "Charles Augustus Milverton," set in 1899 and published in *The Strand Magazine* in 1904. In this story a woman guns down Milverton, the man who had blackmailed her with evidence of an indiscretion.[26] Obviously, Doyle could not have been influenced by the 1907 "blackmail attempt" involving an American who tried to forge Lewis' signature on a compromising letter. Doyle, however, could well have known about Lady Charles and Lady Brooke, who were involved in a Lewis case that also featured the Prince of Wales.

The theme of blackmail does appear in a number of cases, including "A Scandal in Bohemia," 1891; "The Boscombe Valley Mystery," 1891; "Gloria Scott," 1893; "The Reigate Squires," 1893; *The Hound of the Baskervilles*, 1901; "The Second Stain," 1904; and "Black Peter,"

---

25 Sutton Publishing Ltd. (Gloucester, England, 2000) at p. 109

26 Our good friend John Linsenmeyer suggests (email June 19,2011) this description of the murderess in this story could well be a subtle Edwardian description of a Jewess: "the woman, without a word, had raised her veil and dropped the mantle from her chin. It was a dark, handsome, clear-cut face which confronted Milverton—a face with a curved nose, strong, dark eyebrows shading hard, glittering eyes, and a straight, thin-lipped mouth set in a dangerous smile."

1904, and there are references to blackmail in a number of cases Si, George Lewis from Sept 2, where it does not appear as a plot element.[27]

The Bravo Murder case, variously known as The Balham Mystery or Murder at the Priory, in 1876, was the case that made Lewis famous.

The Bravos lived in The Priory, a large, attractive house in Bedford Hill, Balham, London. Charles Bravo took laudanum, a well-known cure for toothache. He and his wife Florence had separate rooms. At about 9:45 p.m. on April 18, 1876, Bravo dashed from his room shouting for hot water to drink. Mrs. Cox, a live-in companion of Florence, rushed to Bravo's aid. He was very ill and soon lapsed into unconsciousness. Florence was called from her sleep and a local doctor was called. The doctor suspected poison but could find no trace. When Bravo came to, he was questioned. He stated that he had taken some laudanum for neuralgia. Florence called in the eminent physician Sir William Gull, one of the most notable doctors of the time and later a favourite Ripper candidate among enthusiasts. He questioned Bravo, who persisted with his story that he had taken nothing but laudanum. Gull told the family that Bravo was dying from poison and he eventually died April 21st, 1876, at age 30. A postmortem examination revealed that Bravo had died from poisoning by antimony, probably administered in a dose of 20 to 30 grains. Lewis describes the case in his own words in an interview in the December 1893 edition of *The Strand Magazine*:

> "There was the Balham mystery," said Sir George, as he remembered some of these "sensations." "I represented the family of the late Mr. Bravo; Sir Henry James, Mrs. Bravo; Serjeant Parry, Dr. Gull; while Mr. Murphy was for Mrs. Cox. A verdict had been obtained that Mr. Bravo had committed suicide and not been poisoned, but the friends of Mr. Bravo not being satisfied, the Court of Queen's Bench did a most unusual thing and ordered a fresh inquest. The jury found a

---

27 "The Yellow Face" [1893], "The Red Circle" [1911], "Lady Frances Carfax" [1911], *The Valley of Fear* [1914] and "The Three Gables" [1926].

new verdict of willful murder against some person or persons unknown.[28]

At both inquests, Dr. Gull was unswerving in his assertion that Bravo had committed suicide.

Lewis' cross-examination of Florence Bravo dragged out every detail of her long-standing relationship with one Dr. James Gully, also a prominent physician, who had become her admirer at the time of the death of her first husband, Alexander Ricardo. After the case, Lewis was called the "torturer" or "Avenging Angel" by the press on account of this cross-examination.[29]

According to a commentary on the interviewers:

> Their awe was probably deepened by the disclosure that Sir George had told *The Strand Magazine* in confidence, the name of the poisoner in the famous Bravo case.[30]

The effect of this case on Lewis' career was significant:

> A ruthless examiner, he was to receive a fee of £1000 for his services, his participation serving as the springboard for a very successful legal career.[31]

In contrast, Doyle's annual income from his medical practice in the 1880s, before he left Portsmouth, was less than £500 and he ran a decent household on that amount.

There are numerous cases in the Canon that involve poison but none parallel the facts in the Bravo Murder case, nor was antimony

---

28 Vol VI, July-December 1893, pp. 655.

29 Juxon: *Lewis and Lewis*; Collins (London, 1983) at p. 136.

30 Reginald Pound, *Mirror of the Century: The Strand Magazine 1891-1950*, (Heinemann, London, 1966), p.87

31 Bernard Taylor and Kate Clarke: *Murder at the Priory*, Grafton Books (London, 1988) at p. 100; See also John Williams: *Suddenly at the Priory*: Penguin Books, (London, 1989). As an aside, Sir Leslie Ward ("Spy") states his study of Sir George was made during the Bravo trial. See Ward: *Forty Years of Spy*. Chatto & Windus (London, undated).

one of the poisons.[32] The Doyle story that does draw some parallels is "The Nightmare Room."[33]

In this melodrama, Lucille is poisoning her husband, Archie Mason, a wealthy young man of affairs. He finds a vial in her jewelry case, which he has analyzed to show it contains 12 grains of antimony. He confronts Lucille and seizes a letter she tries to hide. It was from Captain Campbell, who has begged her to run away with him. Campbell shortly arrives at their flat. They square off at cards to see which will drink the poison. At this point it is revealed that they are making a film and the cameraman stops shooting for the day.

All of the Bravo elements are here—a young woman, a successful businessman, a cuckolded husband and the poisoning of the husband with antimony. As in the real-life Bravo case, the wife is the prime suspect in the poisoning.

The Bravo Murder case has become familiar to succeeding generations. In 2004, Julian Fellowes, well-known writer and television producer, launched the BBC series *Julian Fellowes Investigates A Most Mysterious Murder*, which investigated the case of Charles Bravo.

Lewis also played a prominent role in the Tranby Croft Scandal, also called the Baccarat Case, of 1891.

In 1890 Lieutenant-Colonel Sir William Gordon-Cumming, of the Scots Guards, was accused of cheating while playing baccarat, an illegal game,[34] with the Prince of Wales and other guests of Arthur Wilson, a wealthy ship owner. The game took place at Tranby Croft, Wilson's country home. During the evening, several players observed

---

32 See the following cases: "The Veiled Lodger" – Acid. *A Study in Scarlet* – Alkaloid and acqua tofana and poison (unspecified); "The Dying Detective" – Belladonna; "The Greek Interpreter" – Charcoal fumes; "The Disappearance of Lady Frances Carfax" & "His Last Bow" – Chloroform; "The Sussex Vampire" – Curare and Venom and Poison (unspecified); "The Lion's Mane" – Cyanea; "The Retired Colourman" – Pellet; "The Golden Prince-Nez" – Poison (unspecified); "The Devil's Foot" – Radis Pedis Diaboli; *The Sign of Four* – Strychnine; "The Speckled Band" – Venom. As a matter of interest, George Chapman (Severin Koslowski), suspected by some as Jack the Ripper, was hanged in 1902 for the murders of three women who died by antimony poisoning.

33 Volume 62 *The Strand Magazine*, December, 1921 at pp. 545-459.

34 http://en.wikipedia.org/wiki/RoyalBaccaratScandal

Sir William apparently cheating by altering the amount of the bets he had on the table after he won or lost a hand. Alerted to this, other players watched him more closely the next evening and confirmed his actions. Sir William won a total of £228 during the two days of playing.

The case compelled the Prince to enter the witness box—not for the first time—to testify on the plaintiff's behalf. A word about Gordon-Cumming: he claimed descent from Charlemagne, served with great distinction in the Zulu War and survived the fearful battle of Abu Klea during the Gordon Relief Expedition. He was tall, handsome and, while unmarried, was a tireless and successful seducer of other men's wives. With a huge estate in Scotland and an income of £60,000 a year, he was well qualified to be a friend of the Prince and would often lend the heir to the throne his house in London for an unspecified but fairly obvious purpose. Gordon-Cumming had been forced to sign a paper, to which the Prince of Wales[35] and other guests put their signatures, bearing the following most ambiguous wording:

> In consideration of the promise, made by the gentle-
> men whose names are subscribed, to preserve silence
> with reference to an accusation made in regard to
> my conduct at baccarat on the nights of Monday and
> Tuesday, 8th and 9th September, 1890, at Tranby Croft,
> I will on my part solemnly undertake never to play
> cards again as long as I live.

The letter was given to Lewis for safekeeping. Perhaps if only "gen-tlemen" had been in the know, that promised silence might have been kept; but there were ladies in the house party. When, on the following day, the Prince left Tranby Croft to watch the last day of the Doncaster races, with His Royal Highness spending the night with the 10th Hussars, someone from Tranby Croft began to talk.[36]

---

35 The Prince of Wales was a one-man scandal industry for George Lewis

36 Probably Lady Daisy Brooke, known popularly as "Babbling Brooke" the Prince's soon to be discarded mistress. Refer to our earlier discussion about Lady Brooke and Lady Beresford.

There was only one thing for Gordon-Cumming to do now that the secret was out, and that was to bring an action for libel against his original accusers, Mr. and Mrs. Arthur Wilson, Mr. and Mrs. Lycett Green and Berkeley Levett, one of Gordon-Cumming's own subalterns. The single issue at trial was whether Gordon-Cumming had cheated at the game during the house party. The lawsuit *Gordon-Cumming v. Wilson and others* was opened June 1st 1891 before the Lord Chief Justice, Lord Coleridge, and concluded June 9. Gordon-Cumming lost the case. Lewis was the solicitor instructing counsel for the defence.

Many Sherlockians may find a similarity in that scandal with "The Five Orange Pips," when John Openshaw visits Holmes and Watson seeking advice. He says:

> "I heard from Major Prendergast how you saved him in the Tankerville Club Scandal." "Ah, of course. He was wrongfully accused of cheating at cards."

There is no question of the connection to the Tranby Croft Scandal. Even though "The Five Orange Pips" is set in September 1887, it was first published in *The Strand Magazine* in November 1891, a scant few months after the trial.[37] Doyle also used the theme of a prominent member of society caught cheating at cards in *Rodney Stone*, published in 1891. This story features Lord Avon, who is presumed dead because he has gone into hiding to save the family honour against an accusation of his brother's cheating at cards. In 1894, Doyle adapted *Rodney Stone* into a play, *The House of Temperley*, but expanded the card-cheating theme into a "trial" held in the Committee Room at Watier's gaming club. As a result of the trial, Sir John Hawker is banished from the club after signing a damning letter in which he virtually admitted to cheating at cards.[38] Doyle re-visited this theme with a

---

37 One wonders whether, if Sir George Lewis had acted for Gordon-Cumming instead of the defendants, his name might have been cleared, as Sherlock Holmes had done for Major Prendergast in "The Five Orange Pips."

38 *The House of Temperley, The Play Pictorial*, Vol. 15, No. 90 n.d. [Jan. or Feb. 1, 1910] published on the first of each month. The play opened December 27, 1909 at The Adelphi.

short story, "The End of Devil Hawker," adapted from *Temperley*, published posthumously in *The Strand Magazine* in 1930.[39]

Clearly the card cheating at Tranby Croft, and its effect on the social position of Cumming, had a great influence on Doyle's work. In "The Adventure of the Empty House," published in 1894, Doyle was again to use this theme of a respectable military man being caught cheating at cards and resorting to drastic means to protect his reputation. But this time, instead of a disastrous lawsuit, Colonel Sebastian Moran committed murder.

Sir Charles Russell, counsel for the defendants, focused on Cumming's demeanour in addressing the Court in the Tranby Croft case:

> Sir William Gordon-Cumming's explanation for his strange conduct is that he 'lost his head.' You have seen him in the witness box, cool, clever, and intelligent. There was nothing about his appearance or in his manner in the witness box to show that he 'lost his head' there. Was it the conduct of a man who had 'lost his head,' when he coolly scanned the document presented for his signature and debarring him from ever playing cards again and said: 'Why, this will even prevent me from playing the regimental shilling whist!' He had not 'lost his head' then. He was content so long as secrecy in regard to his conduct was maintained.[40]

Doyle would have been well aware of Cumming's cool composure: Holmes says of Moran, "He was always a man of iron nerve, and the story is still told in India how he crawled down a drain after a wounded man eating tiger."

Another real-life event which may have influenced a Doyle story began in April 1892 at the Kingsclere stables. The Duke of Westminster's

39 Vol. 80, June-Dec. 1930.

40 *New York Times*, June 3, 1891.

horse, Orme (the son of Ormonde and Angelica), was thought to have been poisoned. Professor Williams, a veterinary surgeon, confirmed on April 26 that the horse was suffering from "virulent poison." The Duke of Westminster let it be known that the matter was in the hands of his solicitor, George Lewis. It made the headlines as Orme was the Derby favourite for that year.[41] "The Adventure of Silver Blaze" was published in *The Strand Magazine* for December 1892, a scant eight months after the Orme incident in which Lewis was consulted. Here Colonel Ross, the owner of Silver Blaze,[42] the favourite horse for the Wessex Cup running at 3 to 1 odds, informs Holmes the horse had gone missing.

Ultimately the horse is found and wins the race. The underlying recurring theme is the same in both cases. Someone wants to prevent a horse from winning. While there is no poison as such in "Silver Blaze,"one of the stable lads, Ned Hunter (the one on guard duty the night of the crime), was drugged with powdered opium that someone had put in his supper. Instead of poison, the horse is to be damaged by cutting one of its tendons.

There were other incidents in Lewis' career that might well have formed suitable plot material for Doyle but seem not to have found their way into his work. In *The Strand Magazine* interview:

> I asked the solicitor what was the smartest robbery he had ever met within his experience.
>
> "Well," he answered, "the Hatton Garden diamond robbery was certainly one of the most ingenious. I

---

41 Our thanks to Andrew Lycett for bringing this connection to our attention.

42 Charles Higham in *The Adventures of Conan Doyle*, Pocket Books (New York 1976.) pp. 81-2 refers to the fact that in the *Harper's Weekly* edition of the story, there is reference to the fact the horse is described as being of 'Somomy" stock. He suggests this was a veiled reference to Oscar Wilde and the Marquess of Queensberry's card calling him a "somdomite." Sam Rosenberg has the same comment. See *Naked is the Best Disguise*, Bobbs Merrill (Indianapolis -New York, 1974) at p. 134. However, the card was left at Wilde's club on Feb. 18, 1895, which makes this seem improbable. See Richard Ellman, *Oscar Wilde*, New York: Alfred A. Knopf, 1988, p.438. See also Chris Redmond's brilliant paper "A Study in Gray: More About Doyle and Wilde", published in *Naval Signals* in 1982. Thanks to Peggy Perdue (Violet Westbury, BSI) of the Toronto Reference Library for providing us with a copy of this paper.

acted for the Alliance Marine Insurance Company, but possibly the smartest of modern times was the famous gold robbery. I will tell it in a few words. Some boxes of bar gold were in transit from London to Paris. The boxes were weighed at London Bridge, put into the locker in the guard's van, and locked up. The packages were weighed again at Dover, again at Calais, a fourth time at the station at Paris, and the weight was found to be exactly correct to the turn of a scale. When the boxes were delivered to the owners in Paris and were opened, they contained nothing but shot!"

The guard was in on the robbery. False keys were obtained, and during the transit from London, confederates got into the guard's van, filled the boxes with shot to the exact weight, got out at Dover, took tickets back to town, and the men were in London with the gold before the boxes were opened in Paris! The robbery remained undiscovered for two years, when one of the men turned Queen's evidence. The guard and his accomplices were tried and convicted.[43]

The cleverness of this plot could easily have been in Doyle's mind when he set out to write his two apocryphal Holmes' short stories, "The Lost Special,"[44] and "The Man With the Watches,"[45] both of which turn around deceiving the authorities by using clever tricks involving trains.

Another common acquaintance between Doyle and Lewis was Oscar Wilde. The history of Doyle's dinner with Wilde on August 30, 1889, and the genesis of *The Sign of Four* is well known. It is also well known that the description of Thaddeus Sholto is modelled on Wilde. Doyle, given his connection with Wilde, would have followed Wilde's trials and travails, starting with his improvident lawsuit

---

43 Op. cit. n4, p.655.

44 *The Strand Magazine*, August 1898, Vol. 16, pp.1 53-162, and collected in *Round the Fire Stories*, 1908.

45 *The Strand Magazine*, July. 1898, Vol. 16, pp.13-43, and collected in *Round the Fire Stories*, 1908.

against the Marquess of Queensberry for criminal libel in 1895. As early as July of 1894 Wilde had written to Lewis seeking his advice about the ongoing pressure from Queensberry to stay away from his son 'Bosie.' Here is how Sir George replied:[46]

> Dear Mr. Wilde
>
> I am in receipt of your note. The information that you have received that I am acting for Lord Queensberry is perfectly correct, and under these circumstances you will see at once that it is impossible for me to offer any opinion about any proceedings you intend to take against him. Although I cannot act against him, I should not act against you.

Sir George *did* act against him in a manner of speaking by acting for the Marquess of Queensberry at his bail hearing.[47] After Wilde received Queensberry's note, left at the Albemarle Club, on Feb. 28, 1895, and which started the criminal libel process, Wilde again turned to Lewis for advice, and was reminded that he had been previously engaged by Queensberry. Sir George stated:

> What is the good of coming to see me now? I am powerless to do anything. If you had had the sense to bring Lord Queensberry's card to me in the first place, I would have torn it up and thrown it in the fire, and told you not to make a fool of yourself.[48]

---

46 Richard Ellmann: *Oscar Wilde*, *infra*, footnote 42 at p. 420.

47 After Sir George Lewis appeared at the bail hearing, he resigned the retainer. "Lewis told his client that he could no longer act for him and he must find another solicitor. No doubt this was because Lewis knew Wilde socially and he was unwilling to appear for the defence in a sensational private prosecution brought by a man in whose house he had been a guest." See H. Montgomery Hyde: *Lord Alfred Douglas*, Methuen London Ltd. (London, 1984).

48 H. Montgomery Hyde: *The Trials of Oscar Wilde*, Dover Publications, (New York, 1962), pp. 150-1.

In "The Illustrious Client," Watson states:

> Sir James carried away both Baron Gruner's purloined diary and the precious saucer. As I was myself overdue,[49] I went down with him into the street. A brougham was waiting for him. He sprang in, gave a hurried order to the cockaded coachman, and drove swiftly away. He flung his overcoat half out of the window to cover the armorial bearings upon the panel, but I had seen them in the glare of our fanlight none the less. I gasped with surprise. Then I turned back and ascended the stair to Holmes' room.
>
> "I have found out who our client is," I cried, bursting with my great news. "Why, Holmes, it is"

There is no doubt that the "Illustrious Client" was the Prince of Wales.

Lewis' friendship with the Prince had begun with the lawyer advising him on matters concerned with the royal mistresses. The relationship was to be confirmed—and deepened—during the Tranby Croft Scandal. But several years before that, Lewis had to deal with difficulties arising from another of Edward's passions—horse racing. He tried to renege on a deal made with Lady Stanford to run her two horses under the royal colours and split the winnings. Sir George negotiated a satisfactory outcome. It need hardly be said that the so-called "sport of kings" was just as repugnant to his mother, Queen Victoria, as all of his other pursuits.[50]

It also seems evident that Sir James Damery was modelled on Sir George Lewis. Perhaps the reference to Lewis was a red herring inserted by Doyle to obscure this fact. Even as late as 1922, literate readers would have been well aware of Lewis' reputation and would likely have thought of him as the model for Damery. Or, could this

---

49 See W.S. Baring-Gould: *Time Annotated Sherlock Holmes* p. 689 footnote 23. The explanation given was that his fiancee Mary Morstan was waiting for him.

50 See Juxon at p. 174.

be a 'double blind ' or a 'red red herring'? Could Doyle have inserted the name of Sir George in this passage to alert the reader to the true identity of Damery?

There was every reason for Doyle to have named Sir George Lewis in "The Illustrious Client."

Their lives intersected on numerous occasions, as Lewis was well known in English society. We know Doyle would have known of his career and the events that made him famous. The influence Sir George had on scandalous events of the day was the stuff of legend. The storyteller in Doyle could not resist the temptation to immortalize some of these cases in his fiction.

SHERLOCK HOLMES IN "THE HANDS OF THE JEWS" JEWISH STEREOTYPES IN THE CANON

Presentation to the Bootmakers of Toronto, December, 2012
Canadian Holmes. *Fall 2013, Vol. 36, No. 1 and Winter 2013 / 14 Vol. 36, No. 2.*

I. INTRODUCTION

Hartley and I believe we have almost exhausted all references to real or fictional Jewish characters in the Canon in our five previous Jewish connection papers.[1] However, while we may have dealt with most of the clearly identifiable Jews mentioned by Conan Doyle, there are five canonical phrases which on their face are references to Jews and which appear from the viewpoint of 2012 to be derogatory.

These were contained in the following stories published between the years 1887–1927.

---

1 See: "Who Was That Hebrew Rabbi?" (2011) Vol. 33, No. 4, *Canadian Holmes* at p. 11. "Sherlock Holmes in Jerusalem" (with Joseph Kessel) (2011) Vol. 34, No. 1 *Canadian Holmes* at p. 5. "Who Was Ikey Sanders?" (2012) Vol. 34, No. 2 *Canadian Holmes* at p. 10. "Who Was Old Abrahams?" (2012) Vol. 34, No. 3, *Canadian Holmes* at p. 4. "Oh Sinner Man – Where You Gonna Run to?: Sir Arthur and Sir George", [first part] (2012) Vol. 34, No.4, *Canadian Holmes,* at p.6; [second part] (2012), Vol. 35, No. I , at p.8.

A Study in Scarlet	"The same afternoon brought a grey-headed, seedy visitor, looking like a Jew pedlar…" 1887
"The Cardboard Box"	We had a pleasant meeting together, during which Holmes would talk about nothing but violins, narrating with great exultation how he had purchased his own Stradivarius, which was worth at least five hundred guineas, at a "Jew broker's" in Tottenham Court Road for fifty-five shillings – 1893.
"The Stockbroker's Clerk"	"A touch of the Sheeny" – 1893.[2]
"Shoscombe Old Place"	"He's holding off the Jews till then" "For myself, I am deeply in the hands of the Jews" – 1927.

---

2 Here is all that the OED has to say about "sheeny". It is also used to refer to a shininess of cloth, but clearly that's not the context in which ACD was using it. He could only have meant that Beddington, aka Pinner, had what people would consider to be a Jewish nose.

OED: Sheeny—slang—also "sheenie", "sheeney", "shen(e)y" [of obscure origin : cf. Russ. [characters spelling zhid], Pol., Czech >zid<with semi-circle over z> (pronounced zid) A Jew.] A Jew. 1824 in Spirit Publ. Jrnls. (1825) 85. Orange Battery among the Sheenes [read Sheenies]. Sketches at Bow Street.-- No. V., 1828 *Egan Boxiana* Ser. II. I.632. A good day's play among the Sheenies. 1893 Foreman Trip to Spain 34. A Portuguese Jew (A 'sheeny' as he is termed by the sailors).

attrib. 1888 Kipling's Soldiers Three, In Matter of a Private, You lie, you man-sticker. You sneakin' Sheeny butcher. You lie.

Klinger, *The Memoirs of Sherlock Holmes, Sherlock Holmes Reference Library*, n. 31, p.74, says "A pejorative term for a Jew…Cf. Thackeray, 1847: "Sheeney and Moses are…smoking their pipes before their lazy shutters in Seven Dials." JONES, (p.113). In Volume I of the *New Annotated Sherlock Holmes*, n. 21, p. 481, he expands on this:

A pejorative term for a Jew. Although the precise origin of the word is unknown, some suggest that it comes from the Yiddish expression "miesse meshina", a curse; other sources, such as *Cassell's Dictionary of Slang*, point to the Yiddish *shayner*, which literally means "beautiful" but is more familiarly used to signify a pious person or a traditional Jew (often wearing a full beard). Assimilated Jews, such as those who had emigrated from Germany to England in the early part of the nineteenth century, would use the term to mock those who followed for being old-fashioned and tied to the ways of the old country.

II. BACKGROUND – JEWISH IMMIGRATION TO BRITAIN

The following is a summary of the article on "England" in volume 6 of *Encyclopaedia Judaica*:

There were Jews in England from Roman times, but there was a mass expulsion in 1290 under Edward I. Small numbers of Jews came in through the next the few centuries, most of them transient. There was a small semi-overt Marrano community of approximately 100 in London until 1609.[3] After the readmission of Sephardic Jews during the 1650's under Cromwell, there were various improvements in the status of Jews. The practice of Judaism finally received indirect Parliamentary recognition in the *Act for Suppressing Blasphemy* of 1698. The number of "Jew Brokers" in the City of London was limited to 12. After 1750 the Ashkenazi community was also established, lower in social and commercial status, many occupied in itinerant trading in country areas where the Jewish pedlar became a familiar figure. Emancipation continued throughout the 19th century as various legal disabilities were removed, culminating in 1890. Nathaniel de Rothschild was the first Jew raised to the peerage, in 1885; Sir George Jessel was Solicitor General from 1871; Benjamin Disraeli, a convert to Christianity, was Prime Minister in 1868 and again from 1872-1880. Persecution in Russia from 1881 led to a huge increase in immigration from Eastern Europe. Jews gravitated to one or two trades—creating the ready-made clothing industry. Social and economic pressures, as well as legal impediments, led to many Jews becoming moneylenders and brokers, as well as street pedlars. *The Aliens Immigration Act* of 1905, passed after long, often anti-Semitic agitation, stemmed the tide of immigration. The Jewish population of 65,000 in 1880 increased to 300,000 by 1914. Immigrants formed compact over-crowded ghettos in East London, Manchester, Leeds, Liverpool and Glasgow. In 1901 about 40% of employed Russian-Polish immigrants were tailors, 12-13%

---

3 Contrary to some claims that Shakespeare could not have written *The Merchant of Venice*, because he had never met Jews, there were opportunities for him to do so in London. See James Shapiro, *Contested Will: Who Wrote Shakespeare?* New York: Simon & Shuster, 2010, p.5.

were in the boot trade and 10% in the furniture trade, mainly as cab-inet-makers. The non-Jewish working classes objected—charging that aliens working for low wages on piecework in small workshops would depress wages generally and cause unemployment, put pressure on housing, raise rents, bring disease and crime. Although this was gen-erally found to be untrue, it led to the 1905 *Aliens Act*.

This was the milieu in which the Canon was written and in which references to Jews must be understood. Conan Doyle's reference in "Shoscombe Old Place" to Norberton being in the "hands of the Jews" was a stereotypical description of a man deeply in debt and having to fend off his creditors before they could seize his assets.

III. A BRIEF SUMMARY OF ANTI-SEMITIC REFERENCES TO JEWS IN ENGLISH LITERATURE

It is not possible in a brief summary to set out all of the references to Jews or to Jewish characters in "modern" English literature. For our review we have chosen the period from the publication of *Ivanhoe* by Sir Walter Scott in 1819 to Lord Alfred Douglas in 1926. Here are some comments for you to consider before we turn to Conan Doyle's writings themselves.

Stereotyping can, in the view of some commentators, constitute vir-ulent anti-Semitism:[4]

> "Shoscombe Old Place" [p]ublished in 1927,... is the tale of Sir Robert Norberton who, on account of his debts, takes drastic measures to conceal the death of his sister and benefactor. Because he has "fallen into the hands of the Jews," he finds himself "compelled" to horsewhip Sam Brewer, a well-known Curzon Street moneylender, according to Norberton, a "ras-

---

4 "Fagin & Friends: The Image of The Jew In Victorian Literature and Popular Culture", unpublished talk by Barbara Rusch (n.d.). Reproduced with Barbara's kind permission.

cally fellow," on Newmarket Heath. This raises some troubling questions. If his creditor had been Mr. John Bull, socially prominent bank manager at the Curzon St. Bank, instead of a Jewish moneylender, would he have felt the same compulsion to horsewhip him in public when he attempted to collect on his debt? And would he have gotten away with it? We are not sure Arthur Conan Doyle or his readers ever bothered to ask themselves these questions, so desensitized had they become to such invective, both within the print culture and in real life, especially when it came to attacks on Jewish moneylenders and pawnbrokers. Nor does the fact that it is generally the non-Jew in these cases who has borrowed the money in the first place and is not keeping to his end of the bargain ever seem to enter into the equation …Yet, given their profound influence and ability to rally public opinion, it is indeed disappointing that Charles Dickens and Sir Arthur Conan Doyle succumbed to the powerful cultural mythologies of their day, content to perpetuate existing racial stereotypes rather than rally against them …That many of these great writers, notably Dickens, Arthur Conan Doyle and H.G. Wells, whose undisputed brilliance has been immortalized, shared a utopian vision of a world characterized by social justice and harmony makes their racist attitudes and vitriolic pronouncements all the more disappointing and somewhat mystifying …They belonged to a literary cabal whose vicious portrayals and peculiar brand of racial profiling which pervades their much-loved and critically-acclaimed classics are also a potent form of hate literature, helping to define the public's conception of the Jewish persona and laying the foundations for really professional purveyors of hate, like Joseph Goebbels, on which to build.

We will now refer to a few prominent authors of the period and their publications:

SIR WALTER SCOTT (1771-1832)[5]

Ivanhoe, Sir Walter Scott's historical novel was published in 1819 and was a favourite of Conan Doyle's. Set in 1194, two of the characters include a Jewish moneylender, Isaac of York and his daughter, Rebecca, who suffer frequent injustices. The book was written and published during a period of increasing struggle for emancipation of the Jews in Britain. There are frequent references to injustices against them. Most believe Isaac is Shylock's historical ancestor.[6] The chapter when Isaac is introduced is headed by a quotation from *The Merchant of Venice* "Hath not a Jew eyes?" Gross in *Shylock: A Legend and Its Legacy* writes "Scott's own day-to-day attitude towards Jews was one of tolerance tempered by distance (or perhaps the other way round)". Scott summed up his views in a letter to a friend:

> I think Miss Edgeworth's last work delightful, though Jews will always be to me Jews. One does not naturally or easily combine with their habits and pursuits any great liberality of principle, although certainly it may and I believe does exist in many individual instances. They are money-makers and money-brokers by profession and it is a trade which narrows the mind.

Scott portrays Isaac as unprincipled, grasping and cowardly. He is much more kindly disposed towards Isaac's daughter Rebecca, who is the Jewish paragon in word and deed. He creates a strong positive image of Rebecca.

---

5 For further and more comprehensive reading see Edgar Rosenberg: *From Shylock to Svengali,* Stanford, California: Stanford University Press, 1960 at pp. 234 *et seq.* Anthony Julius: *Trials of the Diaspora,* Oxford University Press, Oxford: 2010. Much of the following commentary about Conan Doyle's literary contemporaries relies on this book. See also John Gross, *Shylock: A Legend and Its Legacy,* New York: Simon and Schuster, 1992.

6 Rosenberg, *ibid* note 5 at pp. 74 *et seq.* and Gross, *ibid* note 5 at pp. 211 *et seq.*

OSCAR WILDE

Oscar Wilde's *The Picture of Dorian Gray* appeared in 1890. His Jewish stage manager Isaacs is a minor character who runs the theatre that Sibyl Vane acts in.[7] His Jewishness is stressed so much and he is so unsympathetically presented that the reader cannot help feeling a bit surprised and even startled. We first meet Isaacs in chapter 4, when Dorian says to Lord Henry:

> A hideous Jew, in the most amazing waistcoat I ever beheld in my life, was standing at the entrance, smoking a vile cigar. He had greasy ringlets, and an enormous diamond blazed in the centre of a soiled shirt. 'Have a box, my Lord?' he said, when he saw me, and he took off his hat with an air of gorgeous servility. There was something about him, Harry, that amused me. He was such a monster.

Dorian's dislike of Isaacs is not simply personal: it has strong anti-Semitic overtones. Nor does it seem to have any limits. Dorian attacks him again and again. A few pages later, for instance, he says:

> On the first night I was at the theatre, the horrid old Jew came round to the box after the performance was over, and offered to take me behind the scenes and introduce me to [Sybil Vane] ... He was a most offensive brute, though he had an extraordinary passion for Shakespeare.

Does this passage do nothing more than unselfconsciously give voice to a sentiment that the majority of the novel's Christian readers would

---

7 Christopher S. Nassaar: "The Problem of the Jewish Manager", Vol. 22 *The Wildean*, January 2003, pp, 29 *et seq*. According to Nassaar, Isaacs is Wilde's response to *Daniel Deronda* by George Eliot, a towering example of the portrayal of the Jewish community in the late 19th century. See also Margaret D. Stetz 'To defend the undefendable': "Oscar Wilde and the Davis Family". *Scholars Special Issue : Oscar Wilde, Jews & the Fin-de-Siecle*, Summer 2010.

endorse—a bodily, as well as moral, loathing echoed by Wilde's narrator, and was this a feeling that Wilde himself shared?

In Gentile circles and in Wilde's own social milieu, close relations with particular Jews (and with Jewish women, in particular)[8] did not guarantee an absence of the kind of negative stereotyping of Jews in general so common in late nineteenth-century Britain.

GEORGE DU MAURIER (1834-1896)

George du Maurier, primarily an illustrator, wrote three novels, the most famous of which is *Trilby* (1894). Edgar Rosenberg in *From Shylock to Svengali*[9] compares Fagin to du Maurier's Svengali in *Trilby* as follows:

> One may conveniently compare Cruikshank's drawing
> of Fagin in his condemned cell in *Oliver Twist* with du

Fagin in prison

> Maurier's drawing of Svengali in the act of hypnotizing Trilby. Detail for detail of two Jews run equally

8 Wilde's female Jewish friends included Sarah Bernhardt and Ida Leverson.

9 Rosenberg, *supra* note 5 at pp. 234 *et seq.*

true to type: the same unkempt hair, the same bushy eyebrows and penetrating stare, the same protruding Hapsburg lip. The noses are beaked in the same way, not so much jutting outward as resting flat against the mustaches, so that the characters may be imagined sniffing into their beards as they converse; the beards, too, are of identical cut, straggling Vandykes. The fingers which Fagin strikes cunningly against the side of his nose and those with which Svengali beckons toward Trilby are the same long, bony, by no means unbeautiful fingers. The shabby clothes, too, are shabby in the same way. The only difference is that Fagin still wears the broad-brimmed hat and the long black kaftan perpetuated by orthodox Jews, whereas Svengali is done

Svengali

up indifferently in the garb of the Parisian bohemian. And their sleeves are a world too wide for their shrunken wrists.

He could well have compared him also to the stage manager, Isaacs, in *The Picture of Dorian Gray*.[10]

---

10 It is interesting to note that in *Oliver Twist* Dickens refers to Fagin as "the Jew" 257 times in 38 chapters. Compare this with Baroness Orczy's *Scarlet Pimpernel, infra* at p. 173.

G.K. CHESTERTON (1874-1936)

G.K. Chesterton faced accusations of anti-Semitism during his lifetime and subsequently. In a work of 1917, titled *A Short History of England*, Chesterton writes that Edward I was "just and conscientious", a monarch never more truly representative of his people than when in 1290 he expelled the Jews, "as powerful as they are unpopular." Chesterton writes that Jews were "capitalists of their age" so that when Edward "flung the alien financiers out of the land," he acted as "both 'knight errant' and 'tender father of his people'".[11] In *The New Jerusalem* (1920), an account of his travels in Palestine, Chesterton made it clear that he believed that there was a "Jewish Problem" in Europe, in the sense that he believed that Jewish culture (not Jewish ethnicity) separated itself from the nationalists of Europe. He suggested the formation of a Jewish homeland as a solution, and was later invited to Palestine by Jewish Zionists who saw him as an ally in their cause.

The Wiener Library (London's archive on anti-Semitism and Holocaust history) has defended Chesterton against the charge of anti-Semitism: "he was not an enemy, and when the real testing time came along he showed what side he was on. Chesterton, like his friend Hillaire Belloc, openly expressed his abhorrence of Hitler's rule almost as soon as it started."[12]

HILLAIRE BELLOC (1870-1953)

Hillaire Belloc was preoccupied with Jews and would tell anyone ready to listen to him what he thought of them. They provoked him. He saw Jewish conspiracies everywhere. According to him the Russian Revolution was a Jewish experiment in Russia. He wrote a series of novels about I.Z. Barnett, a fictional Jewish swindler, who becomes a press magnate and is ultimately elevated to the peerage as Lord Lambeth.[13]

---

11 See Julius, *supra* note 5 at p. 422.

12 http://en.wikipedia.org/wiki/G.K.Chesterton. See also Michael Coren, *Gilbert: The Man Who Was G. K. Chesterton*, London: Vintage, 1990, p.203

13 See Julius, *supra* note 5 at p. 403

H.G. WELLS (1866-1946)

Michael Coren in his biography of H.G. Wells[14] says of him:

H.G. Wells at his desk.

In his fictional writings, Jewish characters occur in surprisingly large numbers, and are invariably stereotypical villains or base caricatures. The first such depiction is in *The Invisible Man*, published as early as 1897. Here we encounter the Jew as landlord, man of property. He is 'an old Polish Jew in a long grey coat and greasy slippers'; one of his two Yiddish speaking stepsons possesses 'staring eyes and thick-lipped bearded face.'

---

14 Michael Coren: *The Invisible Man*; Toronto: Vintage Books, 1993 at p. 214. Coren quotes from other Wells' writings like *Tono-Bungay* (1909), *The New Machiavelli* (1911) and *The Marriage* (1912) all of which can clearly be viewed as anti-Semitic. Coren has tried hard to establish his thesis that G.K. Chesterton was not himself an anti-Semite, while Chesterton's brother, Cecil and Hillaire Belloc, who all moved in the same circles, clearly were acknowledged anti-Semites. We do not find this convincing. The issue is not whether Chesterton was anti-Semitic, but merely how virulent.

T.S. ELIOT (1888-1965)

T.S. Eliot's well-known nonsensical poem "Burbank with a Baedeker: Bleistein with a Cigar" (1919/20)[15] reflects the casual anti-Semitism

T.S. Eliot

that was popular at the time and explains why Conan Doyle could use a derogatory term so casually in "Shoscombe Old Place" without raising any protests.[16] It reads in part:

> A lustreless protrusive eye
> Stares from the protozoic slime

---

15 http://www.bartleby.com/199/14.html – There was another egregious instance in his reference to the undesirability of a large number of "free-thinking Jews" in *After Strange Gods* (1933). Peter Ackroyd gives more details of what appears to be anti-Semitic remarks in unpublished letters between 1917 and 1929. He states in *T.S. Elliot*, Penguin Books Ltd., London: 1993, at pp. 303-4: "All the available evidence suggests then, that on occasion be made what were then fashionably anti-Semitic remarks to his close friends. Leonard Woolf, himself a Jew, has said: "I think T. S. Eliot was slightly anti-Semitic in the sort of vague way which is not uncommon".

16 Emmanuel Litvinoff, the English poet, would have forgiven Eliot this casual anti-Semitism in 1920, but when the poem was reprinted in a 1948 anthology, he became very upset and wrote a poem critical of *Eliot*, which he read to a session attended by Eliot. This incident was reported in the press. This caused Eliot's secretary to deny any suggestion Eliot was anti-Semitic. See Peter Ackroyd: *T.S. Eliot; ibid.*, at p. 303.

At a perspective of Canaletto.
The smoky candle end of time
Declines. On the Rialto once.
The rats are underneath the piles.
The Jew is underneath the lot.
Money in furs.

LORD ALFRED DOUGLAS (1870-1945)

Lord Alfred Douglas was convinced by the *Protocols of the Learned Elders of Zion* that the Jews took positions of power and corrupted the British system.[17]

In 1923, Douglas issued a pamphlet entitled "The Murder of Lord Kitchener—The Truth About the Battle of Jutland and the Jews", claiming that Winston Churchill had been part of a Jewish conspiracy to kill Lord Kitchener. For this he was found guilty of criminally libelling Churchill and was sentenced to six months in prison. Kitchener died on 5 June 1916, while on a diplomatic mission to Russia: the ship in which he was travelling, the armoured cruiser HMS Hampshire, struck a German naval mine and sank west of the Orkney Islands.[18]

In 1924, while in prison, Douglas, in an ironic echo of Wilde's composition of *De Profundis* (Latin for "from the depths"), wrote his last major poetic work, *In Excelsis* (literally, "in the highest"), which contains 17 cantos. The sonnet, which has serious anti-Semitic overtones, opens:

The leprous spawn of scattered Israel
Spreads its contagion in your English blood;

---

17 http://en.wikipedia.org/wiki/Lord Alfred Douglas. *The Protocols* were a notorious forgery concocted in the late 19th century, likely by agents of the Tsar, describing a Jewish plot to control the world. For a history of *The Protocols* and its publication in England, see Hadassa Ben-Itto: *The Lie That Wouldn't Die*, Vallantine-Mitchell, London – Portland, Oregon: 2005.

18 Conan Doyle wrote a sympathetic letter to Churchill after the conviction (now in the Churchill Archives at Cambridge), referring to his own exchange of letters with Douglas (now in the Conan Doyle Collection in Toronto). In spite of this libel claim, Douglas wrote a sonnet in praise of Churchill which appeared in the *Daily Mail* on July 4, 1941. It is reproduced in Douglas Murray: *Bosie*, Hodder & Stoughton, London: 2000 at p. 317.

and ends:

> In hidden holds they stew the mandrake mess
> That kills the soul and turns the blood to fire,
> They weave the spell that turns desire to dust
> And postulates the abyss of nothingness.

Douglas Murray in *Bosie*[19] tells us:

> Though the editing of two newspapers, *Plain English* and *Plain Speech*, had not been a great success, it had at least given Douglas the opportunity to do sustained work. The pitfall was that the papers made him more enemies than friends. Their anti-Semitic content had put many people's opinions firmly against him. Although one of the few specific attacks on Jews came when the famous quatrain
>
> > How odd
> > Of God
> > To choose
> > The Jews.
>
> was published for the first time by Douglas in *Plain English* in 1926. The frequent implications that Jewish conspiracies were being worked at high levels in society made many indignant.

CONTEMPORARY GENRE WRITERS

During the late nineteenth and early years of the twentieth century a number of crime genre writers became popular. Most of these were considered second-rate novelists, but their popularity has survived many more accomplished authors. We cite just three of the more

19 *Ibid.* at p. 233.

prominent, to show how readily their casual anti-Semitism passed without comment.

BARONESS EMMUSKA ORCZY (1865-1947)

The Scarlet Pimpernel, the most famous of her numerous novels, published in 1905, was set in 1792 Paris during the French Revolution. In Chapter XXVI entitled "The Jew" the search is on for a Jew, Reuben Goldstein, last seen with the Scarlet Pimpernel:

> Desgas returned, followed by an elderly Jew in a dirty, threadbare, gaberdine, worn greasy across the shoulders. His red hair, which he wore after the fashion of the Polish Jews, with the corkscrew curls each side of his face, was plentifully sprinkled with grey—a general coating of grime about his cheeks and his chin gave him a peculiarly dirty and loathsome appearance. He had the habitual stoop those of his race affected in mock humility in past centuries, before the dawn of equality and freedom in matters of faith, and he walked behind Desgas with the peculiar shuffling gait which has remained the characteristic of the Jew trader in continental Europe to this day.
>
> Chauvelin, who had all the Frenchman's prejudice against the despised race, motioned to the fellow to keep at a respectful distance.
>
> The Jew, with characteristic patience, stood humbly on the side, leaning on a thick knotted staff, his greasy, broad-brimmed hat casting a deep shadow over his grimy face, waiting for the noble Excellency to deign to put some questions to him.

"The Jew" is never identified by name, but is referred to this way no less than 15 times in the chapter. He is paid to reveal information as to the direction which Reuben Goldstein had driven the Scarlet Pimpernel. Orczy was a noted anti-Semite. Her depiction of 18th century anti-Semitism is an accurate statement about the era; what offends today is her certainty that this was correct.

JOHN BUCHAN (1875-1940)

As Lord Tweedsmuir, Buchan was Governor General of Canada 1935-1940. In *The Thirty-Nine Steps* (1915), Richard Hannay learns from a mysterious American of an international conspiracy of Jewish anarchists and capitalists, at the bottom of which is 'a little white-faced Jew in a bath-chair with an eye like a rattlesnake.' In *Greenmantle* (1916) Hannay continues his Jewish conspiracy theory in describing the German people:

> He may have plenty of brains, as Stumm had, but he has the poorest notion of psychology of any of God's creatures. In Germany only the Jew can get outside himself, and that is why, if you look into the matter, you will find that the Jew is at the back of most German enterprises.[20]

Christopher Hitchens has written of him:[21]

> Like Greene and Evelyn Waugh and many others of the period, Buchan has been accused of anti-Semitism. Two defenses have frequently been offered in these cases: that the alleged anti-Semite harbored a prejudice no greater than was commonplace at the time, and that he had many Jewish friends. A third possibility is that the offending words are uttered by fictional characters and not by the author, is sometimes canvassed. None of these will quite do in Buchan's case. It's not merely that anti-Jewish cliches occur in his books; it's that they occur so frequently. The usual form they take is a reference to Judeo-Bolshevism—the sympathy of Jews, even rich

---

20 *Greenmantle* is the second of the five novels featuring Richard Hannay

21 *The Atlantic Monthly*, March, 2004

ones, for the Russian Revolution. That, however, might be described as political anti-Semitism, just as Buchan's energetic support for the early Zionist movement might be called political philo-Semitism. Paradoxically, perhaps, Buchan greatly disliked as a person the most anti-Jewish and pro-Zionist figure of his day, Arthur Balfour.

AGATHA CHRISTIE (1890-1976)

As one commentator has recently written of Christie's anti-Semitism:[22]

> Jews are "little" or "avid", their lips are "thick and Semitic", and their eyes light up with greed at the mention of money. From *And Then There Were None* (the original title was "Ten Little Niggers ") to *Lord Edgware Dies*, Jews are figures of comedy and contempt, caricatured mercilessly as money-grubbing social climbers.
>
> But would I erase [the stereotyping]? Never: to see anti-Semitism so endemic in the works of a highly-respected and best-selling author is to understand a period of history—and its horrific consequences. Read these detective novels, and you understand how pogroms could go on in Russia and Eastern Europe as late as the 1920s without a squeak from western European governments. Take in Christie's casual anti-Semitism and you see why Jews in Britain clung to ghettos and were suspicious of assimilation. From Oswald Mosley's popularity, through Neville Chamberlain's ambivalence to saving European Jewry, to the "no Jews" admission policy of London gentlemen's clubs: reading the unexpurgated Christie makes sense of what, to contemporary eyes, seems impossible.

22 Christine Odone, *The Telegraph*, December 25, 2012: http://blogs.telegraph.co.uk/news/cristinaodone/100070883/in-terms-of-literary-racism-agatha-christie-is-truly-the-queen-of-crime/

We could cite many other contemporaries of Conan Doyle, whose casual use of anti semitic stereotypes are far more vicious than the essentially benign ones of "Shoscombe Old Place" or his other works.[23]

IV. JEW PEDLARS, JEW BROKERS ET AL –
SOME DEFINITIONS

The list goes on and on but even these few names are enough to suggest that the use of Jewish stereotypes gave authors a great deal of flexibility.

JEW PEDLAR

Felsenstein[24] gives a historical background to the Jew pedlar. He provides an 18th century caricature of a Jew Pedlar with his knickknacks and cheap jewellery which shows him holding up and pointing to a gilt framed portrait of the Queen. He says the word "pedlar" is derived from the German dialect word *schmus*, meaning patter.

Jewish rural pedlars, immigrants from Alsace-Lorraine and the Rhineland, began to appear in England toward the middle of the 18th century, becoming common in most of southern England over next 50 years. Some became street vendors in London and other large cities.

After 1880 10% of the Jews in Glasgow, and higher in Edinburgh, were street pedlars.

JEW BROKER

As noted earlier, by a regulation of 1697, the number of Jewish brokers officially allowed to perform their business at the Royal Exchange was limited to 12 out of a total of 124. This restriction was not rescinded until 1830.

---

23 These include Dorothy Sayers, E. Phillips Oppenheim and R. Austin Freeman, all of whom were best sellers in their time .

24 Frank Felsenstein: *Anti-Semitic Stereotypes 1660 – 1830*, The John Hopkins University Press, Baltimore and London: 1955 at pp. 83 et seq.

HANDS OF THE JEWS

There are more references to Jews in *Rodney Stone* (1896) than in any other of Conan Doyle's fiction. Most of these are in reference to boxing, with a few references to debt and moneylenders.

Although the boxing references use stereotypical descriptions, they are also admiring of the qualities of these Jews.

> There also I saw the keen features of Dan Mendoza, the Jew, just retired from active work, and leaving behind him a reputation for elegance and perfect science which has, to this day, never been exceeded. The worst fault that the critics could find with him was that there was a want of power in his blows, a remark which certainly could not have been made about his neighbour, whose long face, curved nose, and dark, flashing eyes proclaimed him as a member of the same ancient race. This was the formidable Dutch Sam, who fought at nine stone six, and yet possessed such hitting powers, that his admirers, in after years, were willing to back him against the fourteen-stone Tom Cribb, if each were strapped astraddle to a bench. Half a dozen other sallow Hebrew faces showed how energetically the Jews of Houndsditch and Whitechapel had taken to the sport of the land of their adoption, and that in this, as in more serious fields of human effort, they could hold their own with the best.

The moneylender references in *Rodney Stone* are also stereotypical and, although written more than 30 years earlier, are nearly identical to those in "Shoscombe Old Place":

> Of the Captain I knew little, save that he was not of the best repute, and was deep in the hands of the Jews.
> …
> Well, I am going down to Clarges Street to pay Jew King a little of my interest.

...

I knew that, owing to his reckless mode of life, he was firmly in the clutches of the Jews,

...

This will be the last blow to Hume, for I know that the Jews have given him rope on the score of his expectations.

Were these moneylenders even Jewish? As noted earlier, Sam Brewer (not in itself a notably Jewish name) in "Shoscombe Old Place" lived on fashionable Curzon Street.[25] Conan Doyle was clearly not trying to portray him as a lower class or alien type.

"The Jew's Breastplate",[26] is a story about a relic of Solomon's Temple that is being mysteriously damaged each night in its museum case. There are no derogatory references to Jews or the Jewish religion. Except for explaining the Jewish origin and significance of the breastplate, there are no references to Jews or Jewishness—it is just a name for a very valuable object. There is one passage, reminiscent of "The Six Napoleons", where the narrator suggests that the person who is destroying the busts has a hatred for Napoleon:

A curious idea came into my head. "This object is a Jewish relic of great antiquity and sanctity," said I. "How about the anti-Semitic movement? Could one conceive that a fanatic of that way of thinking might desecrate-" "No, no, no!" cried Mortimer. "That will never do! Such a man might push his lunacy to the

---

25 Oscar Wilde mentions Curzon Street in two of his works: in *The Picture of Dorian Gray*, Lord Henry Wotton lives on Curzon Street, and in *Lady Windermere's Fan*, the notorious Mrs. Erlynne lives at 84A Curzon Street. In *Vanity Fair* by William Makepeace Thackeray, Rawdon and Rebecca Crawley live in a very small comfortable house in Curzon Street, Mayfair. In *Mrs. Packletide's Tiger* by Saki, the wealthy Mrs. Packletide has a house on Curzon Street. It is also the location of the Junior Ganymede Club in P.G. Wodehouse's Jeeves and Wooster series of books (*The Code of the Woosters*). In *The Mystery of the Blue Train* by Agatha Christie, Ruth and Derek Kettering also live on Curzon Street: http://en.wikipedia.org/wiki/Curzon _Street.

26 *The Strand Magazine*, February 1899.

length of destroying a Jewish relic, but why on earth should he nibble round every stone so carefully that he can only do four stones in a night?"

Although we must be cautious about concluding that his fictional words are also his personal beliefs, associating anti-Semitism with lunacy surely speaks volumes for Conan Doyle's opinion of anti-Semitism.

Another term often used with reference to Jews is "Semitic". Conan Doyle rarely uses this word, but when he does it is invariably as a description of the facial features of someone he is describing, and always to describe someone who is not Jewish:

> In consultation with him was one who was to prove even more formidable, and for a longer time. Semitic in face, high-nosed, bushy-bearded, and eagle-eyed, with skin burned brown by a life of the veldt it was Delarey, one of the trio of fighting chiefs whose name will always be associated with the gallant resistance of the Boers.[27]
>
> ...
>
> The one, tall, dark, and wiry, with pure, Semitic features, and the limbs of a giant, was Magro, the famous Carthaginian captain, whose name was still a terror on every shore, from Gaul to the Euxine[28]
>
> ...
>
> Then again there is the ethnology of the Red Indians. Some of them are very Semitic in appearance. I should like to have the opinion of some learned linguist as to whether any Indian words could be traced to an ancient Hebrew root....It is impossible to look at a number of them, especially the women, without feeling that they are Asiatic, half Chinese, half Esquimaux. Surely, then,

---

27 *The Great Boer War*, 1900

28 "The Last Galley", *London Magazine*, November 1910, Vol. 25, pp. 242-8,

North America was largely peopled from Behring's
Straits? And yet there is that strain with the Dante
nose and chin. They are not Mongolian or Turanian.
Are they not rather suggestive of the Semite? In that
case there would be some slight corroboration for the
Mormon view. Semites from the south may have inter-
married with Mongols from the north.[29]

V. CONAN DOYLE AND HIS CIRCLE OF FRIENDS

Conan Doyle knew a number of Jewish writers and intellectuals
and was clearly sympathetic to the plight of the Jews. According to
Michael Coren:[30]

Sir Arthur Conan Doyle

---

29 *Our Second American Adventure*, Hodder & Stoughton, London: 1924.

30 *Conan Doyle*, Stoddart Publishing Co. Ltd, Toronto: 1995 at p. 72

One aspect of Irene Adler that does deserve attention is her Jewish-sounding surname. If the choice is deliberate, and it often was with Conan Doyle, it may represent the author's growing interest in Jews and Judaism, as evidenced by his meeting with Jewish intellectuals and spiritualists in Vienna and Jewish writers and thinkers in London. G.K. Chesterton wrote ... that Conan Doyle had referred to the name "Adler" being of Jewish descent.

Conan Doyle was friendly with the Anglo-Jewish novelist and activist Israel Zangwill.[31] He wrote in a letter dated 6 November 1905, on the subject of Jewish suffering and Zionism. This was written in response to a letter from Zangwill after a major series of pogroms in Poland and the western Ukraine. He wrote:

Israel Zangwill

'Pray excuse my delay—I have been exceedingly busy. I have thought much of your scheme for the resettlement

---

31 Zangwill does not appear in the list of attendees at Conan Doyle's wedding on September 17, 1907, nor in Conan Doyle's guestbook, which covers visitors to his home between 1898 and 1912 (we are indebted to Richard Sveum for providing us with a copy of this guestbook). In fact, none of the names in the guestbook appear to be of Jews.

of the refugee Jews—of course I entirely sympathise with it. It seems monstrous and inhuman that on all the face of God's earth there should be no resting place for those unhappy people, who driven out of one land are refused admission into all others. Their position is like the poor non combatants in the middle ages, who were driven out of the besieged city by the garrison but refused a passage through their lines by the besiegers. I would do anything I could to help them to a permanent home. But the more one thinks of it the more the practical difficulties grow—no doubt the British Empire has many tropical or semi-tropical sites vacant for such a colony. There is East Africa—the Highlands of Uganda, Northern Rhodesia, New Guinea and doubtless many other places which I have not thought of.'

Doyle went on to outline the possible problems and concluded his letter with the following:

However it is poor work pointing out difficulties. I admire your pluck in facing them. I wish you heartily every success.

In a speech on Britain's prominent writers delivered June 4, 1914 he said:

The very closest connection exists now between writers of fiction and the practical affairs of life. A very great impetus is given to public causes by the interest which is taken in them by these men who can put them in the proper form…Who stands for Zionism? It is Zangwill. Hardly a man who takes a mere money-making view—who does not venture out into life and employ his talents for the public good.

We make the point that Doyle in supporting the establishment of a Jewish homeland is not necessarily being pro-Semitic. In fact, he could conceivably have been motivated by a desire to see Jewish immigrants diverted from the U.K. to a foreign Jewish homeland, although there appears to be no direct evidence for this.

Andrew Lycett points out that after the Boer War Doyle belonged at the same time to two societies with antithetical purposes:

> No one could fault his patriotism as he organised his rifle club, gave evidence to the Royal Commission on the War, or scurried to a meeting of the Boys' Empire League where, as president, he offered a prize for the best patriotic song. But these preoccupations were taking him into some odd places. For example, he had become a financial supporter of the British Brothers League, which campaigned against alien, by which it meant Jewish, immigration into London's East End. But while the League was Anti-Semitic and is now described as proto-Fascist, Arthur was not anti-Jewish. He supported the burgeoning Zionist movement and, largely through the offices of his friend Israel Zangwill, sat on the London Committee of the General Jewish Colonising Organization.[32]

Doyle's assistance in the Oscar Slater case is well-known. Slater, a German-Jewish immigrant, was wrongfully accused and convicted of murder in Glasgow in 1909. Despite Slater's questionable moral lifestyle and Jewish origins, Conan Doyle took on his case and was instrumental in obtaining his release from prison.

Coren in *Conan Doyle*[33] states:

> Conan Doyle was sympathetic to the Jews, was asked by Jewish friends to try to do something about the

---

32 Andrew Lycett:, *Conan Doyle: The Man Who Created Sherlock Holmes*. Weidenfeld & Nicolson, London: 2007 at p. 278

33 *Supra*, note 30 at pp. 129-130

Slater case and, most important of all, he could not resist supporting the underdog whatever bark he or she had.

After reviewing the names of Conan Doyle's friends and acquaintances, using sources such as reports of his second wedding,[34] the Undershaw guest book and other material, we concluded that Conan Doyle's social circle included very few Jews—unlike Winston Churchill and Edward as Prince of Wales, who were often accused of having too many Jewish friends.[35] Lady Warwick had this to say about Edward's Jewish friends:[36]

> Most of all they disapproved of his close friendships with affluent Jews. We resented the introduction of the Jews into the social set of the Prince of Wales, not because we disliked them individually . . . but because they had brains and understood finance. As a class, we did not like brains. As for money, our only understanding of it lay in the spending, not in the making of it.

The Prince delighted in the company of rich Jews like the Sassoons, the Rothchilds, Baron Maurice von Hirsch and the like. When Edward became king and could not control his spending, he summoned an inner financial circle to his aid. Sir Ernest Cassel, a prominent Jewish banker, was one of these advisors.[37]

Conan Doyle was very friendly with Harry Houdini and had many conversations with him about Spiritualism. It is not hard to assume

---

34 *The Times*, Sept. 9, 1907. We do not have the full list. There were 200-250 people at the Hotel Metropole for the reception, including many authors

35 Coren refers to Doyle's Jewish friends and acquaintances several times, but does not provide any references. He states at p. 197: "In 1929 Conan Doyle helped German refugees to find a home in London and delivered a small series of public lectures, 'The Future of Europe', stressing the tenuous position of the Jews."

36 Christopher Hibbert: *Edward VII: A Portrait*, Penguin Books Ltd., Harmondsworth, England: 1982.

37 Philip Magnus: *King Edward the Seventh*, Penguin Books Ltd., Harmondsworth, England: 1964.

that there may have been conversations that touched on Houdini's Jewishness. Of course, we cannot possibly know Conan Doyle's entire circle of acquaintances, and even with people he did know, including Winston Churchill, it is clear that there must have been undocumented encounters from time to time. Absence of evidence is not usually evidence of absence. However, we can safely conclude that he did not have many close connections with Jews.

We can accept, just on general principles, that Conan Doyle was sympathetic to the plight of the Jews. Conan Doyle always supported the underdog, and much of his writing displays tolerance for minorities. The word "Jew" appears only once in Conan Doyle's autobiography, *Memories and Adventures* (1924) and twice in *Through the Magic Door* (1907), Conan Doyle's thoughts on books and literature. All references are to boxing. The logical inference from this is that Jews and Jewishness really do not matter much to Conan Doyle. He does not think about them a great deal, good or bad, except in connection with subjects like boxing. Occasionally, if an injustice against Jews or their economic and political plight is brought to his attention, he speaks out sympathetically, in keeping with his character.

VI A BRIEF SUMMARY OF PRO-JEWISH REFERENCES TO JEWS IN ENGLISH LITERATURE

There were English writers who clearly demonstrated pro-Jewish views in their writings. To quote from a 1945 essay by George Orwell on anti-Semitism in Britain:

> There has been a perceptible anti-Semitic strain in English literature from Chaucer onwards, and without even getting up from this table to consult a book I can think of passages which if written now would be stigmatised as anti-Semitism in the works of Shakespeare, Smollett, Thackeray, Bernard Shaw, H.G. Wells, T.S. Eliot, Aldous Huxley and various others. Offhand,

the only English writers I can think of who, before the days of Hitler, made a definite effort to stick up for Jews are Dickens and Charles Reade. And however little the average intellectual may have agreed with the opinions of Belloc and Chesterton, he did not acutely disapprove of them. Chesterton's endless tirades against Jews, which he thrust into stories and essays upon the flimsiest pretexts, never got him into trouble—indeed Chesterton was one of the most generally respected figures in English literary life. Anyone who wrote in that strain now would bring down a storm of abuse upon himself, or more probably would find it impossible to get his writings published.[38]

Orwell refers to Dickens and Reade. He could also have cited George Eliot's *Daniel Deronda* as a further example. In another essay on Charles Dickens,[39] Orwell says the following:

It is perhaps more significant that he shows no prejudice against Jews. It is true that he takes it for granted (*Oliver Twist* and *Great Expectations*) that a receiver of stolen goods will be a Jew, which at the time was probably justified. But the "Jew joke", endemic in English literature until the rise of Hitler, does not appear in his books, and in *Our Mutual Friend* Dickens makes a pious though not very convincing attempt to stand up for the Jews. One very striking thing about Dickens, especially considering the time he lived in, is his lack of vulgar nationalism. All peoples who have reached the point of becoming nations tend to despise foreigners,

---

38 George Orwell, "Antisemitism in Britain", *Contemporary Jewish Record*, GB, London, April 1945. Reprinted in *England Your England and Other Essays*, London: Secker and Warburg, 1953; *Such, Such Were the Joys* (1953); Collected Essays (1961); *The Collected Essays, Journalism and Letters of George Orwell* (1968).

39 *A Collection of Essays*, Harvest Books, Orlando: 1981 at p.71.

but there is not much doubt that the English-speaking races are the worst offenders. One can see this from the fact that as soon as they become fully aware of any foreign race they invent an insulting nickname for it.

Orwell might have made similar remarks about Conan Doyle.

There is a wonderful passage in Christopher Hitchens' final column in the February 2012 issue of *Vanity Fair* magazine about Dickens that is along similar lines to Orwell's essay:

> ...he was obviously very impressed when a prominent Jewish lady, Mrs. Eliza Davis, wrote him an anguished letter after the 1838 publication of *Oliver Twist*. She was obviously terribly upset about the character of Fagin and was not even quite willing to concede that some Jews had been involved in the stolen-goods racket. At any rate, Dickens went into the matter and convinced himself that he'd been part of an injustice. He thereupon did three things. He softened the description of Fagin in later versions of the book.[40] When he himself took part in public 'readings" from the story, he downplayed the "Jewish" characteristics of the villain. And he then created a whole new character to order. In *Our Mutual Friend*, we encounter a Jewish moneylender named Mr. Riah, who is friendly and helpful to Lizzie Hexam and Jenny Wren. I admit that I find his personage almost too altruistic to be true, but it says something for Dickens, surely, that he would take someone who had the same occupation as the infamous Shylock, but none of Shylock's vices, and insert him at the heart of business, at a time when vulgar prejudice was easy to stir up. The story isn't as well known as it ought to be.[41]

---

40 Dickens changed the references in the second edition from "Fagin the Jew" to "Fagin."

41 See also Julius, *supra*. note 5 at p. 203 for a discussion of Riah, Dickens' sympathetic Jewish character.

VII. CONAN DOYLE'S USE OF JEWISH STEREOTYPES

First let us consider what a "stereotype" is. A "stereotype" according to the *Oxford English Dictionary* is a basic form of social insight, "a preconceived and oversimplified idea of characteristics which typify a person, situation etc., an attitude based on such a preconception."

While it is difficult, if not impossible, to find any overtly anti-Semitic remark in Conan Doyle's writing, it is not difficult to find stereotypical language referring to Jews in his fictional works that today would be considered derogatory and offensive. Usually these instances are descriptions of Jews, none of whom are important characters—the "Jew pedlar", the "Jew broker" and the Jewish moneylender of the Holmes tales. The many references to Jews in *Rodney Stone* are in the main admiring of the Jewish boxers, and the few references to moneylenders are quite similar to those in "Shoscombe Old Place"—in other words, they are stereotypes. In Doyle's "The Ghosts of Goresthorpe Grange" (1879), the narrator, Dodds wants to acquire a ghost to grace his newly acquired manor. He engages a man named Abrahams for the task:

> [H]ere was a gentleman with a Judaical name... Instead, however, of being the sallow-faced, melancholy-eyed man that I had pictured to myself, the ghost-dealer was a sturdy little podgy fellow, with a pair of wonderfully keen sparkling eyes and mouth which was constantly stretched in a good-humoured, if somewhat artificial, grin.[42]

---

42 According to John Dickson Carr and Owen Dudley Edwards, this story was written in or before 1879. Green and Gibson state that it was sent to *Blackwood's Magazine* under the title of "The Haunted Grange of Goresthorpe." *Blackwood's* neither published it nor returned the manuscript, which is now in the National Library of Scotland with the Blackwood Archives. Conan Doyle apparently rewrote it under the title given above, under which it was published in *London Society*, Vol. 44, pp. 681-682 (1883) and reprinted in the *New York Times*, Dec. 23, 1883. The latter version was then republished in *Dreamland and Ghostland*, George Redway, London: 1887 (Vol. III, pp. 120-150), and subsequently in several other editions under this title and as "The Secret of Goresthorpe Grange."

In the Brigadier Gerard story, "How the Brigadier Held the King", Gerard describes Marshall Massena:

> if, as some said, he had Jewish blood in his veins, he was the best Jew that I have heard of since Joshua's time. If you were in sight of his beaky nose and bold, black eyes, you were not likely to miss much of what was going on.[43]

We must ask ourselves if these stereotypical references, or any of them, are "anti Semitic", or at the least out of tune with the zeitgeist of the era in which they were written. Our conclusion is that they were not anti-Semitic, merely stereotypical and not meant in a derogatory sense. Conan Doyle would have been horrified if someone had suggested to him that they were anti-Semitic. Conan Doyle used these recognizable stereotypes precisely because he knew his readers would be familiar with the characters he described from their context. Particularly in a short story, in which economy of words is essential, such shorthand sketches of minor characters could save him a great deal of elaboration.

If we limit ourselves to the Canon, there are only four direct references to Jews, none of which in our view are anti-Semitic. We can find not one villainous or despicable Jewish character in his entire oeuvre. His general attitude to non-Anglo-Saxons, as expressed throughout his writing career, is the typical patronizing attitude of the British upper class, to which he aspired, but without rancour or dislike— unlike many of the upper class or contemporaries such as Wells and later Chesterton.

---

43 In *Napoleon and His Court* (1924), C.S. Forester wrote: "He was of Italian extraction (many people said Jewish-Italian, and hinted that Massena was a euphonized version of Manasseh) ..." Conan Doyle would have had access to earlier biographical works, which would have made similar claims. The claim can be found in works by authoritative scholars, such as Cecil Roth, but apparently without confirmed sources. It appears to have been fairly common during Massena's lifetime. As far as we can tell, there is no confirmed basis for the suggestion that Massena was Jewish.

In the recently published *The Narrative of John Smith*,[44] a book thought to have been lost, written in 1883 when Conan Doyle was 23, we find the following passage, put in the mouth of an old soldier, but clearly meant to be an exposition of Conan Doyle's own views:

> I should like to see a little more transfusion in the Empire,' he remarked after a pause. 'More black faces in the streets of London and more white ones in the country parts of India. We should find billets in England for a thousand bright Hindoo youths every year, and send out as many of our own young fellows to work at the tea and indigo. It would help us towards consolidating the union between the countries. A few Indian regiments in English garrison towns would have the same effect. As to our parliament, it should be a piebald assembly with every hue from jet to brown, red and yellow, with occasionally a bronze-coloured premier at the head of them. What's the odds how much pigment a man has in his skin, if he has a level head and a loyal heart. Gad, sir, I've seen our British regiments glad enough of their help on the day of battle—why shouldn't we be equally ready to have their assistance at our councils? The Aryan conquerors of England need not be ashamed to take into partnership the Aryan conquerors of India, even though their hide has been a little burned by their long stay in the tropics.

We do point out, however, *Angels of Darkness* (1887)[45] with Splayfoot Dick (a Negro servant) and Ling-Tchu (a Chinese laundryman) as stereotypically unattractive Negroes and Chinese, a work which he deliberately chose not to publish, which also leaves a question mark.

---

44 First published by the British Library in 2011 and edited by John Lellenberg and Daniel Stashower.

45 The Baker Street Irregulars in cooperation with The Toronto Public Library, New York, (2001) – Leslie Klinger, General Editor.

VIII. CONCLUSIONS

This paper is not intended to be a full analysis of Conan Doyle's attitude towards Jews, nor a fulsome study of anti-Semitism in English literature or society. People in Conan Doyle's era simply did not regard expressions of racial or ethnic hostility as politically incorrect. There was no need for people to curb their tongues or keep their discriminatory thoughts to themselves.[46]

In 2010 Jean-Paul Guerlain, the 75-year old French parfumier used the "N" word in a French television interview. He was describing how hard he had worked to build his cosmetic empire. Protests broke out in front of his store on the Champs-Elysees in Paris. Apologising to France's black community, Guerlain said "I am from another generation." He was fined €6,000. We are all held to a different standard today.

Yet if Conan Doyle had similar thoughts, he was remarkably and uncharacteristically reticent about expressing them. We conclude, without being apologists, that Sir Arthur was not anti-Semitic in his personal life and that there is very little trace of what we would today consider anti-Semitic expression in his writing. Terms we would today consider to be anti-Semitic in nature are used as stereotypes, reflective of common terminology and the cultural media of the times.[47]

---

46 See Bill Gladstone "A Russian Jew in Bloomsbury", *Canadian Jewish News*, August 2, 2012. This is a book review of Dalya Diment's "A Russian Jew of Bloomsbury" It describes Samuel Koteliansky's relationship with the Bloomsbury set. He states: "Kot's friendship with D. H. Lawrence thrived despite Lawrences's frequent anti-Semitic remarks. Apparently few people in that era regarded expressions of racial hostility as politically incorrect: there was no need for people to curb their tongues or keep their discriminatory thoughts to themselves."

47 As this book was being prepared for publication, we discovered that Andrew Solberg. in "Sherlock Holmes: Anti-Semite?", *Baker Street Journal*, vol. 51, no. 1 (2001) has come to a similar conclusion, based on a review of how the terms used by Conan Doyle would have been understood when he wrote them.
http://www.bakerstreetjournal.com/images/SH%20Anti-semite%20-%20Solberg.pdf

VAMBERRY THE WINE MERCHANT, COUNT DRACULA AND THE ZIONIST MOVEMENT[*]

Presented to the Bootmakers of Toronto, December 7, 2013

INTRODUCTION

In "The Musgrave Ritual", published in *The Strand Magazine* for May 1893, as Watson and Holmes are sitting by the fire on a wintry evening. Watson asks:

> "There are the records of your early work, then?"... "I have often wished that I had notes of those cases."

Holmes replies:

> "Yes, my boy, these were all done prematurely, before my biographer had come to glorify me." He lifted bundle after bundle in a tender, caressing sort of way. "They are not all successes, Watson," said he. "But there are some pretty little problems among them.

---

[*] The writers wish to thank James Reese for his helpful comments.

> Here's the record of the Tarleton murders, and *the case of Vamberry, the wine merchant*, and the adventure of the old Russian woman, and the singular affair of the aluminium crutch, as well as a full account of Ricoletti of the club-foot, and his abominable wife." (our emphasis)

After due deliberation we have come to the conclusion that "Vamberry" is not a made up name.

We do not believe that Conan Doyle plucked it out of his fertile imagination as he did in the case of "Garrideb" in the "Three Garridebs." There is no doubt that Vamberry is a reference to Arminius Vámbéry, a Hungarian Jewish linguist, traveller and double agent, born March 19, 1832, and died 15 September 1913. We will investigate why Sir Arthur Conan Doyle would have known about Vámbéry, or perhaps even have met him. We will also consider whether "Vamberry" was merely the name of a public figure Conan Doyle inserted into a story, or whether he is there for a reason, such as, for example, the reference to Sir George Lewis in "The Illustrious Client"[1]. Lewis's name was used to explain why Sir James Damery was the real 'fixer' for the Prince of Wales, who was the "client." We will show that the name of "Arminius Vámbéry" was very well-known to the British public and undoubtedly to Arthur Conan Doyle. Vámbéry was one of those persons who, in their own era, were household names, but are barely remembered today. We also hope to show that Vámbéry may have been the inspiration for some of the later activities of Sherlock Holmes.

DATING OF THE CASE OF "VAMBERRY THE WINE MERCHANT"

One notes from "The Musgrave Ritual" that the Vamberry case took place, as Sherlock Holmes states, "before my biographer had come to

---

1 Hartley Nathan & Clifford Goldfarb," Oh Sinner Man – Where You Gonna Run To? Sir Arthur And Sir George", on p. 143 of this volume.

glorify me." While it is understood that Conan Doyle began writing the story in December 1892[2] and it was published in May 1893, the question is when did the case actually take place? One writer[3] suggests the range to be between 1881 and 1887, the latter date being the year in which *A Study in Scarlet* was published. However, if it happened before Watson began to work with Holmes in 1881, the case must have taken place before that year, but after Holmes began his detective career, about 1876-7. H.W. Bell, in *Sherlock Holmes and Doctor Watson: A Chronology of Their Adventures*[4], dates the commencement of Holmes' professional career to the autumn of 1877. He then places the case of Vamberry between that date and 1880.

WHO WAS ARMINIUS VÁMBÉRY?

According to his biography in *Encyclopedia Judaica:*

> VAMBERY, ARMINIUS (1832-1913), Hungarian traveler and orientalist. He was born Hermann Vamberger (erroneously referred to as Bamberger) of Orthodox [Jewish] parents in Dunajska Streda on the island of Schütt, Hungary[5].
>
> Vámbéry attended heder and yeshiva[6] as well as the Protestant elementary school in Dunaszerdahely from age eight. He was a tailor's apprentice for a short time. Due to a dislocated hip, his left leg was para-

---

2 Andrew Lycett: *Conan Doyle: The Man Who Created Sherlock Holmes* Weidenfeld & Nicolson, London 2007 p.84.

3 David Pelgas: "Vamberry or Vambery, A Possible Identification" 4 *Baker Street Journal* (December 1993) 204.

4 Constable & Co. London 1932, pp.12-16.

5 Keter Publishing House Jerusalem Ltd., Vol. 16. Various biographies give different birthplaces and spellings of his family name. According to Ernst Pawel, a biographer of Theodor Herzl, as well as Tom Reiss, a biographer of Kurban Said, Vámbéry's original last name was "Wamberger" rather than "Bamberger." According to his Wikipedia article, Vámbéry was born in Svätý Jur (now in Slovakia), Hungary.

6 Both are Jewish religious schools.

lyzed when he was a small child; he used crutches and later a walking stick for the rest of his life. He never completed high school[7].

Arminius Vámbéry

Possessed of an extraordinary capacity for languages and a phenomenal memory, he mastered numerous European languages and then turned to Arabic, Turkish, and Persian, achieving magisterial fluency and control in these. In his early twenties, fired by the dream of exploring the putative homeland of the Magyars in Asia, he moved to Constantinople where he lived as a tutor of European languages and executed translations from Turkish history. He became a Muslim and entered the service of the Turkish government as secretary to Mehmet Fuad Pasha, five times foreign minister of Turkey. While in Constantinople he earned the esteem of Sultan Abdul-Hamid II[8].

It appears that Vámbéry changed his religions according to his circumstances—to Islam in order to move more freely in the Muslim

7 http://www.yivoencyclopedia.org/article.aspx/Vambery_Armin.
8 *Encyclopedia Judaica*

world, and then to Protestant Christianity in order to secure a teaching position that would have been denied to him as a Jew in Hungary. He may have converted as many as four times[9]. This is in keeping with his mercenary tendencies, which we will mention later.

From 1861-4 he travelled extensively disguised as a Sunni dervish in Central Asia and Persia, and joined a band of pilgrims returning from Mecca. On his return he published his book *Travels in Central Asia*.

Arminius Vámbéry in Dervish Dress

After his return from the long trek in the spring of 1864, he visited London where he was lionized for his triumph as an intrepid adventurer and his impressive polyglot achievement. Then after a stop in Paris, Vambery, who had become a Protestant, accepted an invitation from the University of Budapest to teach oriental languages and in this capacity he served until 1905[10].

---

9 *The Seventh Isaiah Berlin Annual Lecture*, "Diplomacy and Intelligence in the Middle East: How and Why Are The Two Inexorably Interwined?" delivered in London on November 8, 2009.
10 *Encyclopedia Judaica*

In *The Dervish of Windsor Castle*[11], a biography of Vámbéry, we are told that Vámbéry made annual visits to London, including one on April 17, 1880, where he gave "a lecture to a select gathering at the Royal Society of Arts. The title of the lecture was "Russian Influence in Central Asia" and his distinguished audience included a number of baronets and military men."

Tom Reiss, in his biography of Kurbain Said[12], states:

> ... in 1864, when he published his first autobiograph-
> ical account, titled *Travels in Central Asia*, it became a
> bestseller throughout Europe, especially in England,
> where it was read as a valuable military and political
> primer for playing the Great Game for dominance
> of Central Asia. Vámbéry made a triumphant tour
> of London and Paris that year, and the boy who had
> worked polishing shoes on the streets of Budapest until
> he was twelve became a personal friend of the Prince of
> Wales, later King Edward VII, and a frequent guest at
> Windsor Castle. While visiting England, Vámbéry met
> three generations of British royalty: Queen Victoria,
> King Edward VII, and King George V...
>
> Perhaps his most interesting encounter, and one he
> loved to relate as an anecdote to friends, was the time he
> was questioned by then British prime minister Benjamin
> Disraeli on his ethnic origins – the communication of one
> proud, self-conscious "Jewish Oriental" with another.

In 1889, he was presented to Queen Victoria at Sandringham. She found him a 'wonderfully clever man' and he was invited to Windsor Castle[13].

---

11 L. Adler and R. Dalby, Bachman & Turner Ltd, London, 1979 at p 294.

12 *The Orientalist: Solving the Mystery of a Strange and Dangerous Life,* Random House Trade Paperbacks, New York, (2005) p. 232.

13 Keith Hamilton, Historian, Foreign & Commonwealth Office:
http://collections.europarchive.org/tna/20080205132101/www.fco.gov.uk/Files/kfile/TheRecordsofthePermanentUnderSecretarysDepartment_1.pdf

He was in England on a lecture tour in 1885. According to Donald Redmond[14], Vámbéry's name appears in *The Times* four times in 1880, twice in 1881, no less that thirteen times between January and July of 1883 and twice in 1884. Some of these dates refer to a period when Watson was already in partnership with Holmes – from 1881 – and therefore cannot be the dates when Vámbéry might have been Holmes' client or the subject of one of his cases.

Additional research shows Vámbéry's name appeared in *The Times* 43 times between 1889 and 1892[15]. Some of these are letters from Vámbéry, others are notes of lectures given by him, reports from correspondents on his current travels, or letters from correspondents commenting on public statements made by him. He was, in other words, a well-known public figure in England in those days. Vámbéry became known also as a publicist, zealously defending English policy in the East as against that of the Russians. If we are looking for the dates on which he might have come to Conan Doyle's attention, we are better off to focus on the years from 1889 to 1892.

VAMBERRY IS VÁMBÉRY

It is commonly accepted by all commentators that Holmes' Vamberry is Arminius Vámbéry. In the *New Annotated Sherlock Holmes*, Les Klinger writes:

> Vamberry is identified by several scholars with Arminius,
> or Armin, Vámbéry (Hermann Vamberger, 1832-1913),
> a Hungarian professor of Oriental languages at the
> University of Buda-Pesth *and a renowned wine collector.*[16]

Donald Redmond initially proposed that Vamberry was not Arminius Vámbéry, but was selected only as the alias for a real criminal,

---

14 *Sherlock Holmes: A Study in Sources.* McGill, Queens University Press, Kingston and Montreal, 1983 p. 83.

15 14 times in 1889, 8 times in 1890, 10 times in 1891 and 11 times in 1892.

16 Leslie S. Klinger, W.W. Norton & Co., New York and London, 2008, p. 530.

the murderer Arnold Walder.[17] However, Redmond subsequently concluded that "Vamberry the wine merchant" is in fact our man Arminius Vámbéry.[18] Other commentators have also concluded that "Vamberry the wine merchant" is Arminius Vámbéry.[19] Curiously, however, there are at least four pastiches in which Vamberry has nothing to do with our friend Arminius[20], but we dismiss these as pure inventions.

VÁMBÉRY THE DOUBLE AGENT

In 2005 the National Archives at Kew, Surrey, made some of its files accessible to the public. It was revealed, perhaps for the first time publicly, that Vámbéry had been employed by the British Foreign Office as an agent and spy whose task it was to combat Russian attempts at gaining ground in Central Asia and threatening the British position in the Indian sub-continent. Richard Norton-Taylor reported in *The Guardian*[21]:

> His putative usefulness for the British was that he had the ear of the sultan of Turkey, "your friend in Constantinople", as his controller in London described him. He provided information about the weakening Ottoman empire and its relations with the Austro-Hungarian empire and Russia....The papers include letters to Vámbéry from his Foreign

---

17 See "Some Pretty Cases from the Tin Box", *Sherlock Holmes Journal,* 12 No. 1 (Spring 1975), pp. 3-9.

18 "Vamberry the Wine Merchant", *Sherlock Holmes Journal,* 12, Nos. 3-4 (Summer 1976), pp. 76-77.

19 See Evan M. Wilson, in "Vambery, the So-Called Wine Merchant, or the Dervish of Windsor Castle," *Baker Street Journal,* 32, No. 3 (Sept. 1982) pp.140-142; "Sherlock Holmes in Eastern Asia: the Thirty-Six Steps, or Vambery Again", *Baker Street Journal,* 33, No. 2 (June 1983), pp.86-88; and David Pelger in "Vamberry or Vambery, A Possible Identification." *Baker Street Journal,* 43, No. 4 (Dec. 1993) pp. 204-207.

20 Peter Ridgway Watt and Joseph Green, *The Alternative Sherlock Holmes: Pastiches, Parodies and Copies,* Ashgate Publishing Ltd., Aldershot: 2003.

21 "From Dracula's Nemesis to Prototype Foreign Spy", Friday April 1, 2005.

Office handlers, though none of his replies. One, dated 1893, refers to concern in the Commons about the Turkish treatment of Armenians. "Our humanitarian zealots, like our missionaries, are politically inconvenient, but they are not to be suppressed", Vámbéry was told. In 1897, the Foreign Office expressed concern about the sultan's "manoeuvres for the encouragement of Musselman [Muslim] agitation in India and Afghanistan". Vámbéry was always after money and most of the Foreign Office's messages to him refer to arrangements for sending him batches of £50, or £120 in bank notes. Eventually he was given a fixed annuity of £140 plus a pension, despite the view of Lord Salisbury, the Conservative foreign secretary, that a lot of what Vámbéry had to say was "alarmist" and "had done us more harm than good".

It is plausible to state that Vámbéry's trips to London were as much about being debriefed by the Foreign Office and given new instructions – and money – as they were about publicizing the launch of a new book. Perhaps Mycroft was in the audience at his public lectures, to keep an eye on one of England's valuable intelligence assets.

WHAT IS THE CONAN DOYLE CONNECTION TO VÁMBÉRY?

One apparent Doyle/Vámbéry connection is through Bram Stoker, author of *Dracula*. Stoker and Vámbéry were friends. Van Helsing in *Dracula* has conversations with "Arminius." Van Helsing states:

I have asked my friend Arminius, of Buda-Pesth University, to make his record; and ... he must, indeed, have been that Voivode [Prince] *Dracula* who won his name against the Turk.[22]

Bram Stoker

Barbara Belford in her biography of Stoker says:[23]

Stoker met the Hungarian folklore expert at a Beefsteak [Club] supper on April 30, 1890. But there is no evidence that Vambéry initiated the vampire myth.

The authors of *The Dervish of Windsor Castle* are more certain.[24]

It is easy to imagine Vambery in full flow, regaling his new friends with stories of romance and horror from his homeland, and there is good reason to assume that it was he who told Stoker, for the first time, of the

---

22 It is by no means a certainty that this reference is to Vambéry.
   See the discussion at: http://www.ucs.mun.ca/-emiller/A Vambery.htm.
23 *Bram Stoker and the Man who was Dracula*, Da Capo Press, Cambridge, MA 2002.
24 *Op. cit*, n. 11 at p. 462.

name of the historical 'Dracula': Vlad V, a 15th century Prince of Wallachia.

There are quite a few references to their relationship in the *The Dervish of Windsor Castle*. Conan Doyle and Stoker also knew each other well. Conan Doyle sold his play "Waterloo" to Henry Irving in March 1892, when Stoker was his manager at the Adelphi Theatre. So if we can tie Vámbéry to Stoker in 1892 or 1893, it is certainly possible that Doyle met him through Stoker, or at least talked about him with Stoker. We know that Stoker met Vámbéry in 1890 and 1892. Surprisingly, extensive research has so far failed to unearth direct evidence that Conan Doyle and Stoker met in person at any time before 1907[25]. But it is inconceivable that they did not meet many years earlier. Conan Doyle must have attended at least one rehearsal or performance of "Waterloo" in the 1890s. He did not attend the premiere in Bristol on September 21, 1894[26], but he must have attended one of the London performances, as early as May 4, 1895 or in September of that year. Our contention is that Conan Doyle must have met Stoker for the first time no later than March, 1892, when Irving purchased the rights to "Waterloo". Could their conversation at that time have turned to Arminius Vámbéry?

Another strong possibility for an early meeting was over the Stoker/Doyle collaboration on *The Fate of Fenella*, a novel inspired by J. S. Wood. The novel first appeared serially in Wood's weekly magazine, *The Gentlewoman: The Illustrated Weekly Journal for Gentlewomen*, in 1891 and 1892, before appearing in book form in May 1892[27]. Each of the 24 authors wrote one chapter and passed it on to the next person in line. Conan Doyle wrote the fourth chapter, while Stoker wrote the 10[th.]. In her biography of Stoker, Barbara Belford suggests that "Conan Doyle

25 See Brian Pugh, *A Chronology of the Life of Sir Arthur Conan Doyle*, Revised and Expanded Edition, London: MX Publishing 2012. Stoker and his wife visited Undershaw and apparently also attended Conan Doyle's wedding to Jean Leckie: Barbara Belford, *Bram Stoker and the Man Who Was Dracula*, Cambridge, MA, Da Capo Press, 2002 p.311.

26 Clifford S. Goldfarb, *The Great Shadow: Arthur Conan Doyle, Brigadier Gerard & Napoleon.* Ashcroft Press, 1996, p. 68.

27 Hutchinson & Co. London.

convinced Stoker to join him on the project."[28] If that is true, then Conan Doyle had met Stoker before 1892, since Stoker's chapter, "Lord Castleton Explains", was published in the January 30, 1892 issue of *The Gentlewoman.*

When *Dracula* was published in 1897, Conan Doyle wrote to Stoker[29] in the following words:

> I write to tell you how very much I have enjoyed reading Dracula. I think it is the very best story of diablerie which I have read for many years. It is really wonderful how with so much exciting interest over so long a book there is never an anticlimax.

Conan Doyle began writing "The Musgrave Ritual" in December 1892, and it was published in May 1893. Given that Irving gave Stoker *"Waterloo"* to read in 1892, clearly the Doyle/Stoker/Vámbéry connection is established as a reason to mention Vámbéry in the story. It is not surprising that he does not mention Stoker's name in one of the stories published in 1893, as Stoker was not at that date known to the general public.[30]

Vámbéry did publish some works in English prior to 1893 and it is more than conceivable that Conan Doyle could have seen them. Conan Doyle wrote frequent letters to *The Times*, although they did not begin to appear until after 1891.[31] However, it is likely that he was reading the paper well before then and would naturally have seen the numerous letters written by Vámbéry, as well as frequent references to his travels to Asia. Efraim Halevy, former director of the Mossad,

---

28 *Op. cit,* n.25, p.240.

29 Klinger, Leslie S. *The New Annotated Dracula.* W.W. Norton & Co., New York and London 2008, p.xxxii.

30 Graham Moore, *The Sherlockian,* Toronto: Viking Canada, 2010, has paired Stoker and Conan Doyle in a criminal investigation, but it is set much later, in 1900. There is no known evidence of any meetings between Conan Doyle and Stoker at this time, though it is not unlikely.

31 There were two letters from him in 1892. There are seven adventures where *The Times* is either read by Holmes or is otherwise referred to in a story.

Israel's Secret Service, describes Vámbéry's *Travels in Central Asia* as "a canonical opus to this very day."[32]

We can find no direct evidence of a meeting between Conan Doyle and Vámbéry. However, as we have already mentioned, we can at least speculate that Conan Doyle might have heard about Vámbéry from Stoker. Vámbéry was staying at the Athaenaeum Club in London on June 30, 1892, when he wrote a lengthy letter to *The Times* "On Troubles in Afghanistan – Russian Provocation."[33] According to Pugh's *Chronology*, Conan Doyle was at home in South Norwood at that date.[34] Conan Doyle did not become a member of the Athaeneum until 1901[35]. So it is unlikely they would have met in 1892, unless Stoker introduced them. Further research in Conan Doyle' daybooks and journals for this period may shed some light on this possibility. Vámbéry had stayed at the Athaeneum before. In 1865 Charles Dickens met Vámbéry at the Athaenaeum Club and wrote an article about him, "The Hungarian Dervish" in *All the Year Round*.[36]

VAMBERY AND THE ZIONIST MOVEMENT

Efraim Halevy, in his paper[37] states:

> When Theodor Herzl embarked upon the treacherous path leading his people to independence in the Holy Land he quickly reached the conclusion that he would have to... make contact with the powers that be who were in possession of the Holy Land – the rulers of the Ottoman Empire.... Very soon, he realised that he had to reach the Sultan himself; ....

---

32 *Op. cit*, n.9
33 *The Times*, July 2, 1892.
34 *Op. cit*, n.25
35 Lycett, *op.cit*. n.2, 261
36 *Op*. n, 11, p.232.
37 *Op. cit*, n.9

Enter Arminius Vámbéry. [S]imultaneous with his academic duties was recruited and acted as an agent both for the Ottomans and for British Intelligence.

Theodor Herzl (left) and Abdul Hamid II.

He was not a double agent; he acted separately on different issues for different masters. But he was a double dealer and when Herzl approached him and recruited him to obtain an audience with Sultan Abdul Hamid the second, he asked for and received a hefty sum for the service performed. By the time he was working for Great Britain, he was not only collecting and passing information, he was also involved in combating Russian attempts to gain ground in Central Asia, where they posed a potential threat to the British position on the Indian sub continent.....

Herzl did see the Sultan ultimately in the month of May 1901 but...Vámbéry had not been properly briefed and had not adequately prepared either Herzl or the Sultan for the fateful meeting. From a professional point of view, Herzl was no match for double dealing Vámbéry....

In many respects, Vámbéry was a model for generations to come. He often assumed the ways and religion
of his targets; he earned their trust and respect.

Vámbéry did have a genuine interest in the Zionist cause. When
Israel Zangwill sought support in 1906 for establishment of a Jewish
home in unoccupied territories, he received and reprinted a number
of letters:

> What is most notable about the letters reprinted ... is
> that they are by no means all favorable. Arminius
> Vambery, Professor of Oriental Languages at the
> University of Budapest, and a Jew, contributed the lon-
> gest and most detailed letter of support ... Yet Arthurs
> [sic] Conan Doyle ... had difficulty imagining Jews as
> farmers ... [38]

WHY WINE?

If we accept for the sake of argument that Vámbéry had a wine connection, then it is logical that the wine would be Tokaji.

Tracy in *The Encyclopaedia Sherlockiana*[39] defines "Tokay" this way:

> Tokay, a rich, heavy wine, somewhat sweet in taste
> and very aromatic, produced in northern Hungary.
> Thaddeus Sholto offered Mary Morstan a glass (*The
> Sign of the Four*). Holmes and Watson enjoyed Tokay at
> Von Bork's house, which was said to be *Imperial Tokay*
> from Franz Joseph's special cellar at the Schoenbrunn
> Palace ("His Last Bow").

38 Meri-Jane Rochelson, *From A Jew in the Public Arena: The Career of Israel Zangwill*, Wayne State
University Press, 2008, p.160. The letters were published in *Fortnightly Review*, New Series.
Vol. 79 (Old Series: Volume 85) (1906), p. 633.

39 Doubleday & Company Inc, Garden City, New York, 1977 at p. 362.

Tokaji wines (generally spelled "Tokay" in English), are produced in the Tokaj wine region (also Tokaj-Hegyalja wine region or Tokaj-Hegyalja) of Hungary. There is a strong Jewish connection here, as many of the vineyards were leased by Jews from the beginning of the 18th century[40].

Catherine the Great who ruled Russia during the 18th Century, so prized her Tokay that she detailed a special troop of Cossacks to guard her private stock.[41] In addition to Tokay, various other wines are referred to in the Canon.[42] There is a reference to James Windibank, a "traveller in wines" in "A Case of Identity", but no one seems to have taken the trouble to identify him with any type of wine. On the other hand, Vámbéry and Tokay are a natural fit, especially given the dates of publication of the two stories in which Tokay is mentioned: 1890, when Vámbéry was in his heyday in London, and 1917 shortly after he died.

In addition, given the extent to which Tokay was revered and the fact Holmes and Watson drank Tokay said to be from the special cellars of Emperor Franz Joseph (1830-1916), one would expect only a high-class merchant, especially a Hungarian like the well-known Vámbéry, would be given the privilege of distributing Tokay.

In *Dracula:*

> The Count himself came forward and took off the
> cover of a dish, and I fell to at once on an excellent

---

40 Only in the first half of the eighteenth century did Jews who had emigrated from Poland arrive in Tokaj. They leased vineyards, whose products and exports made them very rich. Their neighbors' jealousy was the reason that in 1798 the Jews were forbidden to produce high-quality wine, including high quality kosher wine, which only Christians were permitted to produce. In 1800 the Jews also were forbidden to lease or buy vineyards in the Tokaj area. Only in one area, in the district of Zemplen, were the Jews permitted to hold poor quality vineyards. Nevertheless, the district representatives in Parliament claimed that the Jews concentrated all wine exports in their own hands. On the contrary, the municipality supported the Jews. A few local landowners who were interested in the development of Tokaj also supported them. And really, the Jews of Tokaj didn't disappoint them. The reputation of Tokaj wine is a credit to the Jews. Translation of the "Tokaj" chapter from Pinkas Hakehillot Hungary, Edited by: Theodore Lavi. Published by Yad Vashem, Jerusalem, 1975 http://www.jewishgen.org/yizkor/pinkas_hungary/hun310.html

41 See Alec Waugh: *Wines and Spirits,* Time-Life Books, New York, 1968.

42 *Op. cit,* n. 31.

roast chicken. This, with some cheese and a salad and a bottle of old Tokay of which I had two glasses, was my supper.

These wines (and our man Vamberry) are not to be confused with the modern wines produced in California by 221B Cellars and sold through Vamberry the Wine Merchant in High Holborn Street, London[43].

In the final analysis, while it is tempting to say that, because Vámbéry came from Hungary, the land of Tokay, and, as noted, Les Klinger calls him a "wine collector"[44], we have no direct evidence to show he was a "wine merchant". Why would Holmes refer to a well-known public figure, deliberately misdescribing him as a "wine merchant", and imply that he had consulted Holmes on a case of importance? Perhaps the answer is that Mycroft Holmes knew Watson's avid readers included many of the titled heads of Europe, who might be put off the scent of Vámbéry as secret agent by such a reference. They might believe that his connections to the Sultan Abdul Hamid II (ruled 1876–1909) were simply to assist him in choosing the best wines to purchase for entertaining his non-Muslim visitors[45]. It would not have been difficult for Mycroft to convince Watson to do him this patriotic service.

Incidentally, the Sultan of Turkey is no stranger to Sherlock Holmes. In "The Blanched Soldier" Holmes states:

> I also had a commission from the Sultan of Turkey which called for immediate action, as political consequences of the gravest kind might arise from its neglect.

This is, of course, the same Sultan that Vamberry knew so well.

---

43 http://www.221bcellars.com/

44 Klinger, who 'plays the game' in this publication, does not tell us where he found the otherwise new and convenient information that Vámbéry was a wine collector.

45 Vámbéry would not have been the first Jew to sell wines to a Turkish Sultan. In 1566 Sultan Selim granted Joseph Naxos a monopoly on the importation of wine through the Bosporus: Cecil Roth, *House of Nasi: The Duke of Naxos*, Philadelphia: Jewish Publication Society of America, 1992.

WHY "VAMBERRY" AND NOT "VÁMBÉRY" AND WHY WINE MERCHANT?

If Conan Doyle, through Stoker, or on his own, had actually met Vámbéry in London sometime between 1890 and 1892, it is not unlikely that they might have enjoyed a glass of this wine and a pleasant chat at the Athaeneum. Conan Doyle often used the names of his friends or acquaintances in his work.[46] One of the senses of "merchant" in the Oxford English Dictionary is a "paid agent", which would describe Vámbéry's role for the Foreign Office. So the reference to someone well-known to the public for his travel lectures and biography as a "wine merchant" would be a subtle and private acknowledgment of a pleasant meeting.

The whereabouts of the manuscript of "The Musgrave Ritual" is unknown even to Randall Stock, the expert on ACD's manuscripts[47]. A glance at it might show that Conan Doyle used the proper spelling of "Vámbéry", but the same typesetter who set the text for *The Strand Magazine* chose the phonetic English version, rather than proper Hungarian one. Occam's razor tells us the simplest explanation is the most likely. The accents over the "á" and "é" may have confused the typesetter. In addition, the reference may not have been to "wine merchant" at all. Conan Doyle, after all, was relying on Watson's notes here, and Watson was a medical doctor, a profession notorious for the illegibility of its penmanship (Conan Doyle himself being a notable exception).

We have been allowed by the owner, a distant relative of one of us, who wishes to retain her anonymity, to copy a portion of the first page of the notebook in which Watson wrote up the tale. Here, for the first time, is what he actually wrote – "Vamberry, the wise Magyar gent". While Watson would know that a magyar was a Hungarian, you wouldn't expect a working typesetter to be aware of that. So, doing his best to unravel Watson's untidy script, "wine merchant" seemed to fit, especially since the name included the word "berry".

---

46 Donald Redmond: *"A Study in Sources"* Op. cit. n.14.

47 http://www.bestofsherlock.com/sherlock-manuscripts.htm

WHERE IS THE SHERLOCK HOLMES — VÁMBÉRY CONNECTION?

Sherlock Holmes returns from Reichenbach Falls in 1894. In "The Empty House" Holmes explains to Watson where he has been for the last three years in these well-known words:

> I travelled for two years in Tibet, therefore, and amused myself by visiting Lhassa and spending some days with the head Llama. You may have read of the remarkable explorations of a Norwegian named Sigerson, but I am sure that it never occurred to you that you were receiving news of your friend. I then passed through Persia, looked in at Mecca, and paid a short but interesting visit to the Khalifa at Khartoum, the results of which I have communicated to the Foreign Office. Returning to France, I spent some months in a research into the coal-tar derivatives, which I conducted in a laboratory at Montpelier, in the south of France.

Let us compare Holmes with Vámbéry:

1. The "Musgrave Ritual" is published May 1893. Relevant contemporary cases are "The Greek Interpreter" (September 1893), "The Naval Treaty" (October –

November 1893) and "The Final Problem" (December 1893), all of which can be connected. For example, "The Final Problem" leads to Holmes wandering in Asia, maybe relying on information from Vámbéry as to conditions he would encounter.

2. The first mention of Mycroft in his connection to the British secret service is "The Greek Interpreter" (September 1893).

3. Both Holmes and Vámbéry travelled through Persia and either visited Mecca in the case of Holmes, or met pilgrims returning from Mecca in the case of Vámbéry.[48]

4. Both went travelling in the Middle East in disguise. Vámbéry travelled as a Sunni dervish and we can assume Holmes was in disguise. Travelling in that part of the world as an Englishman would have been instant death unless Holmes was in a disguise to blend in with the locals. Holmes was a master of disguise.

5. Both needed to speak the local dialect, which was easy for Vámbéry and conceivable for Holmes, given his linguistic skills: Holmes studied Cornish in "The Adventure of the Devil's Foot" (December 1910). There is reference to his "receiving a consignment of books upon philology." He could have received these years before. Chaldean (better known as Aramaic) is a Semitic language spoken in the Middle East.

6. Vámbéry was a British agent. Holmes, in his Sigerson persona, and elsewhere during the Great Hiatus years, was undoubtedly a British agent, as well.[49]

---

48 We have to mention the possibility Doyle was using Sir Richard Burton's travels in 1853 as his background for Holmes' trek back to London but Vámbéry had to be more visible to Doyle than Burton.

49 See our paper "Sherlock in Jerusalem" in this volume.

7. Holmes, in "The Naval Treaty" was dealing with a secret treaty, the exposure of which could have significant consequences. Vámbéry also engaged in high level diplomatic intrigues.

8. Vámbéry and Holmes both knew and had business to conduct with the Sultan of Turkey:

> I had also a commission from the Sultan of Turkey which called for immediate action, as political consequences of the gravest kind might arise from its neglect.[50]

CONCLUSION

It is not by accident that Conan Doyle inserted the name "Vamberry/Vámbéry" in "The Musgrave Ritual". Vámbéry was a role model for Sherlock Holmes. We are convinced that Conan Doyle had met Vámbéry. The reference to Vamberry in "The Musgrave Ritual" could only be a subtle greeting to a new friend from the Athaeneum Club, Arminius Vámbéry, with whom he had enjoyed a glass of fine Tokay.

To further demonstrate that this was no accident, we refer once again to the words of Donald Redmond:[51]

> It seems highly probable that the mention of 'Vamberry' the 'club foot' of Ricoletti, and even the 'old Russian woman; in "The Musgrave Ritual." and the facile but slightly improbable tale recited by Sherlock Holmes in "The Empty House." of three years' wanderings in Tibet, Egypt and points between, were all inspired by familiarity with—not to say resentment of,—the bombast of Professor Arminius Vámbéry.

---

50 Sherlock Holmes, "Blanched Soldier", *The Strand Magazine*, October, 1926.
51 Op. *cit*, n.14.

London has not forgotten Arminius Vámbéry, with Vambery Road in SE18.

To conclude we would like to toast Vamberry the wine merchant with a glass of Tokay.

EGÉSZSÉGETEKRE!![52]

---

52 Pronounced "eg' —ggee – she' — gge – teck' – re" It means "to your good health"

REGINA VS. MORAN

by John Linsenmeyer

Central Criminal Court, London, 1ˢᵗ to 3ʳᵈ October 1894, upon a charge of willful murder

The following summary of the proceedings at the Old Bailey before the Hon. Mr. Justice Wills and a jury was prepared by the editor from contemporary accounts in the *Middlesex Legal Intelligencer* and the daily press, and annotated by him. Leading for the Crown was the Rt. Hon. Sir John Rigby, QC, MP, Attorney General of England and Wales, and with him Mr. Horace Avery (instructed by the Director of Public Prosecutions).

Leading for the defense was Sir Hartley Clifford, QC, and with him Mr. Arthur Gill (instructed by Lewis and Lewis).

The Attorney General opened on Monday the first by telling the jury that the Crown would prove that Col. Sebastian Moran, late Indian Army, murdered the late Hon. Ronald Adair at 427 Park Lane, Westminster, by shooting him with a silent appliance seized from the prisoner several days later. The motive was to prevent the victim from taking any action further to the accused's cheating at cards at the Bagatelle Club. Sir Hartley responded that there was no evidence of cheating, that the accused was a brave officer and sportsman of sterling character, that the Crown's theory of the motive was ridiculous and the claimed mechanics of the crime were physically and scientifically impossible.

The Crown's first witness was Mr. Hector Moriarty, Coroner for the Westminster District. He testified that he examined the deceased on the morning of Monday, 2nd April 1894 and observed the body of a healthy male approximately 31 years of age, who had sustained a devastating and instantly lethal wound to the head from what appeared to be a heavy revolver bullet. On cross examination, the Coroner testified that, while he was not especially experienced in gunshot wounds, those being rare in his district, the bullet was so fragmented that it appeared to have been either hollow-pointed or else cross-cut or notched so as completely to expand upon impact. He removed all or almost all of the fragments at the autopsy, and found them to be of pure lead weighing approximately 240 grains, or something over half an ounce at 437.5 grains to the ounce.

The second Crown witness was Inspector G. Lestrade of the Criminal Investigation Department of the Metropolitan Police, who testified that he was called in the middle of the night of 31st March by the uniform inspector at Marylebone Police Station and advised of the murder at 427 Park Lane. He established that the deceased had returned from his card club at 10:20 pm on the Friday, and immediately gone to his sitting room on the second[1] floor approximately 20 feet above the street level and, for reasons unknown, locking the door behind him. Upon the return of the victim's mother and sister at 11:30, and being unable to raise him, the door was broken down and his body found lying near the table with a terrible bullet wound to the head. On the table were two 10-pound bank notes and 17 pounds 10 shillings in coin, arranged in separate little piles. No weapon was found in the room. The window was open and there were no ladder marks or footprints in the blooming crocuses or soft earth 20 feet below to indicate any ingress or egress from the locked room via the window.

On cross-examination, Inspector Lestrade said that there were no other bullet holes anywhere in the room, and that neither he nor anyone to his knowledge attempted to determine the angle or distance

---

1 In British usage, the second floor is the American third floor (the English bottom main floor being the 'ground floor').

from which the fatal shot was fired. He added that he was not familiar with firearms and had never carried one. He said that there was no cheque, cash or notation on the deceased's table in the amount of 420 pounds, or 210 pounds either. He had not investigated to determine if there was any ill-feeling on anyone's part from the victim breaking an engagement to a Miss Woodley.

The third witness was Dr John H. Watson, late Army Medical Department and the well-known colleague of the famous Baker Street detective Mr Sherlock Holmes. Dr Watson testified that the pneumatic weapon offered in evidence by the Crown had been taken from the prisoner in his presence. Upon Sir Hartley Clifford's objection, His Lordship ruled that, since no charges[2] had been laid at the time the weapon was taken,[3] he would not allow any inquiry into the circumstances of its seizure.

The final witness for the day was Lord Balmoral, member of the Bagatelle Club. He, along with Mr Godfrey Milner, now in South Africa,[4] regularly played whist with the prisoner and the deceased, who often played together. In early March, he and Milner had collectively lost the sum of 420 pounds in one sitting, very high stakes for the deceased but perhaps less so for the prisoner, whom the witness

---

2 It is unclear whether Holmes was acting from modesty or from profound legal knowledge when he made the statement quoted in note 3 below. Under English law as of 1894, it is clear that Col. Moran could not have been prosecuted for "the attempted murder of Mr. Sherlock Holmes" as suggested by Inspector Lestrade. In *Rex -v- Lovell*, 2 M. & Rob. 39 (Spring Assizes 1837, Taunton) before Baron Gurney, it was established that Lovell had fired a gun into a room of one Chinnock's house where he assumed Chinnock was, but it turned out that the target was in a different room. Lovell was acquitted because "a man could scarcely be said to be shot at, who was not near the place where the gun was fired." See also "Was it Attempted Murder", pp. 59-69 in *The Baker Street Briefs* by Judge S. Tupper Bigelow, BSI, (Metro Toronto Library)

3 Of course the jury was unaware of the circumstances under which the airgun had been seized, or that Sherlock Holmes had emphatically told Inspector Lestrade that he "did not propose to appear in the matter at all" and had insisted that the only charge laid against Moran be the Adair murder. ("The Empty House", herafter "EMPT". Nota bene: references to Dr Watson's account of the matter will be paginated to *The Oxford Sherlock Holmes*, volume *The Return*.

4 As to Milner's absence, history is silent as to whether his October 1894 presence in South Africa was by reason of some relationship to the Government's proconsul in the Cape Colony, Alfred Milner. For whatever reason, he did not appear as a witness.

described as a "much tougher customer" than Adair. On cross-examination, Lord Balmoral testified that he never had the slightest suspicion of cheating by either. Lord Balmoral added that, since marked decks were impossible because the Bagatelle Club provided the cards and kept them 'fresh', he could not imagine how one partner rather than both partners could cheat at whist. Dishonesty at whist consists of improper or 'illegal' signals between partners as to the contents of their hands,[5] so His Lordship did not see how the accused could have cheated without the conscious complicity and cooperation of the victim. The accused could not have cheated alone.

On October second, the Crown's first and only witness was Sergeant Wilfred Smith, Armourer of the Metropolitan Police. He testified that he had examined the fragments of the bullet recovered from the victim's head by the coroner, and that in his opinion they came from a single soft revolver bullet, that is, of pure lead, and probably to judge by its fragmentation it was a dum-dum bullet. Smith explained that this term refers to hollow-pointed or soft-nosed projectiles, so named because they were manufactured at the Indian Army's Dum-Dum Arsenal near Calcutta. The term can also apply to bullets in effect 'home made' by cross-notching the tips to replicate the effect of hollow points in manufactured ammunition.

On cross-examination, Sergeant Smith stated that he was unable to say whether the bullet was home-made or manufactured, since it was so fragmented. He was also unable to say whether it had been fired from the pneumatic weapon in evidence, because he had no familiarity with air powered arms. He said that the Metropolitan Police used RIC revolvers firing a ".450 Adams" lead bullet, Webley revolvers firing a .455 inch lead bullet, and single-shot Martini-Henry ex-Army rifles firing a heavy .577 bullet. In his opinion, the bullet fragments most closely resembled a revolver bullet, and were certainly similar to the intact soft lead bullet placed in evidence, but beyond that he could not say. He could not identify the weapon from which either bullet had

---

5 This can readily be seen by reference to *The Oxford Dictionary of Card Games* or any edition of Hoyle. Is it significant that Scarlet O'Hara, Phileas Fogg (who played at Conan Doyle's own Reform Club) and Horatio Hornblower all made good money at whist?

been fired, though he might have been able to express an opinion if there were empty cartridge casings by examining the striker or hammer marks on the detonator.[6]

To general surprise, Sir Hartley Clifford did not apply to dismiss the Crown's case, but immediately called his first witness, Constable Henry Puddle of the Marylebone Station, Metropolitan Police. He testified that he was assigned to walk Park Lane on the evening tour (6 pm to 2 am) on Friday, 30th March. He recalled nothing unusual that night until an alarm was raised at no. 427 around 11:30 pm by reason of a man found shot to death. He immediately notified his sergeant, and both entered the room and found the victim; he was then sent to guard the entrance. He believed that the duty inspector notified the CID and Inspector Lestrade arrived a little after midnight. Prior to 11:30, there was the normal pedestrian and vehicular traffic on Park Lane; it was a Friday night and the Lane was fairly busy. At no time did he observe the prisoner, whom to the best of his knowledge he had never seen until this day.

On cross-examination by the Attorney General, the Constable testified that there was no report of a shot at any time. Gunshots were rare; the only one he recalled in his ten years at Marylebone Station was several years ago when a foreign gentleman examining a shotgun at Messrs Purdeys in South Audley Street somehow loaded and discharged a gun out the Mount Street shop window and this was the occasion of a major commotion, even of excited claims that the Fenians were coming. He would have expected a similar commotion had there been a gunshot on the evening of 30th March.

The next witness for the accused was Mr Herbert Lemesurier, Assistant Clerk of the Works for Westminster, London County Council, who testified as the to the breadth of Park Lane opposite no. 427, and

---

6 Regardless of Smith's unfamiliarity with airguns, as of 1894 there was no reliable method of firearms identification. More of this anon, but even the comparison microscope (which would be invented decades later) would not have sufficed to make any reliable comparison test of a bullet which had totally broken up on impact. See, e.g. Major Sir Gerald Burrard, *Identification of Firearms and Forensic Ballistics*, p. 170 (a bullet can be "so deformed as to render all examination abortive"). Herbert Jenkins, London, 1934.

the absence of any building or platform from which a level trajectory into the 20-foot high murder room could be obtained, closer than the trees on the far side of Lovers Walk within Hyde Park, a total distance of approximately 110 yards from the second floor window. There was no cross-examination.

Sir Hartley then called Mr William Wellington Greener, the famous gunmaker and author of St Mary's Row, Birmingham and 29 Pall Mall, London. After qualifying as an expert in firearms and ballistics (at which time Mr Greener presented the Judge and leading counsel with copies of his book *The Gun and Its Development*[7] for easy reference), Mr Greener was shown the airgun in evidence and asked[8] whether a heavy revolver-type lead bullet could have been propelled with lethal force by that gun, and he replied that it could not. He explained that it was simply impossible to generate sufficient pressure with a hand pump and an easily portable weapon to do so. While it is possible to achieve "an extraordinary degree of accuracy . . .with a carefully sighted airgun *at short ranges*" such implements are really only practicable "for indoor target practice."[9] The reason is clear: airguns are limited to very small caliber projectiles, by reason of the "ballistic coefficient." The resistance of the atmosphere to the passage of the projectile increases both with the sectional area and shape of the projectile, and with its velocity. The 'coefficient' is thus proportional to its weight and inverse to its area.[10] In simple terms, then, a large revolver bullet requires far more in the way of propelling force to achieve lethality.

---

7 This classic, first published in London by Cassels, Petler and Galpin in 1881, is amazingly still in print. The page references herein are to the Firearms Classics Library's 1995 reprint of the 1891 illustrated edition, cited hereafter as "Greener." W.W. Greener was a prolific and well-respected author: besides his classic (which he handed to the Judge and counsel) he also wrote *The Science of Gunnery/Rifles, Cannons and Sporting Arms* (1858), *Modern Breech Loaders* (1883), *Modern Shotguns* (1888) and—after his trial testimony in the Adair murder case *Sharpshooting for War and Peace* (1900).

8 In the interests of clarity and conciseness, the elaborate hypothetical questions required by the legal praxis of the 1890s to be propounded to experts have been condensed to provide only the substance.

9 Greener, p. 519

10 *Ibid.*, p. 678

That this is unavailable in airguns like the Crown's exhibit is shown by the chamber pressure in 'modern' firearms; current (1894) military rifles with their high muzzle velocities are subject to chamber pressures of anywhere from 15 to 20 tons per square inch,[11] and revolvers would impose at least half that, say 10 tons per square inch. The most powerful airguns ever made, those of Messrs Townsend & Reilly which must be pumped up by a separate pump, involve no more than pressures of 4-500 pounds—not tons -per square inch.[12] It is absurd to think that airguns, which at the high end involve muzzle values of perhaps 22 or 23 foot-pounds of energy and projectiles of 20 or so caliber could propel a 425- plus grain heavy lead bullet, even of the 'dum-dum' or hollow-point type, with sufficient accuracy and velocity to break up on impact and devastate human cranial bones.[13] An airgun 'cane' such as the weapon in evidence would of course be substantially less powerful and the limitations just testified to would apply all the more emphatically.[14]

The witness was then asked to assume that the fatal shot had been fired from some perch on the far side of Lovers Walk, at least 325 feet from the victim; this, he replied, was utterly impossible with any

---

11 *Ibid*, pp. 735-738

12 Mr Greener was absolutely correct in this. See Volume II *The Annotated Sherlock Holmes* at pp. 344-5 (Baring-Gould [ed.] quoting William Percival on airguns. Note also that at the great Sherlock Holmes Exhibition in London in 1952, a leading firearms expert Major Hugh B.C. Pollard (1888-1966, author of numerous firearms books and regular expert witness in HM Courts of Justice) wrote in the catalogue to that exhibition that the weapon seized from Moran and displayed at the exhibition was "an airgun walking cane" in which "the butt section is an air reservoir which can be pumped up by means of a small diameter air pump to a pressure of some sixty pounds" Note to EMPT [Oxford] no 20 at p. 336

13 EMPT 5 and the coroner's evidence described above.

14 Pollard, op. cit. in note 12 above. Major Pollard's comments from examining the weapon in 1952 are especially compelling in light of his enormous prestige and experience. Pollard was an extraordinary character: combat in the World War; Irish police duty during "The Troubles," and various exploits with Francisco Franco and others; and up to his death expert witness of preference, at least after the retirement of the West End gunmaker Robert Churchill, in civil and criminal cases alike. He was, like Greener, a prolific author: his monumental *History of Firearms* (1936) has been updated and expanded; he also wrote *The Secret Societies of Ireland* (1922), *The Gun Room Guide* (1930), *British and American Game Birds* (1939) etc.

hand-held and hand-pumped pneumatic weapon. He also testified that it was impossible to determine with any precision whether the fragmented fatal bullet and the sample bullet offered in evidence by the Crown had been fired from the same weapon.[15]

On cross-examination, the Attorney General asked the witness to assume that the fatal shot had been fired from the sidewalk on Park Lane below the study window. Mr Greener replied that, unless the victim had been leaning out the window at the time of the fatal shot, and some person in the house dragged him back to the table, the angle for such a shot was impossible. The witness was then asked whether it was not reasonable to expect an exceptional degree of marksmanship from a famous *shikari* such as the prisoner, and Mr Greener replied that it was not. The hunt for maneating or other tigers in the Indian jungles is almost invariably a close range matter, where jungle-craft and steady nerves are more important that long-range marksmanship. Mr Greener referred to the prisoner's two books on the subject, *Heavy Game of the Western Himalayas* and *Three Months in the Jungle*, both of which he had read and recommended to Sir John Rigby to provide a more detailed review of the subject. An exchange then followed which occasioned some amusement in the Court, at the expense of the Attorney General who is well known for a somewhat bristling temperament; it deserves verbatim quotation from the transcript:

---

15 Even were the fatal bullet not fragmented (see Burrard quoted in note 6 above), Greener is of course correct that in the state of firearms identification technology as of 1894, a definitive comparison of bullets was not possible. See Volume II *The Annotated Sherlock Holmes*, p. 349, note 51: "In 1894, ballistics was unknown at Scotland Yard" and Holmes's statement that "The bullets alone are enough to put his head in a noose" is simply wrong. In 1930, the great American firearms expert Lt.Col. Calvin Goddard wrote an analysis of the Chicago St Valentine's Day massacre, proving that accusations of police participation were false, based on the comparison microscope technology, published in the *American Journal of Police Science*, 1930, to show what progress 30 or 40 years would bring. There is a good summary (available on the Internet) in the paper "The History of Firearm and Toolmark Examination" by Dr James Hamby, et al, published in the *Association of Firearm Examiners Journal* (vol. 31, no. 3, summer 1999. revised April 2008). Suffice it to say that as of 1894, the only reliable comparisons would have come from separate microscopic examinations of the striker marks on the cartridge casing, and none such were found in the Adair matter.

The Attorney General: Well, then, Mr Greener, you say this fatal bullet could not have been fired by the airgun. So, sir, how can you account for the death of Ronald Adair on that Friday evening without a shot being heard, if not by a silent airgun?

The Witness: Sir John, at the beginning of this century when your predecessors in the Cabinet were fearful of Napoleon invading England, the First Sea Lord told them 'I do not say the Frenchman will not come. I only say he will not come by sea.' I cannot say how Adair came to be shot in the head. I only say he was not shot by this airgun.

The Attorney General: My Lord, I ask for the protection of the Court. This witness is fencing with me.

The Court: Come, come, Sir John, the witness's analogy is both historically and legally correct. Mr Greener was not called to solve the death of Adair. He was called to help me and the jury by his expert opinion as to whether the fatal shot could have been fired by this appliance. He says it could not. And he is correct in his suggestion that he was neither called, nor for that matter is competent, to say what or who killed Adair.

The witness was then excused, and there was a stir in the courtroom, quickly silenced by His Lordship, as Sir Hartley called the accused's last witness: General the Lord Roberts of Kandahar, VC, KG, etc. Despite his diminutive size, the general cut an impressive figure entering the court in full-dress scarlet. Lord Roberts appeared as a character witness, and briefly described his career, including command of Her Majesty's forces in the Cabul campaign, at the fight at the Sherpur cantonment outside Cabul, and in the Battle of Charasiab. Following the Afghan Wars, he was Commander in Chief

Madras (which included oversight of the Bangalore Pioneers) from 1883 to 1885, and then Commander in Chief—India from 1885 to 1893. Lord Roberts was personally acquainted with the defendant, and as his commanding officer wrote the specific 'mentions in dispatches' honouring him for his exceptional bravery and competence at Charasiab and Sherpur. Lord Roberts was not in the habit of mentioning officers in dispatches if he was either unacquainted with the officer or had any reservations as to his character. Lord Roberts knew Colonel Moran to be an officer of courage, honesty and intelligence, as well as a distinguished *shikari* or big-game hunter and author of books on sporting topics.[16]

The Attorney General's first question was whether the General had been friendly with the prisoner at school, and Lord Roberts replied that since he was eight years older than the Colonel, they did not overlap at Eton—or afterwards, since he attended the East India Military College at Addiscombe and was commissioned initially into the Bengal Artillery, while the Colonel went on to Oxford and was commissioned into the engineers. All his acquaintance with the Colonel was in the course of military duty, both active service in Afghanistan and in cantonment duty at Bangalore.[17] The next question as to the General's awareness of any gambling or other improprieties was met with "Rubbish! Were you not listening to me?" and the witness was excused.

On the third day of the trial, counsel and then the Court summed up the evidence for the jury. His Lordship drew the jury's particular attention (while reminding them that it was for the jury to evaluate it) to the evidence that the claimed motive for the murder, preventing dis-

---

16 It is hard to imagine the impact such testimony by Lord Roberts would have had on an 1894 (all male, of course) English jury. He was not only a soldier of proven personal heroism, having won the Victoria Cross, his Army's highest decoration for valour in the face of the enemy; he was also a very successful commander in the field and was enormously popular personally.

17 Roberts was born in Cawnpore in 1832, the son of an Indian Army officer. *Roberts in India*, Robson [ed.], Army Records Society 1993 at pp. xi-xii. That volume contains, inter alia, a detailed report (datelined Bangalore, 10 October 1884) from Roberts to his friend Lord Napier, former military member of the Viceroy's Counsel and commander in chief, concerning developments in the Pioneer Regiments and other matters of 'Bangalore' interest (op. cit., document no. 209, at pp. 309-14.)

closure of card cheating, was described by the witness Lord Balmoral as improbable since any cheating would appear by reason of the nature of whist to have involved the deceased as well. His Lordship also invited the jury carefully to consider the evidence as to the capability (or lack thereof) of the airgun admittedly seized from the prisoner.

After a deliberation of not more than fifteen minutes, the jury returned a verdict of 'not guilty' and requested that the prisoner be discharged expressly without a stain on his character, which request His Lordship granted and Colonel Moran returned to his home in Conduit Street a free man.

AUTHORS' BIOGRAPHIES

HARTLEY R. NATHAN

Hartley, a practicing lawyer in Toronto, was born in Toronto, obtained his B.A. from the University of Toronto, his LL.B. from Osgoode Hall Law School as a gold medalist, and his Master of Laws from University College, London, obtained his Queen's Counsel in 1982 and was admitted to the Hong Kong bar as a foreign lawyer in 1997. Hartley is a partner in Minden Gross LLP, specializing in corporate-commercial law and is one of Canada's leading experts on company meetings. He is the author of *Nathan's Company Meetings* (10th ed.), (co-authored with Cliff Goldfarb). He is one of the founders of The Bootmakers of Toronto, of which he was Meyers (or President) in 1974. He served a second term in 1975. Hartley has been a frequent speaker at Bootmakers' meetings and at Baker Street Irregular Dinners. He has had many of his papers published in the *Baker Street Journal*, the *Baker Street Miscellanea* and *Canadian Holmes*. His first major paper "John H. Watson M.D. Discovered at Last" in 1972 proved conclusively that Dr. Watson lived in Toronto. It made the Toronto newspapers and helped bring the Bootmakers to prominence. He became a Master Bootmaker in 1982 and was investitured in the BSI in 1980 as "The Penang Lawyer". He is the author of *"Who Was Jack the Ripper?"* (The Battered Silicon Dispatch Box, Eugenia, Ontario, 2011).

He is married to Marilyn who was his faithful Mrs. Hudson during his two terms as Mr. Meyers, has a daughter, a son and two grandchildren, all of whom do their best to tolerate his Sherlockian activities.

CLIFFORD S. GOLDFARB

Cliff was born and raised in Toronto. He graduated from the University of Toronto with a B.A, followed by a J.D. degree from the Faculty of Law and a Master of Laws from the London School of Economics. Cliff is a partner in the Toronto law firm Gardiner Roberts LLP, practicing in the areas of charities and non-profits and business law. He is Past Chair of the Ontario Bar Association's Charity and Not-for-Profit Section and was the 2012 winner of its AMS-John Hodgson Award for excellence in charity and not-for-profit law. With Hartley Nathan, he is the co-author of *Nathan's Company Meetings* (10th ed.). Cliff became a Bootmaker at its second meeting and served as Meyers in 1979. He became a Master Bootmaker in 1983 and was investitured in the BSI as "Fordham the Horsham Lawyer" in 1984. He has a strong interest in the non-Sherlockian works of Sir Arthur Conan Doyle and is a co-founder and Chairman of the Friends of the Arthur Conan Doyle Collection at the Toronto Public Library. He is the author of *The Great Shadow: Arthur Conan Doyle, Brigadier Gerard and Napoleon* (Calabash Press, Ashcroft, B.C., 1996) and the introduction to *The Complete Brigadier Gerard* (Barnes & Noble Library of Essential Reading Series, 2005), as well as numerous papers and articles. Cliff is married to Doris and has two wonderful children and a growing cast of grandchildren, of whom he is inordinately proud. The family indulges him in his non-lucrative activities.

AWARDS

Hartley and Cliff were awarded The True Davidson Memorial Award for the best paper presented at a Bootmakers meeting for three of the papers presented here, "Who was that Hebrew Rabbi?"

in 1984; "Who Was 'Ikey' Sanders?" in 2004; and "Sherlock Holmes in Jerusalem" (with Joseph Kessel) in 2006. Their paper "Oh Sinner Man, Where You Gonna Run To? Sir Arthur and Sir George" won the 2012 Derrick Murdoch award for the best paper published in *Canadian Holmes*.